PROFESSIONAL PRACTICE in
Crime Prevention
and
Security Management

I0121704

Edited by **Tim Prenzler**

www.
AUSTRALIANACADEMIC**PRESS**
.com.au

First published 2014
Australian Academic Press Group Pty. Ltd.
18 Victor Russell Drive
Samford Valley QLD 4520
Australia
www.australianacademicpress.com.au

National Library of Australia Cataloguing-in-Publication entry

Title:	Professional practice in crime prevention and security management / edited by Tim Prenzler.
ISBN:	9781922117243 (paperback) 9781922117250 (ebook)
Notes:	Includes bibliographical references.
Subjects:	Crime prevention. Crime prevention and architectural design. Criminology. Crime analysis. Security sector--Management. Security systems industry--Management. Private security services--Management. Industries--Security measures.

Other Authors/Contributors:
                Prenzler, Tim, editor.

Dewey Number: 364.4

Cover design by Maria Biaggini, The Letter Tree

Typesetting by Australian Academic Press

This book is dedicated to the memory of
Annie Holzwart,
1891–1911
A beautiful young woman,
she was cruelly murdered.

Contents

About the Authors

Rick Draper is the CEO of Amtac Professional Services, a security consulting firm based in Brisbane, Australia.

Matthew Manning is a lecturer in the School of Criminology and Criminal Justice, Griffith University, Brisbane, Australia.

Mateja Mihinjac is a tutor in the School of Criminology and Criminal Justice, Griffith University, Brisbane, Australia.

Tim Prenzler is a professor in the School of Criminology and Criminal Justice, and a chief investigator with the Australian Research Council Centre of Excellence in Policing and Security, Griffith University, Brisbane, Australia.

Danielle Reynauld is a lecturer in the School of Criminology and Criminal Justice, Griffith University, Brisbane, Australia.

Jessica Ritchie is a tutor in the School of Criminology and Criminal Justice, Griffith University, Brisbane, Australia.

Rick Sarre is a professor in the School of Law, University of South Australia, Adelaide, Australia.

Eric Wilson is a tutor in the School of Criminology and Criminal Justice, Griffith University, Brisbane, Australia.

Gabriel T.W. Wong is a PhD student in the School of Criminology and Criminal Justice, Griffith University, Brisbane, Australia.

Preface

This is a book of research, policy and practice aimed primarily at a practitioner audience. My purpose in putting this edited collection together is to provide a clear and up-to-date guide to what works and what constitutes best practice across a range of crime prevention and security management applications and issues. The book fills a gap in the literature in regard to the integration of environmentally-based crime prevention science and applied security work.

I have two particular target audiences in mind for the book: crime prevention project managers and security managers. If these groups find the book useful for enlarging the scope of their work and its positive effects, then I will feel I have achieved something of value. Another target group is policy officers. We need more sophisticated government and corporate crime prevention policies that produce results, and this book will provide a resource for advancing that process. I am also hoping that tertiary-level students of crime prevention and security studies will find the book engaging and beneficial. Academic crime prevention sources can be obscure and tedious. The book should provide an easy entree into the field and help convey some of the main principles, methods and sources — with guidance for further secondary research. Finally, I hope that academic colleagues will find the book useful, whether for research purposes, teaching or both.

The first part of the book is concerned with theory and evaluated practice. Chapter 1 elaborates on the key lessons from situational crime prevention and associated opportunity theories, including routine activity theory. The role of the security industry in applying situational methods is also touched on, and a number of issues and controversies around situational prevention are addressed in favour of a democratic and egalitarian approach to regulation and management. Chapter 2 provides an exposition of the role of Crime Prevention Through Environmental Design (CPTED) in successful crime reduction projects; and chapter 3 argues the case for improved financial impact assessments, with a practical model to assist in analysing the financial dimensions of projects. The final two chapters in this part (chapter 4 and chapter 5) provide summaries of a wide range of exemplar case studies of successful crime prevention across the areas of violent crime and disorder, and property and financial crime — illustrating what can be achieved through a systematic, theoretically-informed, approach to crime problems.

The second part of the book is focused on best practice in security management. Chapter 6 shows how rational choice and routine activity approaches can enhance traditional security management methods by integrating situational techniques within a comprehensive, systematic and multilayered approach to security. Chapter 7, on physical security, develops this theme, focusing in particular on the key role of the security survey. Chapter 8 is concerned with personnel dimensions of security, including attention to different forms of human guardianship and the value of rule setting.

The third part is concerned with the knowledge and strategies required to take the security industry further into the new era of professionalism. The first chapter in part 3 (chapter 9) maps the size and growth of the industry internationally and in Australia, and discusses the implications for policing and crime prevention partnerships. Chapter 10 outlines the legal context of security work, focusing on Australia, covering statute and case law. The chapter also highlights areas where modifications to the law would facilitate the public interest dimension of security services. The next chapter (chapter 11) recounts major legal breaches and outlines an industry risk profile for unethical conduct, making the case for better regulation. The final chapter (chapter 12) evaluates existing regulatory systems. It also describes a 'smart regulation' model designed to make use of practitioner knowledge and triangulated conduct indicators to ensure licensing-based government regulation is as efficient and effective as possible. Smart regulation should support a highly professional industry that makes an optimal contribution to crime prevention.

Tim Prenzler

PART ONE

Effective Crime Prevention: From Theory to Practice

Chapter 1

Situational Crime Prevention: Theories, Impacts and Issues

Tim Prenzler and Eric Wilson

Situational crime prevention has been the most important theoretical framework for understanding and designing effective crime reduction strategies. This chapter examines the contribution of the theory to success in applied settings. In addition, associated theories of rational choice, routine activity and problem oriented policing are examined. Implications for the security industry are considered, along with the problem of the 'security gap' in modern society. The chapter concludes by analysing a number of criticisms that have been made of situational prevention. Issues of displacement, inconvenience and inequality need to be taken into account when planning and evaluating crime prevention projects. However, these potential problems should not be seen as inevitable and should not inhibit project managers and security managers from making the most of situational prevention techniques.

Opportunity Theories

Situational crime prevention is founded on the rational choice theory of crime. A key text here is Cornish and Clarke's (1986) edited book *The Reasoning Criminal: Rational Choice Perspectives on Offending*. Rational choice theory sits with a group of opportunity-based approaches to crime including 'environmental criminology' (concerned with the physical environment of crime), 'routine activity theory' and 'deterrence theory'. This perspective has considerable longevity but was boosted by scientific research in the 1970s (Clarke, 1997). In *The Reasoning Criminal*, Cornish and Clarke (1986) stated:

> The synthesis that we had suggested — a rational choice perspective on criminal behaviour — was intended to locate criminological findings within a framework particularly suitable for thinking about policy-relevant research. Its starting point was an assumption that offenders seek to benefit themselves by their criminal behaviour; that this involves the making of decisions and choices, however rudimentary on occasion these processes might be; and that these processes exhibit a measure of rationality, albeit constrained by limits of time and ability and the availability of relevant information. It was recognised that this conception of crime seemed to fit some forms of offending better than others. However, even in the case of offenses that seemed to be

> pathologically motivated or impulsively executed, it was felt that rational components were also often present and that the identification and description of these might have lessons for crime-control policy. (pp. 1–2)

Studies of offender decision-making were a major source of support for this approach. For example, interviews with persons who engaged in burglary to feed a drug habit showed they weighed different environmental cues about access and escape routes, what might be worth stealing inside premises, and the likelihood of different types of guardians being present (Macintyre, 2001). The role of rational decision making in crime was also supported by studies of the types of locations of crimes, the targets of crime, and times of the day or the week when offences occurred — all indicating that crime is rarely random and that offenders avoid detection and seek to minimise effort and maximise rewards (Clarke, 1997; Cornish & Clarke, 1986). Further support was provided by studies which observed how ordinary people often broke rules in situations where they were tempted to cheat or commit a crime and thought they would not be observed or identified (Gabor, 1994).

Some elements of rational choice theory can be seen in the 'classical' school of criminological thought developed in Enlightenment Europe in the 17th and 18th centuries (Curran & Renzetti, 2001, chapter 1). This approach set itself against the brutal punishments of the time, arguing they were not only inhumane but ineffective. Instead, reformers believed that the right combination of 'severity, certainty and swiftness' of punishment would deter would-be criminals, most of whom engaged in a cost–benefit analysis of the risks and potential rewards entailed in criminal conduct. The problem with this approach was that it put too much faith in the criminal justice system to ensure 'certainty and swiftness'.

Rational choice differs from classical theory in identifying the more complex conditions under which offenders will decide to act. This includes a focus on perceptions of the probability of apprehension. A key element here is observability. For example, Clarke (1997, p. 6) refers to studies in the 1920s showing children were more likely to be dishonest when they were subject to less supervision, and that property crime rates were higher during winter when there was more cover provided by longer hours of darkness. Traffic law enforcement provides a good example of the idea of modifying an environment to change human perceptions and the opportunity structure for crime (Bates, Soole, & Watson, 2012). Random speed testing and random breath testing are designed to make drivers feel that noncompliance could be detected at any time. However, rational choice theorists are also interested in the ways in which environmental changes can simply make it more difficult or impossible to break the law. Examples from traffic law enforcement include speed bumps, bollards and barriers that force drivers to slow down or stop drivers entering prohibited areas. Ignition immobilisers or vehicle confiscation can also be applied to repeat offenders who are unresponsive to increases in the likelihood of detection and punishment.

Rational choice theory was developed at a time when criminology was dominated by sociological theories of crime focused on inequality and poverty (Curran & Renzetti, 2001, chapter 4). Equality of opportunity and the redistribution of wealth were seen as the solutions to the crime problem. However, crime rates escalated despite post-war prosperity and the rise of the welfare state. Anti-crime programs, focused on reducing poverty and improving social capital, were poorly managed and largely ineffective. Crime also continued to rise despite the preferences of many governments for more police and tougher sanctions. Imprisonment and offender rehabilitation programs also appeared to be ineffective, prompting the promulgation of a 'nothing works' thesis in criminal justice (Martinson, 1974).

The intersection of rising crime rates and failed crime policies provided the setting for the development of routine activity theory. Cohen and Felson's (1979) groundbreaking article, 'Social Change and Crime Rate Trends: A Routine Activity Approach', published in *The American Sociological Review*, correlated increasing crime rates with increasing freedom and the availability of consumer goods. The researchers highlighted the proliferation of opportunities for crime, famously asserting that (Cohen & Felson, 1979, p. 589):

> Structural changes in routine activity patterns can influence crime rates by affecting the convergence in space and time of the three minimal elements of direct-contact predatory violations:
>
> 1. motivated offenders,
> 2. suitable targets, and
> 3. the absence of capable guardians against a violation.

The long post-war economic boom generated enormous increases in the number of lightweight, high-value, easily transportable goods that could be stolen. There was much more cash in circulation and more valuables in the possession of more people. The rapid growth in motor vehicle ownership created a major new target for thieves and a means of accessing targets and escaping crime scenes. In addition, more people worked away from home during the day, including increasing numbers of women; while workplaces were abandoned at night in the commute back to the suburbs. People also went out more and travelled more, exposing themselves to robbery and assault. There were more people living alone who were more vulnerable to burglary, robbery and assaults.

This separation of guardians from targets was a key factor in the escalating crime problem. In many countries, crimes reported to police increased three- and four-fold between the 1960s and 1990s (Van Dijk, 2008, 2012). In Australia, between 1973/74 and 1995/96, the total volume of crime reported to police increased by 121% as a rate per 100,000 population, while violent crime increased by 373% (Makkai & Prenzler, 2012, p. 56). The crisis in crime prompted numerous calls for more police and more punitive sentencing, and these calls were reflected in a general trend towards increased police-population ratios and harsher sentences (Pratt, 2005). Public policing was 'a seemingly forever growing industry' (Silvestri, 2012, p. 3)

Rational choice and routine activity theories challenged the police monopoly on crime control. Analysis of crime opportunities highlighted the extremely limited capacity of police to provide a preventive presence or an effective interdiction through rapid responses to crimes in progress. Felson (1998) estimated the extent of police coverage of premises in Los Angeles County if patrol officers were deployed to capacity. He concluded that this would give each location 15 seconds of protection in 24 hours. Doubling the number of police would therefore provide 30 seconds of protection: 'like putting two drops in a bucket instead of one' (p. 9).

Opportunity theories also showed how many businesses and organisations exposed themselves to crime. Walker (1994, p. 17), for example, described how retail stores 'almost invite shoplifting' with wide access, minimal staffing and open display of products. Felson described how many modern schools 'produce' crime by poor building design, poor student-to-teacher ratios and poor supervision (1998, p. 97). Manufacturers produced goods with little regard for their security, making crime prevention the responsibility of consumers who lack the means to protect their purchases.

Analysis of the factors that make a 'suitable target' assisted in understanding crime rates in greater depth than was permissible through the reporting of aggregate data. For example, crime rates across nations and jurisdictions are inflated by multiple offences committed against the same victims — including organisations and places as 'victims'. This phenomenon of repeat victimisation informed the concept of 'risky facilities'. Researchers such as Eck, Clarke, and Guerette (2007) focused on the concept of 'place management' as a major explanation for this phenomenon. Place managers can be responsible, often unconsciously, for management practices that are 'crime enablers' (Eck et al., 2007):

> The concentration of crime at a few facilities can seldom be dismissed as a random fluke or 'just a lot of targets' or active offenders … Comparing the way similar facilities with different crime levels are managed can test crime enabling. If compared to low crime facilities, the high crime locations have fewer rules, lax enforcement, easy access, poor security, and other features that help offenders detect targets, commit crimes, and get away … If the high crime facilities have many targets or more highly desirable targets (either hot

products or repeat victims) compared to low crime facilities, but managers do little to enhance target protection, this also suggests place management is at the heart of the problem (p. 240).

Research has identified many dramatic cases of repeat victimisation. Eck et al. (2007) cited examples such as motel crimes in Chula Vista, California, where 19% of local motels were responsible for 51% of calls to police; and shoplifting in Danvers, Connecticut, where 20% of stores were responsible for 85% of incidents. A United Kingdom (UK) study in Merseyside found that 43 schools were subject to eight or more burglaries in one year, and 57 retail/manufacturing facilities were subject to four or more burglaries (Bowers, Hirschfield, & Johnson, 1998). Repeat victimisation occurs in part because a successful crime will motivate offenders to return to the same location; often with a short time frame, such as a month (Bowers et al., 1998).

A useful way of picturing crime opportunities is with the 'crime triangle', developed by Clarke & Eck (2003), shown in Figure 1.1. The inner triangle summarises the three primary ingredients for crime: an offender, a target, and a place where the crime occurs. The outer triangle shows key human agents who can facilitate or inhibit crime by their actions. A 'manager', as we saw earlier, has responsibility for conduct in a specific location, 'such as a bus conductor or teacher at a school' (Clarke & Eck, p. 27). A 'handler' is someone who has a relationship with a potential offender and can exercise some control or influence over their behaviour. Handlers include teachers, parents and friends. 'Capable guardians' are 'usually people protecting their own belongings' or those of other people (p. 26).

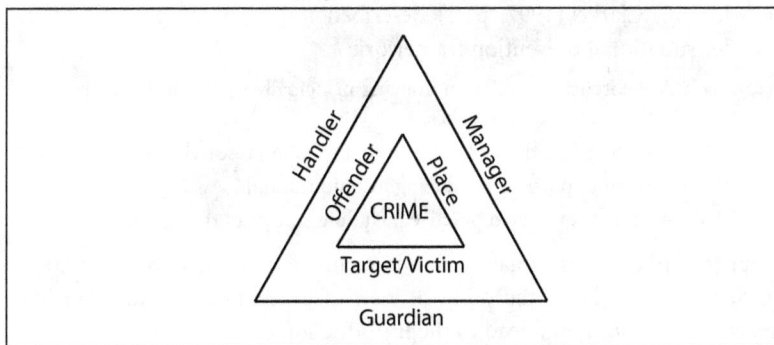

Figure 1.1
The crime triangle. Source: Clarke & Eck, 2003, p. 27. (Used with permission.)

Situational Crime Prevention

Opportunity theories focused on the role of situational factors in crime causation and led to the development of the idea of situational interventions to prevent crime. The key text here is *Situational Crime Prevention: Successful Case Studies* (Clarke, 1997), first published in 1992. Clarke's introduction is arguably the most important manifesto in the science of crime prevention. Following the themes developed above in relation to opportunity theories, Clarke (1997) stated:

> Situational crime prevention departs radically from most criminology in its orientation ... proceeding from an analysis of the circumstances giving rise to specific types of crime, it introduces discrete managerial and environmental change to reduce the opportunities for those crimes to occur. Thus it is focused on the settings for crime, rather than upon those committing criminal acts. It seeks to forestall the occurrence of crime, rather than to detect and sanction offenders. It seeks not to eliminate criminal or delinquent tendencies through improvement of society or its institutions, but merely to make criminal action less attractive to offenders. Central to this enterprise is not the criminal justice system, but a host of public and private organisations and agencies — schools, hospitals, transit systems, shops and malls, manufacturing businesses and phone companies, local parks and entertainment facilities, pubs and parking lots — whose products, services and operations spawn opportunities for a vast range of different crimes. (p. 2)

More specifically, Clarke (1997) defined situational crime prevention as follows:

> Situational prevention comprises opportunity-reducing measures that (1) are directed at highly specific forms of crime, (2) involve the management, design or manipulation of the immediate environment in as systematic and permanent way as possible, (3) make crime more difficult and risky, or less rewarding and excusable as judged by a wide range of offenders. (p. 4)

In addition, Clarke (1997. p. 6) described four key components of the broader situational prevention framework:

1. A theoretical foundation drawing principally upon routine activity and rational choice approaches,
2. A standard methodology based on the action research paradigm,
3. A set of opportunity-reducing techniques, and
4. A body of evaluated practice including studies of displacement.

Opportunity theories explain crime in terms of a calculation about effort, risk and reward. From the point of view of prevention, a routine activity analysis of crime should lead to the introduction of 'routine precautions' to prevent crime (Felson, 1998, p. 139). This can involve simple and obvious actions by individuals, such as locking doors, keeping wallets out of reach of thieves, and avoiding dangerous areas. Routine precautions can also be adopted in a more systematic fashion by organisations, through the application of regular security risk assessments, security management interventions, and system tests (see chapter 6).

Situational prevention is focused on fitting interventions to specific circumstances, and this can only be determined through primary research. The 'action research' component refers to practical problem solving and practitioner-researcher collaboration, with the involvement of stakeholders in the applied research process. Clarke (1997, p. 15) sets out five stages required for the implementation of a situational prevention project:

1. Collection of data about the nature and dimensions of the specific crime problem.
2. Analysis of the situational conditions that permit or facilitate the commission of the crime in question.
3. Systematic study of possible means of blocking opportunities for these particular crimes, including analysis of costs.
4. Implementation of the most promising, feasible and economic measures.
5. Monitoring of results and dissemination of experience.

Monitoring should attempt to include all crime-related incidents pre- and post- intervention, stakeholder experiences and opinions, and financial costs. In a model project, the classic scientific method is followed with a matching control group to ensure changes in the experimental group are not wrongly attributed to the interventions. This is not always possible however. A number of instructive crime prevention case studies are 'natural experiments', where authorities make changes outside a scientific paradigm. In these cases, an association between interventions and outcomes can still be identified with good incident data and the presence of post hoc 'controls' that review possible alternative explanations for project outcomes (Clarke, 1997, p. 35).

Finally, the 'set of opportunity-reducing techniques' is summarised in Table 1.1., with 25 techniques grouped under five major strategic areas: 'Increase the effort', 'Increase the risks', 'Reduce the rewards', 'Reduce provocations' and 'Remove excuses'. These approaches can also be structured in terms of a hierarchy of 'hard' and 'soft' approaches. Harder methods involve various forms of 'target hardening', denial of access, and threats of arrest and punishment. Examples include locks, fences, barriers, street closures, security guards and police. Softer approaches 'assist compliance' by communicating rules, reducing frustration, and making it easy for people to obey the rules. Examples include:

- providing entertainment when people are queuing reduces irritability and conflict
- providing food and entertainment at licensed premises reduces boredom, intoxication and the likelihood of violence

Increase the Effort	Increase the Risks	Reduce the Rewards	Reduce Provocations	Remove Excuses
1. Target harden • Steering column locks and immobilisers • Anti-robbery screens • Tamper-proof packaging	6. Extend guardianship • Take routine precautions: go out in group at night, leave signs of occupancy, carry phone • "Cocoon" neighborhood watch	11. Conceal targets • Off-street parking • Gender-neutral phone directories • Unmarked bullion trucks	16. Reduce frustrations and stress • Efficient queues and polite service • Expanded seating • Soothing music/muted lights	21. Set rules • Rental agreements • Harassment codes • Hotel registration
2. Control access to facilities • Entry phones • Electronic card access • Baggage screening	7. Assist natural surveillance • Improved street lighting • Defensible space design • Support whistleblowers	12. Remove targets • Removable car radio • Women's refuges • Pre-paid cards for pay phones	17. Avoid disputes • Separate enclosures for rival soccer fans • Reduce crowding in pubs • Fixed cab fares	22. Post instructions • "No Parking" • "Private Property" • "Extinguish camp fires"
3. Screen exits • Ticket needed for exit • Export documents • Electronic merchandise tags	8. Reduce anonymity • Taxi driver IDs • "How's my driving?" decals • School uniforms	13. Identify property • Property marking • Vehicle licensing and parts marking • Cattle branding	18. Reduce emotional arousal • Controls on violent pornography • Enforce good behavior on soccer field • Prohibit racial slurs	23. Alert conscience • Roadside speed display boards • Signatures for customs declarations • "Shoplifting is stealing"
4. Deflect offenders • Street closures • Separate bathrooms for women • Disperse pubs	9. Utilize place managers • CCTV for double-deck buses • Two clerks for convenience stores • Reward vigilance	14. Disrupt markets • Monitor pawn shops • Controls on classified ads. • License street vendors	19. Neutralize peer pressure • "idiots drink and drive" • "It's OK to say No" • Disperse troublemakers at school	24. Assist compliance • Easy library checkout • Public lavatories • Litter bins
5. Control tools/weapons • "Smart" guns • Disabling stolen cell phones • Restrict spray paint sales to juveniles	10. Strengthen formal surveillance • Red light cameras • Burglar alarms • Security guards	15. Deny benefits • Ink merchandise tags • Graffiti cleaning • Speed humps	20. Discourage imitation • Rapid repair of vandalism • V-chips in TVs • Censor details of modus operandi	25. Control drugs and alcohol • Breathalyzers in pubs • Server intervention • Alcohol-free events

Figure 1.2
Twenty five techniques of situational prevention.
Source: Center for Problem-Oriented Policing (2013). (Used with permission.)

- visible, accessible, free public toilets help prevent public urination
- the availability of rubbish bins helps prevent littering

- frequent and clear speed limit signs help prevent inadvertent speeding and remind wilful speedsters of the law and their obligations.

Intermediate measures include denial of benefits, deflecting offenders, natural surveillance and informal guardianship.

Applications: Intervention Projects

Perhaps the greatest strength of situational crime prevention lies in its expanding 'body of evaluated practice'. The second edition of *Situational Crime Prevention: Successful Case Studies* included 23 studies where opportunity-based analyses of crime problems led to the successful introduction of situational interventions. A number of these cases are described in various amounts of depth in following chapters of this book. Below are brief summaries of three of Clarke's (1997) case studies.

- In the United States (US) at Gainesville, Florida, convenience store robberies were reduced by 81% from 97 in 1986 to a low of 18 in 1990 (Hunter & Jeffery, 1997). A key intervention legislated by the city council was that stores which opened between 8 pm and 4 am had to have two clerks on duty. It is likely that this improved guardianship was supported by strategies that included lighting in car parks, cash minimisation, and improved visibility into stores and within stores.
- In the UK in the early 1980s, the Finsbury Park area of London experienced a significant problem with street prostitution; 'curb crawling' by male customers; and associated problems of disorder, harassment, crime and traffic congestion. In 1983, 666 women were arrested for solicitation in an intensified crackdown. Pimps and brothel keepers were also arrested. This appeared to reduce the problem, although previous experience indicated the effects of police crackdowns were not sustainable. A series of meetings between police, local residents and the local authority led to agreement on modifications to a traffic management plan that would limit access to the area. In 1985, the introduction of restricted access through road closures led to 'a remarkable transformation ... Soliciting and curb-crawling virtually disappeared, and the area was transformed from a noisy and hazardous "red-light" district into a relatively tranquil residential area', with no evidence of displacement (Matthews, 1997, p. 78). The overall crime rate fell by 42% in one year.
- Another US study by DiLonardo (1997) measured the impact of electronic article surveillance (EAS) by comparing inventory shortage rates. In the apparel sections of eight stores without EAS, losses increased 30% over 5 years. In stores that installed EAS, losses decreased by 17%. In a separate 9-year study with one store, in one year losses fell from 7.0% to

1.4% following the installation of EAS. The system was then removed and losses went up to 7.7%. Reinstallation resulted in an immediate fall to 2.9%. The 7.7% loss was put at US$616,000 and the 2.9% loss put at US$238,000 — a difference of US$378,000. EAS installation was costed at $105,000, which allowed for a substantial overall saving of US$273,000.

It is clear from these examples that situational crime prevention techniques are highly adaptive. Other diverse examples of effective situational crime prevention include:

- In Greater Manchester, UK, in the early 2000s, concerns about automatic teller machine (ATM)-related crime led to a scheme in which a small 'personal space zone' was painted on the ground around selected machines. Robbery around the experimental sites declined by 66% from an average of 27 in the 6 months pre-intervention down to 9.2 in the 6 months post-intervention (Holt & Spencer, 2005).

- In the early 1990s, following increases in ATM-related robberies, city councils in Los Angeles and New York legislated security standards that included lighting, 'safety reminders' to customers, and warnings about security measures (Guerette & Clarke, 2003). Additional modifications included transparent windows, reduced vegetation, cameras and mirrors. Over an 8-year period in New York, ATM robberies declined by 78% from 380, in the peak year, to 82. In Los Angeles, robberies declined by 88% from 152 to 18.

- In 1999, the Australian welfare distributor Centrelink began assigning covert video surveillance of suspected fraud cases to private investigation firms. In the first year of operation, 1,063 cases were completed, with 70% leading to A$3.9 million targeted for recovery. In 2008/09, 1,023 surveillance operations were completed, with 589 or 57.5% considered 'actionable', leading to annualised gross reductions in payments of $5.5 million and debt of A$21.2 million (Sarre & Prenzler, 2011, p. 97). Analysis indicated that for every dollar spent on the program, Centrelink saved A$27 in losses.

- In Australia, between 1981 and 1996, there were 13 mass shootings involving five or more victims, with a total of 104 victims killed (Chapman, Alpers, Agho, & Jones, 2006). Following the 1996 Port Arthur massacre, in which 35 people were killed, in an example of 'controlling tools/weapons', the National Firearms Agreement legislated tight restrictions on gun ownership, including prohibitions on automatic and semi-automatic weapons. More than 700,000 weapons were destroyed, largely through a buy back scheme. Chapman et al. (2006) found that in the 10.5 years after the agreement was introduced, up to late-2006, there were no mass shootings. In the

US, with very few restrictions on gun ownership, in the 10-year period 1997 to 2006, there were 17 mass shootings involving five or more victims, with 121 fatalities (Follman, Aronsen, & Pan, 2012).

Related Approaches

Situational crime prevention overlaps with a number of other approaches to crime reduction. Three of these are outlined briefly below.

Crime Prevention Through Environmental Design

Crime prevention through environmental design (CPTED) is a form of situational prevention focused on physical settings. The CPTED method is concerned with designing open malls, parks, streets, buildings, entrances and rooms in ways that facilitate 'defensible space' and 'territoriality'. Key texts include C. Ray Jeffery's (1971) *Crime Prevention Through Environmental Design*, and Oscar Newman's (1972) *Defensible Space: Crime Prevention Through Urban Design*. CPTED is the subject of the next chapter in this book.

Problem-Oriented Policing and Problem-Oriented Partnership Policing

Problem-oriented policing (POP) was developed by Herman Goldstein and articulated in a 1979 article 'Improving Policing: A Problem-Oriented Approach', in the journal *Crime and Delinquency*, and a 1990 book *Problem-Oriented Policing*. Like 'community policing', POP involves police adopting a consultative approach to solving crime-related community problems, rather than simply reacting to crime by attempting to arrest offenders. POP advocated an information-driven approach, and the process aspects of situational crime prevention can be seen in the police problem-solving 'scan, analyse, respond, assess' model (SARA model; Eck & Spelman, 1987). The importance of partnerships with groups outside police led to the term 'problem-oriented and partnership policing' (POPP).

Crime Mapping

Computer-aided crime mapping is useful to show graphically how crime patterns occur across space and time; including stable, fluctuating and evolving patterns (Anselin, Griffiths, & Tita, 2011). Situational crime prevention operates on the assumption that the more crime is concentrated at particular times or places, the more amenable it is to effective interventions. 'Hot spot analysis' is a related term that targets highly concentrated areas of crime.

Product Design Against Crime

There is work focused on building crime prevention features into products (Ekblom, 2011). Examples include fixed hanger tops in hotel wardrobes that prevent full removal and pilfering of hangers, wetsuit pockets for car keys, nonreusable syringes preventing sharing of needles, backpacks made from cut-resistant materials, table hooks for handbags at cafés and restaurants, and personal identity number (PIN) access to mobile phones and computers.

Crime Prevention and the Security Industry

Situational crime prevention drew in part on established security management techniques, and it informed advances in security management (see chapter 6). The work of Clarke and other pioneers of situational prevention acknowledged the role of security providers — both private and public sector — in contributing to successful crime reduction interventions through guardianship, surveillance and place management. A range of associated professions have also contributed to successful crime reduction initiatives, including police, architects, town planners and product designers, business and facilities managers, business and resident associations, and crime prevention project managers. More recently, information technology (IT) security specialists have become essential to defending against computer-based crime. Partnerships between members of these groups have been particularly important for maximising yields in crime prevention projects (see chapters 4 and 5).

The impact of the security industry is increasingly evident in national and international crime data. The situational crime prevention literature consists largely of discrete case studies — consistent with the recommended approach — focused on specific locations or types of crime. In the 1990s, there were few studies available that included national or international data. Some notable exceptions included the work of Webb (1994), showing the benefits of steering column locks on motor vehicle theft; and fraud reduction initiatives in Sweden (see chapter 5). A number of national crime experience surveys also correlated burglary rates with home security devices — mainly 'target hardening' devices such as door and window locks and security grills. These data indicated that the presence of security measures accounted for lower rates of attempted and successful burglaries (Van Dijk, 2008).

Property crime rates began to fall consistently in many countries from the late-1980s into the 1990s; followed by smaller falls in violent crimes around the turn of the century (Van Dijk, 2008, 2012). Falls in crimes reported to police were reflected in crime experience surveys. A variety of theories were put forward to explain these trends, including economic theories and theories related to improved policing and greater imprisonment. From a global perspective, Van Dijk (2012) argued that the trends appeared to operate largely independently of economic cycles, police innovations, and imprisonment rates. While changes in policing and imprisonment may have relevance in some locations (e.g., the alleged 80% crime drop in New York City [Zimring, 2012]), they do not provide an explanation for crime trends at the global level. The most likely explanation is the growth of situationally-based 'self-protection' measures and 'responsive securitization'. In Van Dijk's words (2012):

> Investments in self-protection have since the 1970s been a mass phenomenon, impacting on almost all aspects of society. A prime example is the huge increases in private security guards and alarm centres ... But responsive securitization is not limited to human surveillance by security guards. Measures to prevent crime have become ubiquitous in all corners of modern society. Harnessing new technology, security provisions have been built into homes, cars, stores and parking lots, public transport and public/social housing, schools and hospitals, offices and other work places, entertainment venues and sports stadiums, airports and seaports, and to warehouses and transportation terminals. (p. 11)

The Security Gap

Despite the idea that security is pervasive in modern society, research indicates that many businesses and households lack adequate protection. Business crime surveys in the 1990s highlighted low rates of adoption of security measures (Bowers, 2001; Van Dijk, 1997). As we saw, there has been a long-term trend towards more security, but significant vulnerabilities often remain. A fairly recent British Chambers of Commerce (2008) survey found that 44% of respondents had never sought advice about how to reduce crime (p. 20). Research has also shown that businesses typically upgrade security or obtain security advice only after being victimised, and that insurance against losses is generally inadequate (Prenzler, 2009).

In Australia, there have been a number of surveys that include questions about the use of security devices. A survey of Australian businesses in the mid 1990s found a low uptake of security. Only 47% of respondents had spent money on crime prevention. Of these, 47% invested in 'special lighting', 43% in 'after-hours security', 41% in 'window protection' and 36% on 'alarm systems' (Australian Institute of Criminology [AIC], 2002, p. 48). A 1999 survey in New South Wales found that only 47% of dwellings could properly secure all entry points (Australian Bureau of Statistics [ABS], 2000, p. 5). Significantly, 'lone parent households and persons living alone' were the household types least likely to live in a dwelling in which all entrances could be secured' (ABS, p. 3). A survey in Western Australia in 2004 found that only 42% of households had deadlocks and 45% had security screens on all external doors (ABS, 2005, p. 4). Rented dwellings generally had lower levels of security.

Issues

It seems that few innovations are introduced without complications and controversy. Situational crime prevention has its share of detractors and potential pitfalls and drawbacks that need to be taken seriously. The following subsections briefly analyse these issues and provide some rejoinders and possible solutions.

Displacement

Displacement presents as a major potential problem with situationally-based interventions. Making crime more difficult in one place may simply drive offenders to nearby areas or other types of crime. Displacement makes situational interventions unfair as well as unproductive from a wider social perspective. Research has shown that displacement can occur in some cases (Clarke, 1997). However, it is more often the case that there is no evidence of displacement — as offenders are often limited in their scope and easily discouraged from further attempts at crime. Research has also shown the existence of a 'multiplier' or 'halo effect' in some cases, where the crime reduction effects of interventions are extended to neighbouring areas due to the broader deterrent effect on would-be offenders (Van Dijk, 2012, p. 17).

An Inconvenient Fortress Society?

Another partially valid concern is that situational crime prevention entails, at best, annoying and inconvenient security devices and, at worst, a 'fortress society' of high walls, barbed wire, omnipresent closed-circuit television (CCTV) and vicious guard dogs (Clarke, 1997, p. 37). It is true that many manifestations of crime prevention can be annoying, frustrating, ugly, and even threatening and oppressive. However, other security innovations, such as entry-phone systems and transparent fencing, can be unobtrusive and enhance convenience. In residential complexes, CPTED principles, discussed in the next chapter, emphasise the importance of aesthetics and convenience in developing territoriality, 'image' and manageable spaces that create crime-prevention outcomes from an improved sense of community.

Inequality

Situational crime prevention has also been criticised for failing to address the deep causes of crime in social inequality, poverty and unemployment (Clarke, 1997). It is probably true to say that statements about the focus of situational crime prevention sometimes appear to exclude other crime prevention methods. However, early childhood interventions aimed at improving family integration, school performance and social capital can generate large reductions in crime; and some offender rehabilitation and management programs have also shown significant reductions in reoffending rates (see chapter 3). The obvious point must be that crime is multi-dimensional and needs to be addressed from a variety of directions. The many successes of situational prevention underscore the large contribution it can make within a broad approach. Situational interventions are particularly suitable for agents that have a mission for crime prevention but face challenges in changing dispositional factors in the offender population. A store owner can do little about the long-range motivations of shoplifters and burglars, but they can do a lot to prevent crime on their premises.

Of course, a major benefit of successful situational interventions is that they reduce the demand on the public justice system. Primary prevention also reduces the negative experiences of potential offenders (and their families) with the criminal justice system. Van Dijk (2012) has emphasised the role of security in preventing the escalation of crime and the development of criminal careers. This includes a social justice outcome for potential offenders as well as victims. Car theft and burglary, for example, often serve as 'stepping stones' to more serious crimes for young males (Van Dijk, 2012, p. 17). The idea that relatively minor crimes like joy riding in stolen vehicles and domestic burglary are the entree to more serious crimes and criminal careers is a commonplace of criminology. However, what has received much less attention is the fact that the prevention of these crimes can steer young people away from a criminal lifestyle. Property crime prevention by security services therefore has an often unacknowledged role in preventing more serious property crimes, and also preventing crimes of violence such as robbery and armed robbery.

The cost of security can entail significant disadvantage. However, governments can address the problem of capacity to pay through subsidised security, as well as security in government housing, public transport, public hospitals and public schools. Van Dijk has emphasised the widening gap worldwide between victimisation of the rich and poor relative to their ability to afford security, with little or no prospect of the public police bridging the gap (Van Dijk, 2012):

> The results of the International Crime Victim Survey show that across twelve Western nations the lowest income groups have stepped up their household security to a lesser extent than the middle and upper classes. They cannot afford to ... The survey also shows that the lowest quartile have benefitted less from the falls in burglary victimisation than the rest of the population. (p. 17)

With this phenomenon in mind, Van Dijk (2012, p.17) argues that 'situational crime prevention is not just a matter of efficiency. It is also a matter of social justice'.

Conclusion

This chapter has outlined the main claims of situational crime prevention to generate large reductions in a wide range of crimes. The benefits for prevention of an opportunity perspective on crime are developed in more detail in the following chapters of this book. It should be clear from the evidence presented so far that situational crime prevention has a great deal of untapped potential. A multipronged attack on crime — developmental, social, criminal justice and situational — has the potential to make enormous inroads into the large problem of criminal victimisation in modern society.

References

Australian Bureau of Statistics. (2000). *Home security precautions, New South Wales.* Canberra, Australia: Author.

Australian Bureau of Statistics. (2005). *Home safety and security, Western Australia.* Canberra, Australia: Author.

Anselin, L., Griffiths, E., & Tita, G. (2011). Crime mapping and hot spot analysis. In R. Wortley & L. Mazerolle (Eds.), *Environmental criminology and crime analysis* (pp. 97–116). Abingdon, England: Routledge.

Australian Institute of Criminology. (2002). *Crimes against business: A Review of victimisation, predictors and prevention.* Canberra, Australia: Author.

Bates, L., Soole, D., & Watson, B. (2012). The effectiveness of traffic policing in reducing traffic crashes. In T. Prenzler (Ed.), *Policing and security in practice* (pp. 90–109). Houndmills Basingstoke, England: Palgrave-Macmillan.

Bowers, K. (2001). Small business crime: The evaluation of a crime prevention initiative. *Crime Prevention and Community Safety: An International Journal, 3*(1), 23–42.

Bowers, K., Hirschfield, A., & Johnson, S. (1998). Victimization revisited: A case study of non-residential repeat burglary on Merseyside. *British Journal of Criminology, 39,* 429–452.

British Chambers of Commerce. (2008). *The invisible crime: A business crime survey.* London.

Center for Problem-Oriented Policing. (2013). *Twenty five techniques of situational prevention.* Retrieved from http://www.popcenter.org/25techniques/

Chapman, S., Alpers, P., Agho, K., & Jones, M. (2006). Australia's 1996 gun law reforms: Faster falls in firearm deaths, firearm suicides, and a decade without mass shootings. *Injury Prevention, 12,* 365–372.

Clarke, R.V. (Ed.). (1997). *Situational crime prevention: Successful case studies.* Guilderland, NY: Harrow and Heston.

Clarke, R.V., & Eck, J. (2003). *Become a problem solving crime analysis in 55 small steps.* London, England: Jill Dando Institute for Crime Science, University College London.

Cohen, L., & Felson, M. (1979, August). Social change and crime rate trends: A Routine activity approach. *American Sociological Review, 44,* 588–608.

Cornish, D.B., & Clarke, R.V. (Eds.). (1986). *The reasoning criminal: Rational choice perspectives on offending.* New York, NY: Springer-Verlag.

Curran, D.J., & Renzetti, C.M. (2001) *Theories of crime.* Boston, MA: Allyn and Bacon.

DiLonardo, R.L. (1997). The economic benefit of electronic article surveillance. In R. Clarke (Ed.), *Situational crime prevention: Successful case studies* (pp. 74–82). Guilderland, NY: Harrow and Heston.

Eck, J., Clarke, R.V., & Guerette, R. (2007). Risky facilities: Crime concentration in homogenous sets of establishments and facilities. *Crime Prevention Studies, 21,* 225–264.

Eck, J., & Spelman, W. (1987). *Problem-solving: Problem-oriented policing in Newport News.* Washington, DC: National Institute of Justice.

Ekblom, P. (2011). Designing products against crime. In R. Wortley & L. Mazerolle (Eds.), *Environmental criminology and crime analysis* (pp. 195–220). Abingdon, England: Routledge.

Felson, M. (1994). *Crime and everyday life.* Thousand Oaks, CA: Pine Forge Press.

Felson, M. (1998). *Crime and everyday life.* Thousand Oaks, CA: Pine Forge Press.

Follman, M., Aronsen, G., & Pan, D. (2012). *US mass shootings, 1982–2012.* Data from Mother Jones' investigation. Retrieved from http://www.motherjones.com/politics/2012/12/mass-shootings-mother-jones-full-data.

Gabor, T. (1994). *Everybody does it! Crime by the public.* New York, NY: Macmillan.

Goldstein, H. (1979). Improving policing: A Problem-oriented approach. *Crime and Delinquency, 24,* 236–258.

Goldstein, H. (1990). *Problem-oriented policing.* New York, NY: McGraw-Hill.

Guerette, R., & Clarke, R. (2003). Product life cycles and crime: Automated teller machines and robbery. *Security Journal, 16,* 7–18.

Holt, T., & Spencer, J. (2005). Little yellow box: The targeting of automatic teller machines as a strategy in reducing street robbery. *Crime Prevention and Community Safety: An International Journal, 7,* 15–28

Hunter, R.D., & Jeffery, C.R. (1997). Preventing convenience store robbery through environmental design. In R. Clarke (Ed.), *Situational crime prevention: Successful case studies* (pp. 191–199). Guilderland, NY: Harrow and Heston.

Jeffery, C.R. (1971). Crime prevention through environmental design. Beverly Hills, CA: Sage.

Macintyre, S.D. (2001). *Burglar decision making*. (Doctoral dissertation). School of Criminology and Criminal Justice, Griffith University, Brisbane, Australia.

Makkai, T., & Prenzler, T. (2012). The nature and prevalence of crime. In H. Hayes & T. Prenzler (Eds.), *An introduction to crime and criminology* (pp. 52–70). Sydney, Australia: Pearson.

Martinson, R. (1974). What works? — Questions and answers about prison reform. *The Public Interest, 35*, 22–54.

Matthews, R. (1997). Developing more effective strategies for curbing prostitution. In R. Clarke (Ed.), *Situational crime prevention: Successful case studies* (pp. 74–82). Guilderland, NY: Harrow and Heston.

Newman, O. (1972). *Defensible space: Crime prevention through urban design*. New York, NY: Macmillan.

Pratt, J. (Ed.). (2005). *The new punitiveness: Trends, theories and perspectives*. Cullompton, England: Willan.

Prenzler, T. (2009). *Preventing burglary in commercial and institutional settings: A place management and partnerships approach*. Washington, DC: ASIS Foundation.

Sarre, R., & Prenzler, T. (2011). *Private security and public interest: Exploring private security trends and directions for reform in the new era of plural policing. Report for the Australian Research Council*. Adelaide: University of South Australia.

Silvestri, A. (2012). Austerity, spending cuts and the 'frontline'. In A. Silvestri (Ed.), *Critical reflections: Social and criminal justice in the first year of the collation government* (p. 12). London, England: Centre for Crime and Justice Studies.

Van Dijk, J. (1997). Towards effective public-private partnerships in crime control: Experiences in the Netherlands. In M. Felson & R.V. Clarke (Eds.), *Business and crime prevention* (pp. 97–124). Monsey, NY: Criminal Justice Press.

Van Dijk, J. (2008). The world of crime. Thousand Oaks, CA: Sage.

Van Dijk, J. (2012, June). *Closing the doors*. Stockholm prizewinners lecture 2012. Paper presented at the Stockholm Criminology Symposium, Stockholm.

Walker, J. (1994) Trends in crime and criminal justice. In D. Chappell & P. Wilson (Eds.), *The Australian criminal justice system: The mid 1990s* (pp. 1–36). Sydney, Australia: Butterworth-Heinemann.

Webb, B. (1994). Steering column locks and motor vehicle theft: Evaluations from three countries. *Crime Prevention Studies, 2*, 71–89.

Zimring, F.E. (2012). *The city that became safe: New York's lessons for urban crime and its control*. New York, NY: Oxford University Press.

Chapter 2

Crime Prevention Through Environmental Design: Evolution, Theory and Practice

Mateja Mihinjac and Danielle M. Reynald

This chapter provides a brief overview of the theoretical framework of crime prevention through environmental design, or CPTED (pronounced *sep-ted*). As a proactive situational crime prevention approach that relies on (manipulation of) physical design, CPTED strategies are aimed at minimising criminal opportunities while simultaneously enhancing opportunities for surveillance and crime detection. These strategies are not only focused on reducing victimisation at specific places, but also on minimising fear of crime at places. This chapter will sketch the evolution of CPTED, beginning by outlining the six core components that CPTED interventions rely on, and will highlight ways in which they overlap and reinforce each other. CPTED techniques do not rely exclusively on the physical environment, as they are aimed at increasing opportunities for place management and guardianship in order to maximise the potential for crime control at places. Despite some limitations and critiques related to its conceptual framework and implementation, the empirical literature demonstrates that CPTED techniques can be highly effective. This suggests the utility of situational approaches such as CPTED compared to generally more intrusive and traditionally offender-focused alternatives. Most significantly, we conclude that continued development of CPTED rests on the more explicit incorporation of place managers and guardians as primary users of the practical tools to maximise crime control, which CPTED provides.

Crime Prevention Through Environmental Design: Definition and Description

Crime prevention through environmental design (CPTED) is a place-based crime prevention approach that relies on manipulation of the physical environment in order to affect the behaviour of space users. This is based on the premise that it is easier to alter the environment than it is to change people, as this can have a strong indirect influence on people's behaviour (Jeffery, 1971). More specifically, CPTED focuses on encouraging the protection of potential victims, targets and target areas by using environmental design to increase opportunities for surveillance and effective management and control of places. By manipulating cues from the physical environment to discourage illegal and disruptive behaviours, while simultaneously promoting the intended use of space by legitimate users, CPTED has become a viable physical environment intervention (Lab, 2010; Schneider, 2010). With this in mind, CPTED rests on the core premise that 'the proper design and effective use of the built environment can lead to a reduction in the fear of crime and the incidence of crime, and to an improvement in the quality of life' (Crowe, 2000, p. 7).

There are two main crime control dimensions that CPTED makes use of: environment and design. While the *environment* dimension focuses on 'people and their physical and social surroundings', *design* is concerned with 'physical, social, management, and law enforcement directives' (Crowe, 2000, p. 35). The six core components that comprise CPTED (see Figure 2.1) are borne out of the unification of these two dimensions. These CPTED crime control techniques, which will be elaborated on later in this chapter, are:

1. natural surveillance
2. territorial reinforcement
3. natural access control
4. target hardening
5. activity support
6. space/image management.

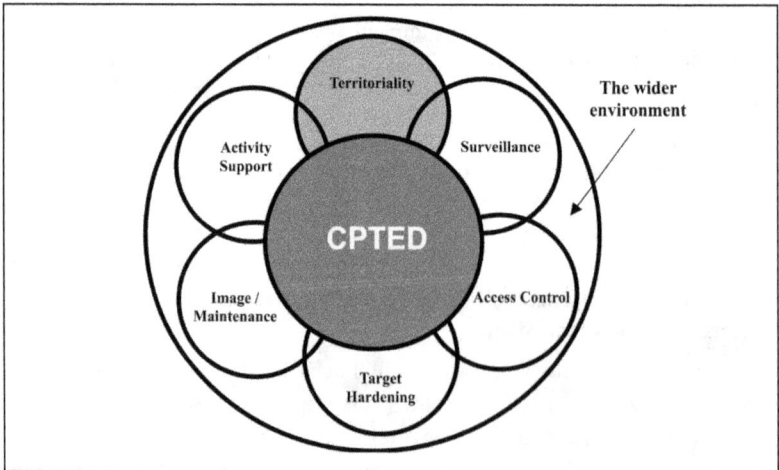

Figure 2.1
First-generation CPTED crime control techniques — key concepts.
Source: Adapted from Moffatt (1983, p. 23) in Cozens, Saville, & Hillier (2005, p. 330).

CPTED is not only concerned with physical settings, but requires a number of procedural considerations such as a well-designed and effectively implemented policy and political will. Managerial considerations are equally essential. These include the effective execution of context-specific interventions that are designed to promote the efficient management/maintenance of places and informal guardianship at places. Thus, CPTED relies not only on informal users, owners and managers of space, but also on policy makers and crime prevention practitioners to provide clear directives for implementing design principles that can create an environment conducive to legitimate behaviour while discouraging crime and related activity.

Crime Prevention Through Environmental Design and Situational Crime Prevention

CPTED falls under the umbrella of the situational crime prevention (SCP) approach. CPTED strategies are therefore designed to proactively control criminal opportunities and are rooted in the theoretical framework provided by the opportunity theories of crime (Felson & Clarke, 1998, p. 4): crime pattern (offender search) theory, the rational choice perspective and the routine activity approach (for more information on these theories see Chapter 1). Anchored in these theories, CPTED principles are based on the rationale of minimising criminal opportunities and enhancing opportunities for detection, which are inherent in the design and layout of the built environment. CPTED can thus be considered an SCP technique aimed at executing the crime prevention strategies of 'increasing the risks' of getting caught for offenders and 'increasing the effort' required for offenders to successfully commit crime (Clarke, 1997). CPTED principles are designed to affect these strategies at specific places through the manipulation of the design, materials and layout of buildings, streets etc. CPTED strategies can therefore be effective at both larger spaces (such as residential neighbourhoods or entertainment districts), and at more specific locations — such as houses, bars, school etc. (e.g., Armitage, Monchuk, & Rogerson, 2011; Cozens & Love, 2009; Schneider & Kitchen, 2007). A context-specific understanding of places, their dynamics, characteristics and crime patterns are (therefore) crucial for tailoring effective CPTED strategies at places in response to the specific crime problems at hand.

CPTED as a Multidisciplinary Approach

Another defining feature of CPTED as an SCP technique is that its principles draw on knowledge from multiple (related) disciplines. The environment and design dimensions of CPTED speak to these influences and provide an indication of the importance of physical environments and the usage of space. The main disciplines that CPTED draws on are described below.

Environmental criminology. The main focus of environmental criminology is on crime opportunity reduction through the manipulation of situational and physical characteristics of specific environments. This is achieved by incorporating the principles from the three aforementioned opportunity theories of crime that, together, explain (a) how offenders' search patterns are influenced by a physical setting (Brantingham & Brantingham, 1981); (b) how their decisions to offend are performed in relation to environmental cues and constraints when choosing a target (Cornish & Clarke, 1986); and (c) how the elements of place management and guardianship affect the evaluation of criminal opportunities (Cohen & Felson, 1979).

Urban studies and new urbanism. This discipline focuses on urban city designs and the infrastructure of cities for work, entertainment, movement, transportation and other activities, with the goal of making contemporary cities safe, sustainable and enjoyable (Australian Council for New Urbanism, 2006; Davey, Mackay, & Wootton, 2009; McMahon, 2012). Safety and sustainability of urban environments are often considered to be mutually exclusive (Davey et al., 2009). While enclosed street layouts are believed to promote safety, permeable designs that encourage free traffic flow are believed to provide increased criminal opportunities (Beavon, Brantingham, & Brantingham, 1994; Johnson & Bowers, 2010). Davey and colleagues (2009), however, concluded that through proper design, safety and sustainability can coexist.

Environmental psychology. Environmental psychology specifically draws on the 'environment-organism(mind)-behaviour' model of how we interact with and react to our immediate environments (Jeffery & Zahm, 1993, p. 339). This model focuses on how the environment can be designed in a way that influences information and decision-making, resulting in predictable behaviour and movement patterns. For example, the internal layout of nightclubs subconsciously affects movement patterns and can be designed specifically to direct the flow of patrons to prevent crowding and related aggression (Homel & Clark, 1995). Understanding the link between the design and behaviour is therefore crucial if behaviour is to be controlled through manipulation of the environment.

Key Crime Prevention Through Environmental Design Components: Techniques for Crime Prevention

Users of space, legitimate or illegitimate, are directly influenced by their immediate surroundings. CPTED aims to influence the behaviour of users through the six main interrelated principles that have the power to affect both crime and perceptions of safety. These were depicted in Figure 2.1. Although researchers draw on various conceptual frameworks, discussing as many as seven or eight interrelated concepts (Cozens et al., 2005; Ekblom, 2011; Moffatt, 1983) or as little as three (Crowe, 1991, 2000), the following six principles are the most consistently cited across the literature.

Surveillance

In his theory of defensible space, Newman (1972) defines natural surveillance as 'the capacity of physical design to provide surveillance opportunities for residents and their agents' (p. 78). Thus, this principle focuses on creating opportunities *to see* and *be seen*. Opportunities for natural surveillance can be created through the design of open layouts for places, and clear lines of sight by trimming trees and bushes that might conceal visibility, positioning windows and access points to properties overlooking public and semi-public spaces (Jacobs, 1961; Newman, 1972). These natural surveillance strategies aim to promote informal surveillance of places by relying on users of those places to either directly intervene or contact formal guardians such as the police, or place managers like security officers or others whose formal duty is to protect people and property they are responsible for.

Reynald's (2009, 2011) guardianship in action studies support the idea that lower property crime levels can be explained in part by enhanced opportunities for surveillance. These studies used real-life observations of surveillance opportunities at residential properties, as well as related features of territorial definition and image/maintenance of properties. These physical environment observations were compared with observed levels of active guardianship by residents (their availability, observed monitoring and interventions), as well as levels of property crime (Reynald, 2009). Unobstructed opportunities for natural surveillance in residential streets were associated with increased levels of active guardianship by residents and lower levels of property crime (see also Hollis-Peel, Reynald, van Bavel, Elffers, & Welsh, 2011; Hollis-Peel, Reynald, & Welsh, 2012).

With the development of private security, this natural surveillance principle has been extended to include organised and mechanical surveillance approaches (Welsh & Farrington, 2009), which encompass the allocation of security guards and CCTV installations. Such security management practices are most often implemented in business and commercial settings and at public events with frequent partnerships between private and public policing (Prenzler & Sarre, 1998).

The majority of recent studies evaluating the effectiveness of surveillance have predominantly focused on mechanical and technical forms of surveillance, including lighting and CCTV. These studies confirm that these forms of surveillance also promote a sense of safety. While lighting has the potential to increase use of space after dark (Farrington & Welsh, 2006; Painter & Farrington, 1997, 1999), CCTV is most effective at preventing crime in smaller settings (Ditton & Short, 1999; Welsh & Farrington, 2006).

Territoriality

This principle focuses on the control of places using place boundaries and clear signs of ownership. Territoriality has been defined as 'the capacity of the physical environment to create perceived zones of territorial influences' (Newman, 1972, p. 51). Newman (1972, 1996) argues that this makes places more easily 'defendable'. According to this principle, effective design should provide a clear demarcation of public, semi-public and private spaces. Several studies on residential properties confirm the importance of clear signs of ownership for the prevention of burglary (Brown & Altman, 1983; Brown & Bentley, 1993). In general, research has shown a common overreliance on 'hard' approaches including the use of high walls and fences, and gated communities that promote fortressing (e.g., Ellin, 1997). This may have a negative effect on natural surveillance opportunities (Newman, 1972; Reynald, 2009). Rather, more subtle approaches, such as symbolic barriers through material use or signage, have been found to be equally effective while simultaneously discouraging social exclusion and promoting informal guardianship (Blakely & Snyder, 1997; Ellin, 1997). Merry (1981) and Schneider (2010) also highlighted the importance of social factors and conditions for effective territorial influence, claiming that design is a 'necessary but not sufficient condition for crime prevention' (Merry, 1981, p. 420). They argued that community cohesion and community participation are important elements of manifesting territorial influence over places in order to mobilise the community and to avoid socially exclusive practices.

Access Control

This principle is designed to direct or restrict movement and access to places or facilities. Cozens et al. (2005, p. 335) explain that opportunities for crime can be reduced by 'denying access to potential targets and creating a heightened perception of risk in offenders'. Once again, by engaging the community to control access to places through informal surveillance, more subtle and favourable approaches to access control can be used where viable to avoid overreliance on hard approaches.

Such approaches have been tested on a neighbourhood level in which property crime was found to be higher in through streets with nonrestricted traffic flow compared to less permeable streets where traffic flow was reduced by designing one-way streets and cul-de-sacs while also encouraging community members to informally supervise their immediate surroundings (Armitage et al., 2011; Beavon et al., 1994; Johnson & Bowers, 2010). In addition to being used in larger spaces like neighbourhoods, access control can also be applied at smaller units of space, such as facilities. Access to commercial facilities, for instance, can be controlled through the use of technical approaches such as swipe card access, face recognition, fingerprint comparison, security alarms, and so on (Bowers, 1989).

Target Hardening

Similar to access control, this principle is concerned with restricting access to places, facilities or buildings through (typically) highly visible approaches such as locks, doors and hardened materials. While access control can operate at a broader place-based level, target hardening operates at a micro-target level. In fact, Cozens et al. (2005) have questioned whether target hardening should be included as a distinct principle under CPTED. Target hardening relies on a hard physical definition and is commonly criticised for promoting a 'fortress' mentality (Ellin, 1997, p. 40). In spite of this, target hardening approaches have been demonstrated to be beneficial under certain circumstances, such as in providing clear cues to burglars about accessibility of property targets (e.g., Cromwell, Olson, & Avary, 1991; Pease, 1991).

Activity Support

This is an underlying principle of effective space management and ensures that space will be managed so that desired activities can be supported and promoted while unwanted activities are discouraged (Cozens et al., 2005). This is often achieved by providing a combination of activities in the same area to encourage informal surveillance and, in turn, foster a sense of safety (Crowe, 2000). For example, placing an ATM or other cash handling facility so that it is juxtaposed with highly used spaces ensures that ATM users are overlooked by other users of space who can act as potential guardians. This can provide (a sense of) safety to users (Cozens et al., 2005). Similarly, entertainment districts mixed with shopping areas, or a children's play area in the vantage point of the cafes, can serve the same function. In essence, this principle relies on the strategic design of space and effective place management to create and maintain facilities that promote intended use while increasing opportunities for informal guardianship.

Image/Maintenance

This principle highlights the importance of ensuring that places are well maintained and manifest a positive image (Newman, 1972). According to this principle, place managers should ensure that any signs of damage or incivilities are eliminated so that the positive image of a place attracts legitimate users and discourages illegitimate ones. This positive image, in turn, motivates the community to engage with these spaces and use them as intended in order to maintain the positive image. This fosters a sense of ownership and in turn increases informal surveillance by encouraging people's presence. Moreover, by inspiring the community to maintain a positive image, social disorder can be reduced and community cohesion promoted (Crowe, 2000; Jacobs, 1961). For example, it has been demonstrated that regular maintenance of public transportation systems and removal of signs of incivilities promotes use of services and in turn reduces the negative perception of these facilities (Carr & Spring, 1993; Sloan-Howitt & Kelling, 1997). This principle is also supported by the 'broken windows theory' (Wilson & Kelling, 1982), which suggests that a positive image of space is an important characteristic for crime prevention as it also sends a message to potential offenders that a place is owned and well controlled.

The Evolution of Crime Prevention Through Environmental Design

The roots of contemporary CPTED can be traced back to Jane Jacobs and her concept of encouraging 'eyes upon the street' in order to increase surveillance and minimise crime through informal supervision (Jacobs, 1961, p. 45). Jacobs became a great proponent of more open cities, increased use of public space and mixed land use that would encourage a steady flow of activity throughout the day. Having knowledge of architecture and urban design, she also encouraged designs and layouts that would promote natural surveillance opportunities.

Following Jacobs was the work by American architect Oscar Newman who explicated the 'defensible space' theory as a means of making both private and shared communal spaces of residential environments safer (Newman, 1972, p. 3). Newman's theory was based on a study of crime levels in the increasingly popular high-rise, low-cost, public housing projects in urbanised cities of the US. In his New York City based study, he found that high-rise design was associated with higher crime levels than the low-rises, as the high-rises contained a greater proportion of areas that were undefended because they were lacking in clear ownership, such as hallways, elevators, stairwells and lobbies (Newman, 1972). He concluded that these undefended areas should be avoided in favour of creating more defensible residential spaces. Such residential areas and their uses, he maintained, could be protected from crime and related activity through the incorporation of natural surveillance, territoriality and image/milieu principles. Despite some criticisms concerning Newman's disregard for socio-economic differences between the studied communities (Repetto, 1976) and his oversimplification of the defensible space principle (Mawby, 1977), this theory and its proposed principles were extremely influential in reinforcing the link between crime and environmental design. All of these defensible space principles are intimately related to contemporary CPTED techniques: the natural surveillance principles are the same, the territoriality-related principles have substantial overlap, and image/milieu from defensible space is identical to the image/maintenance principle from CPTED.

These original environmental theorists laid the foundation for the development of CPTED. This advancement can be attributed to American criminologists C. Ray Jeffery and Timothy Crowe. While Jeffery first coined the term 'CPTED' (Jeffery, 1971), Crowe, having been influenced by early CPTED and related crime prevention developments (see Figure 2.2), highlighted the importance of the central space management concepts: 'natural access control', 'natural surveillance' and 'territorial reinforcement' (Crowe, 2000, pp. 36–37). It is important to note that advances in modern technology and the expansion of the private security industry have instigated the broadening of these concepts beyond their 'natural' roots, to include organised and mechanical/technological dimensions of existing mechanisms. In fact, it may be argued that greater attention is currently given to more recently developed mechanical/technological techniques than to the original natural methods.

Criticisms that CPTED promoted fortified cities contributed to the development of the '2nd generation CPTED' (Saville & Cleveland, 1997) or 'social CPTED' (Mallett, 2004, p. 4), which emphasises the importance of previously neglected social characteristics of the neighbourhood, social cohesion and 'collective efficacy' (Sampson, Raudenbush, & Earls, 1997, p. 920). In addition to the importance of physical environment, 2nd generation CPTED focuses on the importance of fostering strong social ties in communities and relies on more explicit techniques to encourage community cohesion and collective participation in crime prevention. In essence, the principles proposed by 2nd generation CPTED promote residents' engagement in social problems, including crime prevention, by mobilising communities to effectively address their own problems (Saville & Cleveland, 1997).

While 2nd generation CPTED is not without its critics, technology enthusiasts have already begun thinking about further developments to usher in '3rd generation CPTED', focusing on the use of modern green technologies to foster safer living environments in an environmentally sustainable manner (United Nations Interregional Crime and Justice Research Institute [UNICRI], 2011). Thus, in addition to relying on security features of the original CPTED, building of eco-friendly liveable cities that promote use of public spaces and informal surveillance is expected to also decrease fear of crime and perception of safety by relying on less invasive environmental features. While 3rd generation CPTED does not yet have a strong theoretical basis, its implementation is believed to have the advantages of achieving the same outcomes as proposed by the first two generations, while simultaneously addressing the shortcomings of environmental determinism and unsustainable practices. Despite these ongoing developments that are on the horizon, CPTED in practice remains heavily reliant on the principles proposed by the early theorists.

Criticisms

While CPTED has evolved over time, some criticisms of the approach have also endured. A common criticism of CPTED is that of displacement, which is a routine critique of situational prevention approaches in general (see chapter 1). Critics claim that because situational measures are place-, situation- or target-specific, their implementation prevents crime in individual settings by displacing it to other places, times and/or targets, with motivated offenders seeking other suitable opportunities (Barr & Pease, 1992; Reppetto, 1976). However, this criticism has been dulled by the fact that empirical studies have shown displacement by opportunistic criminals to be rare (Eck, 2002). In fact, the opposite phenomenon, the 'diffusion of benefits', whereby the positive effects of the intervention extend beyond the target areas, is often found to be a more common consequence of situational approaches (Chainey & Ratcliffe, 2005, p. 19; Clarke, 1995, p. 122). For example, improved street lighting can reduce the incidence of crime and fear of crime not only in the targeted area but also in adjacent areas, thus also proving to be cost-effective (Painter & Farrington, 1999). Although the consequences of displacement, if it occurs, are rarely alarming, to prevent potential negative consequences, well-implemented strategies are crucial (Barr & Pease, 1990, 1992). Moreover, crime prevention strategies and programs need to be monitored throughout the course of their existence to detect potential complications, such as displacement, that may arise as a result of interventions.

As previously highlighted, CPTED has also been criticised for over-emphasising the role of the physical environment in determining behaviour, and under-emphasising the importance of the social context. In fact, this criticism stimulated the development of 2nd generation CPTED. As a social problem, crime cannot be effectively dealt with by relying on the physical environment alone (Altes & van Soomeren, 1998; Dovey, 1998; Mallett, 2004). The idea of human guardianship has always been implicit in CPTED. Original defensible space theorists made clear that places could not be made defensible against crime without capable and willing residents and users of space (i.e., informal guardians), even if they have *defensible* physical design

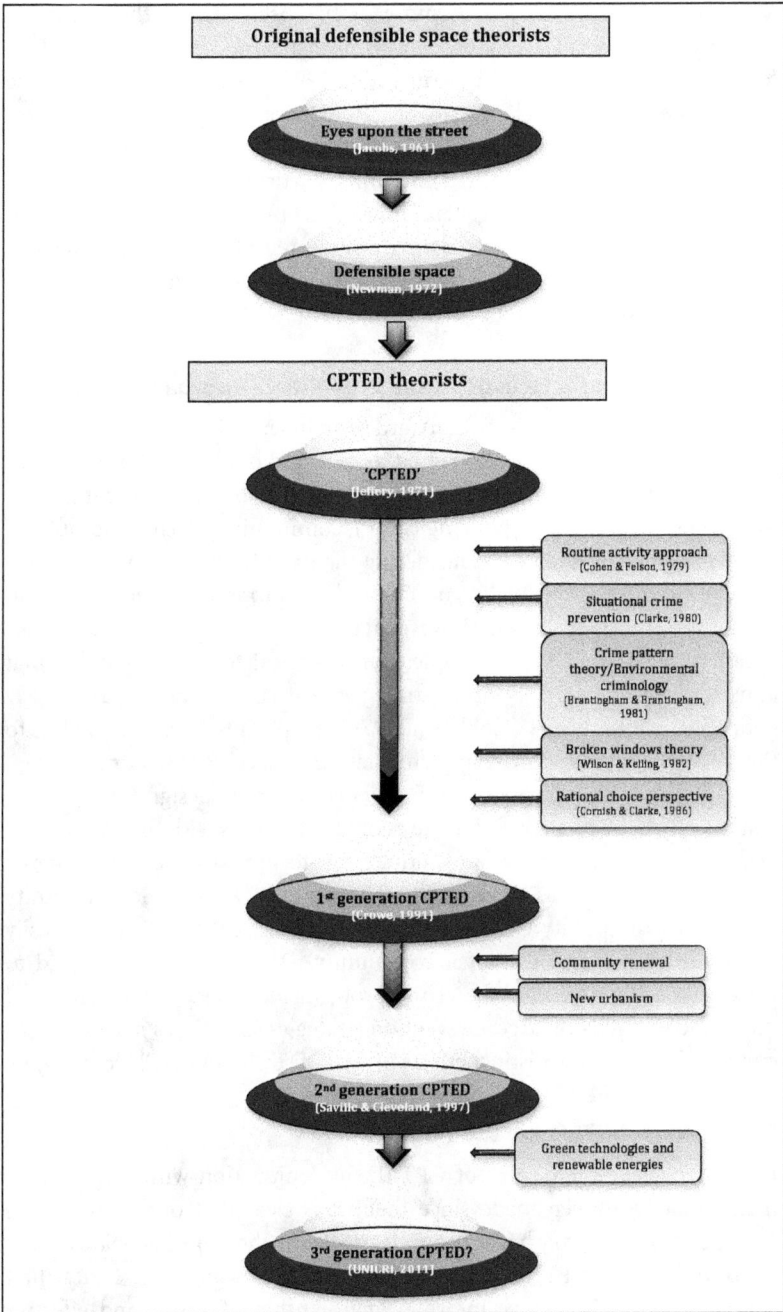

Figure 2.2
Timeline of CPTED developments and theoretical influences.

features (Jacobs, 1961). Furthermore, it has been argued that narrowly focusing on physical features of the environment could potentially result in fortressing and 'architecture of fear' (Ellin, 1997; see also chapter 1). These criticisms drove the developments of CPTED away from its alleged overre-liance on 'environmental determinism' (Porteous, 1977, p. 135) and towards a renewal of Jacobs' ideas of community participation. The community building strategies that 2nd generation CPTED proposes, and which Jacobs called for, may provide more lasting crime prevention effects, while also improving the quality of life by socially inclusive rather than exclusive prac-tices (Altes & van Soomeren, 1998; Ellin, 1997).

CPTED as Part of a Holistic Crime Prevention Approach

Although CPTED has been put forward as an independent crime prevention approach, it is rarely implemented on its own and is often applied as part of a suite of crime prevention initiatives (Ekblom, 2011). These commonly include problem oriented policing (POP), community policing and public–private partnerships (PPP). Considering the complexity of crime problems and the need for contextually and culturally appropriate crime prevention approaches, this is beneficial. However, it can pose implementation and eval-uation difficulties. POP, for example, is an analytical approach for police that aims to devise crime prevention strategies that correspond to particularly defined crime problems (Goldstein, 1979, 1990). This approach is akin to that of CPTED in which the implementation of specific situational mecha-nisms is aimed at controlling the problems caused by design features. The community policing approach focuses on partnerships with the community and other agencies outside law-enforcement to provide solutions to perti-nent crime problems as identified by the members of a specific community (Office of Community Oriented Policing Services, 2012). CPTED is easily implemented as part of a larger community policing strategy designed to target a specific aspect of the crime problem identified. Being subsumed under the umbrella of larger prevention strategies sometimes makes it diffi-cult to disentangle the distinct effects of CPTED techniques (Ekblom, 2011).

Conclusions: CPTED for the Future

Looking back at the origins of CPTED, in conjunction with the develop-ments that have been made since then, it is clear that one of the paths forward for this approach is to more clearly define the role of people as crime controllers in the CPTED model. Good physical design is the critical first step in encouraging active informal guardianship of places and effective place management. Equally important is the enforcement of 'responsibilisa-tion' strategies that encourage users and managers to exercise care and control over shared public and semipublic places (Reynald, 2011). In light of this, one of the critical steps forward in the continued development of CPTED is a greater incorporation of the notion that community engagement is vital for the effective functioning of CPTED as a crime prevention approach. This may be achieved through community building and socially inclusive practices that mobilise the community in sharing responsibility for crime prevention and associated problems that could undermine the quality of life. Such communities extend beyond the residential context and residential guardians. The community of a place often includes transient users of that space, residents of the place and place managers. While physical features of the environment offer passive tools through which guardianship and place management can be affected, active engagement in supervision of places, and the management and maintenance of places, is necessary to regulate the usage of places to discourage criminal opportunities (Clarke & Eck, 2005, p. 14; Felson, 2008, p. 74).

References

Altes, H.J.K., & van Soomeren, P. (1998, December). *CPTED and community building: The next phase.* Paper presented at the 3rd International CPTED Conference, Washington, DC.

Armitage, R., Monchuk, L., & Rogerson, M. (2011). It looks good, but what is it like to live there? Exploring the impact of innovative housing design on crime. *European Journal on Criminal Policy and Research, 17*(1), 29–54.

Australian Council for New Urbanism. (2006). *Australian new urbanism: A guide to projects* (2nd ed.). Melbourne, Australia: Ecologically Sustainable Design Pty Ltd.

Barr, R., & Pease, K. (1990). Crime placement, displacement, and deflection. *Crime and Justice, 12,* 277–318.

Barr, R., & Pease, K. (1992). A place for every crime and every crime in its place: An alternative perspective on crime displacement. In D.J. Evans, N.R. Fyfe, & D.T. Herbert (Eds.), *Crime, policing and place: Essays in environmental criminology* (pp. 196–216). London, England: Routledge.

Beavon, D.J.K., Brantingham, P.L., & Brantingham, P.J. (1994). The influence of street networks on the patterning of property offenses. In R. V. Clarke (Ed.), *Crime prevention studies, Vol. II* (pp. 115–148). New York, NY: Willow Tree Press.

Blakely, E.J., & Snyder, M.G. (1997). Divided we fall: Gated and walled communities in the United States. In N. Ellin (Ed.), *Architecture of fear* (pp. 85–99). New York: Princeton Architectural Press.

Bowers, D.M. (1989). Access control and personal identification systems. In L.J. Fennelly (Ed.), *Handbook of loss prevention and crime prevention* (pp. 364–378). Stoneham, MA: Butterworth-Heinemann.

Brantingham, P.L., & Brantingham, P.J. (1981). Notes on the geometry of crime. In P.J. Brantingham & P.L. Brantingham (Eds.), *Environmental criminology* (pp. 27–54). Beverly Hills, CA: Sage.

Brown, B., & Altman, I. (1983). Territoriality, defensible space and residential burglary: An Environmental analysis. *Journal of Environmental Psychology, 3*, 203–220.

Brown, B.B., & Bentley, D.L. (1993). Residential burglars judge risk: The role of territoriality. *Journal of Environmental Psychology, 13*, 51-61.

Carr, K., & Spring, G. (1993). Public transport safety: A community right and a communal responsibility. In R.V. Clarke (Ed.), *Crime Prevention Studies* (pp. 147–155). Monsey, NY: Criminal Justice Press.

Chainey, S., & Ratcliffe, J. (2005). *GIS and crime mapping.* Chichester, England: Wiley.

Clarke, R.V. (1995). Situational crime prevention. *Crime and Justice, 19*, 91–150.

Clarke, R.V. (1997). Introduction. In R.V. Clarke (Ed.), *Situational crime prevention: Successful case studies* (pp. 1-43). Guilderland, NY: Harrow and Heston.

Clarke, R.V. (1980). 'Situational' crime prevention: Theory and practice. *The British Journal of Criminology, 20*(2), 136–147.

Clarke, R.V., & Eck, J.E. (2005). *Crime analysis for problem solvers in 60 small steps.* Washington, DC: Office of Community Oriented Policing Services.

Cohen, L.E., & Felson, M. (1979). Social change and crime rate trends: A Routine activity approach. *American Sociological Review, 44*(4), 588–608.

Cornish, D., & Clarke, R. (1986). Introduction. In D.B. Cornish & R.V. Clarke (Eds.), *The reasoning criminal: Rational choice perspectives on offending* (pp. 1–16). New York, NY: Springer-Verlag.

Cozens, P., & Love, T. (2009). Manipulating permeability as a process for controlling crime: Balancing security and sustainability in local contexts. *Built Environment, 35*(3), 346–365.

Cozens, P.M., Saville, G., & Hillier, D. (2005). Crime prevention through environmental design (CPTED): A Review and modern bibliography. *Property Management, 23*(5), 328–356.

Cromwell, P.F., Olson, J.N., & Avary, D.W. (1991). *Breaking and entering: An Ethnographic analysis of burglary.* Newbury Park, CA: Sage.

Crowe, T. (2000). *Crime Prevention Through Environmental Design: Applications of architectural design and space management concepts.* Oxford, England: Butterworth-Heinemann.

Crowe, T.D. (1991). *Crime Prevention Through Environmental Design: Applications of architectural design and space management concepts.* Stoneham, MA: Butterworth-Heinemann.

Davey, C., Mackay, L., & Wootton, A. (2009). Designing safe residential areas. In R. Cooper, G. Evans & C. Boyko (Eds.), *Designing sustainable cities* (pp. 139–162). Oxford, England: Wiley-Blackwell.

Ditton, J., & Short, E. (1999). Yes, it works, no, it doesn't: Comparing the effects of open-street CCTV in two adjacent Scottish town centres. In K. Painter & N. Tilley (Eds.), *Surveillance of public space: CCTV, street lighting and crime prevention, Crime prevention studies, Vol. 10* (pp. 201-223). Monsey, NY: Criminal Justice Press.

Dovey, K. (1998, September). *Safety and danger in urban design.* Paper presented at the Australian Institute of Criminology and Victorian Community Council Against Violence Conference on Safer Communities: Strategic Directions in Urban Planning, Melbourne, Australia.

Eck, J.E. (2002). Preventing crime at places. In L.W. Sherman, D.P. Farrington, B.C. Welsh & D. Layton MacKenzie (Eds.). *Evidence-based crime prevention* (pp. 241–294). New York, NY: Routledge.

Ekblom, P. (2011). Deconstructing CPTED ... and reconstructing it for practice, knowledge management and research. *European Journal on Criminal Policy and Research, 17*(1), 7–28.

Ellin, N. (1997). Shelter from the storm or form follows fear and vice versa. In N. Ellin (Ed.), *Architecture of fear* (pp. 13–45). New York, NY: Princeton Architectural Press.

Farrington, D.P., & Welsh, B.C. (2006). Improved street lighting. In B.C. Welsh & D.P. Farrington (Eds.), *Preventing crime: What works for children, offenders, victims, and places* (pp. 209–224). Dordrecht, the Netherlands: Springer.

Felson, M. (2008). Routine activity approach. In R. Wortley & L. Mazerolle (Eds.), *Environmental criminology and crime analysis* (pp. 70-77). Cullompton, England: Willan.

Felson, M., & Clarke, R.V. (1998). *Opportunity makes the thief: Practical theory for crime prevention.* London, England: Home Office.

Goldstein, H. (1979). Improving policing: A Problem-oriented approach. *Crime and Delinquency, 25,* 236–258.

Goldstein, H. (1990). *Problem-oriented policing.* New York, NY: McGraw-Hill.

Hollis-Peel, M.E., Reynald, D.M., van Bavel, M., Elffers, H., & Welsh, B.C. (2011). Guardianship for crime prevention: A Critical review of the literature. *Crime, Law and Social Change, 56*(1), 53–70.

Hollis-Peel, M.E., Reynald, D.M., & Welsh, B.C. (2012). Guardianship and crime: An International comparative study of guardianship in action. *Crime, Law and Social Change, 58*(1), 1–14.

Homel, R., & Clark, J. (1995). The prediction and prevention of violence in pubs and clubs. Retrieved from *http://www.griffith.edu. au__data/assets/ pdf_file/0016/13327/prediciting.pdf.*

Jacobs, J. (1961). *The Death and life of great American cities.* Harmondsworth, England: Penguin.

Jeffery, C.R. (1971). *Crime Prevention Through Environmental Design*. Beverly Hills, CA: Sage.

Jeffery, C.R., & Zahm, D.L. (1993). Crime prevention through environmental design, opportunity theory, and rational choice models. In R.V. Clarke & M. Felson (Eds.), *Routine activity and rational choice: Advances in criminological theory, Vol. 5.* (pp. 323-350). New Brunswick, Canada: Transaction.

Johnson, S.D., & Bowers, K.J. (2010). Permeability and burglary risk: Are cul-de-sacs safer? *Journal of Quantitative Criminology, 26*(1), 89–111.

Lab, S.P. (2010). *Crime prevention: Approaches, practices and evaluations.* New Providence, NJ: LexisNexis/Anderson.

Mallett, J. (2004, September). *The Queensland community crime prevention program and CPTED*. Paper presented at the 9th Annual International CPTED Association Conference, Brisbane, Australia. Retrieved from http://www.veilig-ontwerp-beheer.nl/publicaties/the-queensland-community-crime-prevention-program-and-cpted/view?searchterM = CPTED%20brisbane.

Mawby, R.I. (1977). Defensible space: A Theoretical and empirical appraisal. *Urban Studies, 14,* 169–179.

McMahon, S. (2012). Urban design. In S. Thompson & P.J. Maginn (Eds.), *Planning Australia: An overview of urban and regional planning* (pp. 294–330). New York, NY: Cambridge University Press.

Merry, S.E. (1981). Defensible space undefended: Social factors in crime control through environmental design. *Urban Affairs Quarterly, 16*(4), 397–422.

Moffatt, R.E. (1983). Crime prevention through environmental design — a management perspective. *Canadian Journal of Criminology, 25*(4), 19–31.

Newman, O. (1972). *Defensible space: Crime prevention through urban design.* New York, NY: Macmillan.

Newman, O. (1996). *Creating defensible space.* Washington, DC: U.S. Department of Housing and Urban Development.

Office of Community Oriented Policing Services. (2012). *Community policing defined.* Washington, DC: U.S. Department of Justice.

Painter, K., & Farrington, D.P. (1997). The crime reducing effect of improved street lighting: The Dudley project. In R.V. Clarke (Ed.), *Situational crime prevention: Successful case studies* (pp. 209–226). Guilderland, NY: Harrow and Heston.

Painter, K., & Farrington, D.P. (1999). Street lighting and crime: Diffusion of benefits in the Stoke-on-Trent project. In K. Painter & N. Tilley (Eds.), *Surveillance of public space: CCTV, street lighting and crime prevention, Crime prevention studies, Vol. 10* (pp. 77–122). Monsey, NY: Criminal Justice Press.

Pease, K. (1991). The Kirkholt Project: Preventing burglary on a British Public Housing Estate. *Security Journal, 2*(2), 73–77.

Porteous, J.D. (1977). *Environment & behavior: Planning and everyday urban life.* Reading, MA: Addison-Wesley.

Prenzler, T., & Sarre, R. (1998). Regulating private security in Australia. *Trends and Issues in Crime and Criminal Justice, No. 98.* Canberra, Australia: Australian Institute of Criminology.

Reppetto, T.A. (1976). Crime prevention and the displacement phenomenon. *Crime & Delinquency, 22,* 166–177.

Reynald, D.M. (2009). Guardianship in action: Developing a new tool for measurement. *Crime Prevention and Community Safety, 11,* 1–20.

Reynald, D.M. (2011). Translating CPTED into crime preventive action: A critical examination of CPTED as a tool for active guardianship. *European Journal on Criminal Policy and Research, 17*(1), 69–81.

Sampson, R.J., Raudenbush, S.W., & Earls, F. (1997). Neighborhoods and violent crime: A Multilevel study of collective efficacy. *Science, 277,* 918–924.

Saville, G., & Cleveland, G. (1997, December). *2nd generation CPTED: An Antidote to the social Y2K virus of urban design.* Paper presented at the 1st Annual International CPTED Association Conference, Orlando, Florida.

Schneider, R.H., & Kitchen, T. (2007). *Crime prevention and the built environment.* Oxon, England: Routledge.

Schneider, S. (2010). *Crime prevention: Theory and practice.* Boca Raton, FL: CRC Press.

Sloan-Howitt, M., & Kelling, G.L. (1997). Subway graffiti in New York City: 'Getting' up' vs. 'meanin' it and cleanin' it'. In R.V. Clarke (Ed.), *Situational crime prevention: Successful case studies* (pp. 242–249). Guilderland, NY: Harrow and Heston.

United Nations Interregional Crime and Justice Research Institute (UNICRI). (2011). *New energy for urban security: Improving urban security through green environmental design.* Retrieved from http://www.unicri.it/news/files/2011-04-01_110414 _CRA_Urban_Security_sm.pdf.

Welsh, B., & Farrington, D.P. (2009). *Making public places safer: Surveillance and crime prevention.* New York, NY: Oxford University Press.

Welsh, B.C., & Farrington, D.P. (2006). Closed-circuit television surveillance. In B.C. Welsh & D.P. Farrington (Eds.), *Preventing crime: What works for children, offenders, victims, and places* (pp. 193–208). Dordrecht, the Netherlands: Springer.

Wilson, J.Q., & Kelling, G.L. (1982). Broken windows. *The Atlantic Online.* Retrieved from http://www.lantm.lth.se/fileadmin/fastighetsvetenskap/utbildning/Fastig hetsvaerderingssystem/BrokenWindowTheory.pdf.

Chapter 3

Financial Costs and Benefits of Crime Prevention

Matthew Manning and Gabriel T.W. Wong

Traditionally, crime prevention researchers have attempted to answer the question 'what works with respect to controlling and/or reducing crime?' Examples of programs evaluated in this space include developmental, correctional and situational prevention. However, the question 'what is worthwhile?' is rarely addressed. This is an efficacy question and is becoming more prevalent in a discipline that is becoming increasingly multidisciplinary. In this chapter, we introduce the use of economic analysis (EA) and discuss the importance of addressing the efficacy question when evaluating crime prevention programs and assessing public and private security investment decisions. This is achieved by providing an overview of some selected studies that utilise the economic method, highlighting the differences between accounting and economic methods, and summarising various EA techniques. Finally, we introduce a simple method (using cost and outcome analysis [OA]) for conducting EA with respect to security investment decisions.

Evaluation Research in Crime Prevention: Financial Aspects

There is growing recognition by public and private sectors that appropriate crime prevention policies, programs and strategies should be evidence-based and economically efficient (Mclntosh & Li, 2012). This philosophy, however, has only been partially realised because of (a) the difficulty for noneconomists to differentiate between economic and accounting analysis, (b) missing or inadequate economic data, and (c) the absence of a simple method for conducting EA. These shortfalls prohibit government, businesses and individuals from making fully informed decisions between alternative crime prevention options. In addition, they hinder the efficient allocation of resources. Most importantly, however, these shortfalls make it difficult to foresee the economic consequences of investment decisions. Examples of debates of this nature include the financial value of imprisonment (Meyer & Hopkins, 1991), mandatory-sentencing laws (or the 'three-strike' law; Greenwood et al., 1994), and the adoption of the 'Scared Straight' program (Petrosino, Turpin-Petrosino, & Finckenauer, 2000). In summary, the motivation regarding the economic component of these evaluation studies has been to:

1. assess the effectiveness and efficiency of new and existing programs
2. answer questions regarding the allocation of scarce or limited resources
3. ensure the greatest return on investment
4. make decisions regarding further investment
5. assess the impact these strategies have had on individuals and society more generally.

One important question to be addressed when making decisions regarding investment in crime prevention alternatives is 'what are the costs of crime?'. This question is important for both government and individuals. From a governmental perspective, this question looks at the costs of crime from a societal perspective. That is, how much does crime cost society? An answer to this question is helpful with respect to the allocation of government resources. Individuals also benefit from an answer to this question, as crime is also a cost to the individual. The costs of crime to the individual can be direct (e.g., loss of property), indirect (e.g., slowdown in business due to drug dealing on the streets outside the shop), and intangible (e.g., diminution of quality of life).

Costs of Crime in Australia

The Australian Institute of Criminology (AIC) adopted an approach from the United Kingdom (UK) Government Home Office to estimating the costs of crime in Australia (Mayhew, 2003; Rollings, 2008). The costs of crime were disaggregated into three categories: (1) 'costs in anticipation of crime'; (2) 'costs as a consequence of crime'; and (3) 'costs in response to crime' (Mayhew, 2003, p.7; see Table 3.1). The total costs of crime, as estimated by the AIC (Rollings, 2008), were $35.8 billion. This was disaggregated into thirteen categories of crime, shown in Table 3.2. The main problems associated with these analyses were:

1. Criminal justice system (CJS) costs were only available by financial year, and the detailed disaggregation of costs in relation to a particular crime (e.g., shop theft) was not provided.
2. As a national estimation of the costs of crime, the studies were not able to fully consider local data. For example, in the robbery category, there is no definite figure estimating the average property loss per robbery across Australia.
3. They did not provide a consistent approach to estimating the intangible losses from crime. For example the authors used a combination of willingness to pay, compensation awards, and victims' desired compensation methods. Moreover, intangible costs were not calculated for all crime categories or were highly reliant on results from the UK (e.g., Dubourg, Hamed, & Thorns, 2005).

Table 3.1

Some of the Costs of Crime Measured by Mayhew (2003)

Costs	✓ = Taken into account
In anticipation of crime	
Security expenditure	✓
Insurance	✓
Individual precautionary behaviour	✓
Central and local government crime prevention activity	
Community defensive action	
Social costs of fear of crime and precautionary behaviour	
As a consequence of crime	
Property stolen and damaged	✓
Lost output	✓
Health service costs	✓
Intangible costs to victims (emotional and physical impact)	✓
Victim support services	✓
Lost earnings on the part of prisoners	✓
Mental health costs	
Costs of supporting offenders and their families	
'Second generation' costs of offending	
Disinvestment in high-crime areas	
In response to crime	
Criminal justice system (police, prosecution, courts, etc.)	✓
Dealing with offenders (e.g., probation and prison)	✓
Criminal injuries compensation	✓

Source: Mayhew (2003, p.8). (Used with permission.)

The Costs and Benefits of Crime Prevention Programs

In this section we look at studies that have attempted to address the efficacy question (see Table 3.3). The studies are classified according to developmental, correctional, and situational prevention. The main focus of this section is on studies using cost–benefit analysis, with reported cost–benefit (CB) ratios. Analysts calculate a CB ratio by quantifying the benefits in monetary terms and comparing it with quantified costs. The CB ratio is the net gain for every dollar invested in a program, and a higher ratio refers to greater return on investment For example, a CB ratio of 4.05 indicates that for every dollar invested, a return of $4.05 is generated.

Table 3.2

Summary of Costs of Crime in Australia (2005)

Categories	Cost type Estimated cost in 2005 ($m)	Percentage of total costs
Crime types		
Homicide	950	2.7
Assault	1,411	3.9
Sexual assault	720	2.0
Robbery	225	0.6
Burglary	2,229	6.2
Thefts of vehicles	597	1.7
Thefts from vehicles	529	1.5
Shop theft	861	2.4
Other theft	282	0.8
Criminal damage	1,582	4.4
Arson	1,624	4.5
Fraud	8,516	23.8
Drug offences	1,816	5.1
Other costs		
Criminal justice	9,808	27.4
Victim assistance	1,073	3.0
Security	2,999	8.4
Insurance administration	580	1.6
Total	35,802	100.0

Source: Rollings (2008, p .xii). (Used with permission.)

Developmental Prevention

Developmental interventions are aimed at improving children's life chances through improved parenting and school participation programs. Many of these programs have demonstrated ability to pay for themselves and generate financial benefits to society (see Table 3.3). One well-known developmental study that was evaluated using EA was the HighScope Perry Preschool Program (Schweinhart et al., 2005). The Perry Preschool Program provided high-quality preschool education to African-American children living in poverty. Follow-ups of the program included estimates of the economic return on investment at ages 19, 27 and 40. The latest cost–benefit analysis was conducted by Schweinhart et al. (2005). Despite some criticisms of the

Table 3.3

Examples of Studies Examining the Economic Efficiency of Crime Prevention Programs

Strategies	Authors	Description	EA Result[a]
Developmental Prevention			
General parent education	Greenwood et al., 2001	Elmira Prenatal-Early Infancy Project	CB ratio = 4.06
Preschool programs	Schweinhart, et al., 2005	HighScope Perry Preschool Program	CB ratio = 16.14 at age 40 analysis), 7.16 (at age 27 analysis)
Preschool programs	Reynolds, Temple, Robertson & Mann, 2002	Chicago Child-Parent Center Program	CB ratio = 1.66 (4-6 years of participation)
School programs	Aos, Lieb, Mayfield Miller, & Pennucci, 2004	Quantum Opportunities Program	CB ratio = 1.87
Community programs	Aos, Phipps, Barnoski, & Lieb, 2001	Multi-Systemic Therapy	CB ratio = 28.33
Correctional Prevention			
Earned release time from prison	Drake, Aos, & Miller, 2009	Earned early release	CB ratio = 1.88
Treatment	Robertson, Grimes, & Rogers, 2001	Intensive outpatient counselling with cognitive-behavioural therapy	CB ratio = 1.96
Treatment	Caldwell, Vitacco,	Mendota Juvenile Treatment Center Program	CB ratio = 7.18
In-prison substance abuse treatment	Daley et al., 2004	Connecticut's in-prison substance abuse treatment	CB ratio = 5.74 (30 outpatient group sessions within 10 weeks)
Substance abuse treatment, community supervision	Roman, Chalfin, Reid, & Reid, 2008	Anchorage Wellness Court alcohol treatment program	CB ratio = 3.44 (after 24 month follow-up), 1.25 (after 30 months follow-up)
Drug courts	Anton, 2007	Minnesota adult drug court	CB ratio = 5.08

CONTINUED OVER PAGE...

Table 3.3 ...CONTINUED

Situational Prevention

Natural surveillance	Painter & Farrington, 2001	Improved street lighting	CB ratio = 6.19 (Dudley), 5.43 (Stoke-on-Trent)
Formal Surveillance	Gill & Spriggs 2005	CCTV in London Hawkeye (car parks)	CB ratio and cost per crime prevented: 1.27, £620 (high risk car park)
Formal Surveillance	Knight, 1994	Security guard in Glasgow (residential)	CB ratio = 1.31
Target hardening	Bowers, et al., 2004	Alley-gating	CB ratio = 0.96 (after 6 months) and 1.86 (after 12 months)
Target removal, natural surveillance, identifying property, target hardening	Forrester, et al., 1990	Kirkholt Burglary Prevention Project	CB ratio = 5.04

Note:[a] CB ratio = cost–benefit ratio. A CB ratio less than one can be judged to be economically unviable. [b] Readers should note that this is not a systematic review of extensive research. Further, we do not discuss the quality of economic studies.

method (e.g., that the dollar costs attributed to murder were not accurate [Heckman, Moon, Pinto, Savelyev, & Yavitz, 2010]), the approach provides for a fairly comprehensive model. The program cost per participant, which included both operating costs (e.g., staff salary and administration fee) and capital costs (for classrooms and facilities), was put at US$15,166. The program yielded a positive return of US$244,812 for each participant. Every dollar invested in the program thus generated a return of US$16.14. Of the return, US$12.90 was societal benefits, including savings due to avoided victim costs and criminal justice costs, reduced welfare transfers, and increased taxes due to higher earnings of program participants. Further, US$3.24 of the return was benefits to participants, mainly in the form of higher earnings.

Correctional Prevention

Correctional measures affect offender behaviour and reduce crime through deterrence (general and specific), rehabilitation and incapacitation). The majority of EA in this area have focused on the value of mandatory-sentencing laws and drug courts. For example, RAND criticised the economic efficiency of California's 'three-strikes' law. They based their criticism on EA that compared the new law (three-strikes) with other alternatives such as 'Jones' 2nd-strike only' or guaranteed full term imprisonment (Greenwood et al., 1994). Disagreeing with RAND's estimates, Scheidegger and Rushford (1999) argued that the cost of the new law estimated by RAND was inaccurate. They suggested that tough sentencing was economically efficient.

With respect to drug courts, findings demonstrate that they potentially reduce reoffending and generate desirable economic benefits through avoiding costs such as future victimisation, improved health outcomes for the offender, and CJS costs (see Table 3.3). Anton (2007) found that general and drug-related arrests and convictions per person, following completion of drug court program in all three counties when comparing to the control group, were significantly lower. Costs were saved due to the lower costs of drug courts compared to normal court proceedings, and less subsequent arrests and convictions.

Situational Prevention (and Security)

Situational prevention strategies aim to prevent crime by 'increasing the risk and effort', 'reducing the rewards and provocations', and' removing the excuses' of offending (Cornish & Clarke, 2003, chapter 1). For example, findings show that the installation of lockable gates across alleyways at the back of properties could effectively reduce burglary and generate benefits to society via reduced CJS costs (see Table 3.3) and reduced financial losses to victims (Bowers, Johnson, & Hirschfield, 2004). In another cases study, improved street lighting was shown to reduce crime and produce economic returns to crime victims and local councils that exceeded the total costs of the project (Painter & Farrington, 2001). The deployment of security guards in a residential estate was also a high-yield investment, which prevented property losses (e.g., direct losses by victims of crime) and reduced costs to the CJS by deterring vandalism and burglary (i.e., reducing policing, court and corrections costs) (Knight, 1994). With respect to CCTV systems, there are mixed results. Installation of CCTV in high-risk car parks generated desirable benefits but otherwise there was little evidence of beneficial outcomes (Gill & Spriggs, 2005).

One well-known situational prevention project that was evaluated using EA was the Kirkholt Burglary Prevention Project (see chapter 5). Anti-burglary interventions on homes included security upgrades, removing coin-fed meters and a close form of neighbourhood watch (Forrester, Frenz, O'Connell, & Pease, 1990). After 3 years of observation, findings indicated the program contributed to a 75% reduction in burglaries (from 526 to 132 per year) and had a favourable CB ratio of 5.04 (Forrester et al., 1990). The program cost (£298,398) included UK Government Home Office grants, housing department budgets for improving estate safety and security, and the cost of police and probation staff. Program benefits (£1,504,664) included the avoided costs of burglary (e.g., property and electricity meter losses, CJS costs, and housing repair costs; Safe Neigbourhoods Unit, 1993).

The Kirkholt project evaluation was not free from criticism. First, it had a weak before-after design without a comparable control site (Welsh & Farrington, 2000). Second, the mixed contribution of situational and community prevention components made it very difficult, if not impossible, to identify the effects of individual prevention measures on the outcome. Third, evaluators did not remove the effects of inflation or calculate the present value. Nevertheless, the estimation of program benefits and the CB ratio was conservative since some potential benefits (e.g., savings in insurance claims and freed police time) were not included (Forrester et al., 1990).

Economic Costs and the Beneficiaries

The contribution of corporate security to an organisation's financial wellbeing has been an underdeveloped research area (Gill, Burns-Howell, Keats, & Taylor, 2007). There are several factors that explain this. First, there has been an absence of financial data about costs of crime on businesses, since official crime statistics do not separate crimes against businesses out from other crimes. Second, the lack of transparency of resource allocation by organisations hinders the estimation of costs and benefits. Even where an EA has been conducted, precise information about the value and calculation process might not be released due to confidentiality. This has prohibited further review of these EA. Finally, some organisations are not aware of the importance of EA and are reluctant to collect relevant metrics (Gill, Taylor, Bourne, & Keats, 2008).

The Importance of Economic Analysis

So why is EA important? EA produces two important estimates: first, the costs associated with controlling and preventing crime; and second, the benefits derived from crime reduction/prevention strategies. The concept of collecting costs and benefits is not new. Grey's (1979) historical review of the costs of crime ranges from the beginning of the 18th century through to the latter half of the 19th century. Consistently, authors noted the lack of progress with respect to adequately capturing the full costs of crime. Four decades on, the story has changed little. Economists are still working on systematically identifying and valuing the full costs of crime at the individual and societal level.

All the studies in Grey's review acknowledged the importance of EA, arguing that economics is a science that focuses on the allocation of scarce resources in society. Simply, economics is the study of making choices

(Mankiw, 2001). From a crime prevention perspective, the above economic line of enquiry is clear as criminal justice policy decisions always involve a trade-off. That is, there are always choices and these choices all have their own costs and benefits. From a governmental perspective, understanding the costs and benefits of alternatives allows informed decisions to be made that potentially enhance society's wellbeing. The downside of deriving costs and benefits is that if the analysis is inaccurate (due to a poorly developed method) then the results may do more harm than good (Allard & Manning, 2011).

Another important reason for EA is identifying and valuing the intangible costs of crime. Noneconomists question the moral justification and adequate empirical basis for monetising intangible factors such as pain, suffering and loss of quality of life. There are, however, very good reasons for monetising intangible factors. For example, economists are able to compare the relative harm caused by crime — from street crimes such as robbery, violence and homicide — to white-collar crimes — such as corporate, financial and governmental crimes. Economists also value the intangible costs of crime so one can compare the aggregated harm of crime with that of other societal problems, such as social and economic inequality, increases in urban population density, and environmental dilapidation. From a public policy perspective, this is extremely important information because resources are finite and so is public expenditure. As such, governments must make judgements on the relative importance of social issues and make funding distribution decisions based on the relative weights they place on competing societal issues (Manning, in press).

Economic Versus Accounting Costs

Intangible costs are what set an EA apart from a purely accounting exercise. Manning (in press, p. 7) states: 'costs should not be limited to accounting costs, which are based on an account statement. Rather, costs should be economic costs'. Figure 3.1 shows the difference between economic and accounting costs; where economic costs include: implicit costs (a cost that is represented by lost opportunity in the use of one's own resources, excluding cash — the costs associated with a trade-off); and explicit costs (e.g., wages, rent and materials). The clear difference between economic and accounting costs is that accounting costs only include explicit costs and do not consider the costs associated with a trade-off. From an economics perspective, costs are seen as opportunity costs. That is, if the input is not used in one context it could be used in another (Manning, Homel, & Smith, 2006). In other words, the opportunity cost of using an input is its value in its best alternative use.

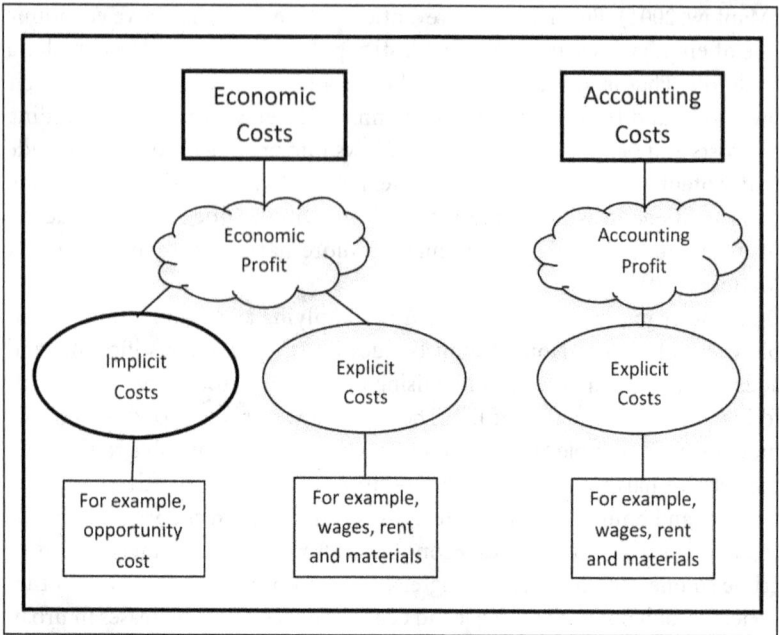

Figure 3.1
Economics versus accounting costs.

Economic costs are superior to accounting costs for a number of reasons. First, accounting budgets do not usually include all the cost information on all the resources used; for example, volunteer time, donated equipment and services, and any other unpaid inputs. Second, inputs that have already been paid for, or are not included in the budget, will not be easily discernible in the accounting spreadsheet. Third, standard accounting budgets may distort the true cost of an input. For example, accounting budgets typically charge the cost of an input to the year in which the cost occurred. If the life of the asset is, for example, 20 years then this cost should be distributed over the life of the asset. Fourth, costs are often embedded in a budget or expenditure statement that is larger than the project in question. For example, costs of an intervention (e.g., police time) may be embedded into the total operational costs of the enterprise and as a consequence these must be categorised according to economic classifications (e.g., variable costs). Finally, accounting documents often represent plans for how resources will be allocated as opposed to classifying expenditures after they have been used. In other words, accounting statements often include budgeted accounts with actuals being left for inclusion until the end of the accounting period (Levin & McEwan, 2001).

Who Are the Beneficiaries?

The discussion so far highlights the important role EA should have in the public policy sector, with a focus on government. However, potential beneficiaries include individuals and firms. As well as classifying by groups, the benefits of EA can also be classified by use. Examples include transparency of resources used by government (e.g., CJS costs to taxpayers or the cost to taxpayers for specific crime prevention projects), developing a business case for private security investment, and as an informative tool to the general public (e.g., understanding the costs associated with being victimised). In the absence of EA, businesses and individuals (potential victims of crime) would need to rely on anecdotal evidence to determine the level and type of private security investment. This would be an extremely inefficient method.

Techniques of Economic Analysis

EA is a generic term used to denote an array of research techniques that have two common components: (1) they examine costs and outcomes (as discussed earlier); and (2) they compare two or more options (e.g., investment in CCTV compared to investment in electronic tagging systems; Manning, in press). Four commonly used techniques of EA are 'cost–savings analysis', 'cost-effectiveness analysis', 'cost–benefit analysis' and 'cost–utility analysis'. The techniques address slightly different decision-making questions. They also represent different degrees of analytical sophistication, require slightly different data, and have different theoretical underpinnings (Manning, in press). The advantages and disadvantages of the four techniques are summarised briefly in Table 3.4.

A Simple Best Practice Model for Crime Prevention Project Managers and Security Managers

The choice of technique will depend on a number of factors. The first is the type of data. For example, data that demonstrate direct outcomes associated with a security investment (e.g., reductions in store shrinkage or employee and customer theft) are easy to use and access compared to data assessing feelings or perceptions of safety (see Manning, in press). The second factor is the ease of converting outcomes to dollars. Some outcomes are extremely difficult to monetise especially if they are nonmarket goods such as happiness or perceptions of personal safety (see Brand & Price, 2000). The third factor is the budget available to conduct an EA. Methods such as cost–savings analysis and cost-effectiveness analysis are significantly cheaper than cost–benefit analysis and cost–utility analysis. The fourth factor is the expertise available. More sophisticated methods such as cost–benefit analysis and cost–utility analysis require the expertise of experienced economists. The

Table 3.4

Economic Analysis Techniques

Type of analysis	Measure of cost	Measure of outcomes	Strengths	Weaknesses
Cost-Effectiveness	Monetary value of resources	Units of effectiveness	Easy to incorporate standard evaluations of effectiveness Good for alternatives with small number of objectives	Hard to interpret when there are multiple measures of effectiveness Only useful for comparing two or more alternatives
Cost–Benefit	Monetary value of resources	Monetary value of benefits	Can judge absolute worth of a project Can compare CB results across a variety of projects	Difficult to place monetary values on salient life benefits
Cost–Savings	Monetary value of resources	Monetary savings resulting from impact of intervention	Good for assessing the savings generated to stakeholders	Difficult to place monetary values on salient life benefits
Cost–Utility	Monetary value of resources	Units of utility	Incorporates individual preferences for units of effectiveness Incorporates multiple measures of effectiveness into single measure of utility	Difficult to arrive at consistent and accurate measures of individual preferences Cannot judge overall worth of a single alternative

Adapted from: Levin & McEwan, 2001, pp. 27-28.

final factor to consider is the question. The research question will determine the technique required. This of course is dependent on budget, and as such one must be mindful of this when developing the research question (Manning, Smith, & Homel, 2013).

Cost Analysis — The Numerator

The first step to conducting EA is the identification and collection of cost data for each option or alternative. This is normally called the 'cost analysis' (CA). CA is a comprehensive description of the type and amount of resources used. A number of choices must be made, including: what costs to

Table 3.5

Example of Resources used for Additional Security in a Retail Firm

Variable (Explicit)	Fixed (Explicit)	Implicit
Personnel (additional security)	Space (for new staff- assuming	Management time
Supplies (uniform, walkie talkie)	no change in premises)	Staff time
Travel for training	Security monitoring systems	Volunteer time
(security courses)	and their upkeep (e.g.,	Other space costs
Utilities (e.g., new staff add	long-term contracts)	
additional electricity costs)	Licences and permits	
Upkeep of equipment	for the business	
(more usage)	Rent (long-term lease)	

consider or the range of costs to be considered; how costs should be esti-mated (e.g., quantities of resources, assignment of unit costs); how nonmar-ket items should be valued; the adjustment of market prices (ensuring that market prices reflect true opportunity costs); the length of time costs should be tracked; the inclusion of unrelated costs (flow-on effects from common practice or options already in place); and, the handling of capital outlays (e.g., equipment, buildings and land; Boardman et al., 2006).

Once these issues have been considered and choices made, a cost analysis methodology can be developed. A format for conducting a cost analysis, adapted from Levin and McEwan (2001), includes the following steps:

Step 1　measuring and valuing fixed costs (explicit costs)

Step 2　measuring and valuing implicit costs or in-kind costs

Step 3　distributing costs among stakeholders

Sept 4　depreciating tangible capital assets

Step 5　categorising all expenditures and costs

Step 6　discounting costs for further analysis such as cost-effectiveness.

To be consistent with the economic principles of measuring all resources involved in producing an option (Step 1 and Step 2), explicit costs (costs that require an outlay of money, for example salaries of employees) as well as implicit costs (input costs that do not require an outlay of money; e.g., vol-unteer time) must be identified. Table 3.5 provides an overview of potential costs for additional security staff employed to prevent stock shrinkage in a retail firm. In the table, explicit costs are separately categorised into fixed and variable costs. Fixed costs are costs that do not change when the numbers of participants increase (e.g., premises — this does not change in the short term). Variable costs are costs that may fluctuate depending on the number

Table 3.6

Worksheet for Estimating Costs

Cost Ingredients	Total Cost	Costs to Investor	Costs to Government Agency	Costs to Private Organisations
Personnel (includes all labour)				
Equipment (includes all durable items)				
Facilities (includes land, office space, parking space)				
Supplies (includes other consumables. Utilities can be included into this category)				
Other costs including in-kind costs				
Total ingredients cost				
User fees				
Cash subsidies				
Net costs				

of participants (e.g., additional security staff, uniforms, equipment, etc.; Foster, Dodge, & Jones, 2003).

When distributing costs among stakeholders (Step 3), a cost worksheet should be used listing all ingredients. This helps to disaggregate costs among stakeholders (see Table 3.6). To depreciate tangible capital assets (Step 4), the 'diminishing value method' as recommended by the Australian Taxation Office (ATO; 2012) can be adopted. Other methods are available and these are normally outlined by relevant taxation bodies (e.g., ATO, 2012). To ensure that all data are collected and easily accessible for later evaluation, it is helpful to categorise all costs (step 5). How one chooses to do this will be determined by the type and makeup of the option one is evaluating. For example, when classifying costs Manning (2004) used the following categories:

1. Personnel (includes all labour)
2. Equipment (includes all durable items)
3. Facilities (includes land, office space, parking space)

4. Supplies (includes other consumables. Utilities can be included in this category)
5. Other costs (including in-kind costs).

The final step in conducting a CA involves discounting all costs (step 6). The basic principle is that costs incurred in the future are less of a burden than costs incurred in the present. Therefore, future costs must be discounted to properly compare them with present costs. The method for comparing alternative investment patterns is by calculating their present value. The calculation of present value uses an interest rate to discount future costs relative to current ones. A full description of how to calculate present values is provided in Levin and McEwan (2001).

Outcome Analysis — The Denominator

The method used in outcome analysis (OA), which constitutes the denominator in EA, will depend upon the technique (this is also dependent on a range of factors as outlined earlier) adopted. For simplicity let's assume that a company wishes to invest in CCTV to reduce stock shrinkage (e.g., theft by customers or employees). The most appropriate technique to use in this case would be cost-effectiveness analysis. The reason for this choice is that the outcome does not need to be monetised and the unit of analysis, in this case, is the number of thefts or stock shrinkage. A noneconomist can easily handle this and it is also a relatively cheap option compared to a full cost–benefit analysis. In addition, the technique only requires the assessment of small number of objectives. For example, one could disaggregate shrinkage by staff and customer.

Initially, a distinction must be made between whether the option/s are independent (the costs and effects of one option are not affected by the introduction of another option) or mutually exclusive (implementing one option means that another cannot be implemented). For the purposes of this discussion we will assume that all options are independent. Cost-effectiveness analysis requires that cost-effectiveness ratios (CER) are calculated for each option and placed in order. A CER is created by calculating the overall costs of the option (CA) and dividing those costs by the effects produced (OA). The calculated ratio indicates the cost required to attain a 1-point increase in outcome (Levin & McEwan, 2001). Thus, the alternative with the lowest ratio is considered the best alternative, to the extent of resources available.

Conclusion

Crime prevention measures that have mild effect but are expensive may not be very favourable compared to other economically viable options. By recognising the advantages of undertaking EA, public and private sectors can make informed decisions on resource allocation by investing in cost-effective alternatives. Some economic techniques such as cost–benefit analysis and cost–utility analysis are extremely sophisticated and require economic expertise to retrieve relevant metrics for outcome evaluation. Evaluators who cannot afford such rigorous analyses, or do not have access to qualified micro-economists may consider adopting less demanding approaches such as the cost–savings analysis and cost-effectiveness analysis.

References

Allard, T., & Manning, M. (2011). Establishing an evidence base: Economic analysis. In A. Stewart, T. Allard & S. Dennison (Eds.), *Evidence based policy and practice in juvenile justice* (pp. 187–205). Brisbane, Australia: Federation Press.

Anton, P. (2007). *Benefit-cost calculations for three adult drug courts in Minnesota.* Saint Paul, MN: Wilder Research.

Aos, S., Lieb, R., Mayfield, J., Miller, M., & Pennucci, A. (2004). *Benefits and costs of prevention and early intervention programs for youth.* Olympia: Washington State Institute for Public Policy.

Aos, S., Phipps, P., Barnoski, R., & Lieb, R. (2001). *The comparative costs and benefits of programs to reduce crime.* Olympia: Washington State Institute for Public Policy.

Australian Taxation Office. (2012). *Guide to depreciating assets 2012-2013.* Canberra.

Boardman, A., Greenberg, D., Vining, A., & Weimer, D. (2006). *Cost-benefit analysis: Concepts and practice.* Upper Saddle River, NJ: Pearson-Prentice Hall.

Bowers, K., Johnson, S., & Hirschfield, A. (2004). Closing off opportunities for crime: An Evaluation of alley-gating. *European Journal on Criminal Policy and Research, 10*(4), 285–308.

Brand, S., & Price, R. (2000). *The economic and social costs of crime.* London, England: Home Office.

Caldwell, M., Vitacco, M., & Van Rybroek, G. (2006). Are violent delinquents worth treating? A Cost-benefit analysis. *Journal of Research in Crime and Delinquency, 42*(2), 148–168.

Cornish, D., & Clarke, R. (2003). Opportunities, percipitators and criminal decisions. In M. Smith & D. Cornish (Eds.), *Theory for situational crime prevention* (pp. 41–96). Monsey, NY: Criminal Justice Press.

Daley, M., Love, C., Shepard, D., Petersen, C., White, K., & Hall, F. (2004). Cost-effectiveness of Connecticut's in-prison substance abuse treatment. *Journal of Offender Rehabilitation, 39*(3), 69–92.

Drake, E. K., Aos, S., & Miller, M. G. (2009). Evidence-based public policy options to reduce crime and criminal justice costs. *Victims and Offenders, 4*, 170–196.

Dubourg, R., Hamed, J., & Thorns, J. (2005). *The economic and social costs of crime against individuals and households 2003/04*. London, England: Home Office.

Forrester, D., Frenz, S., O'Connell, M., & Pease, K. (1990). *The Kirkholt Burglary Prevention Project: Phase II*. London, England: Home Office.

Foster, M.., Dodge, K., & Jones, D. (2003). Issues in the Economic Evaluation of Prevention Programs. *Applied Developmental Science, 7*(2), 76–86.

Gill, M., Burns-Howell, T., Keats, G., & Taylor, E. (2007). *Demonstrating the value of security*. Leicester, England: Perpetuity Research & Consultancy.

Gill, M., & Spriggs, A. (2005). *Assessing the impact of CCTV*. London, England: Home Office.

Gill, M., Taylor, E., Bourne, T., & Keats, G. (2008). *Organisational perspectives on the value of security*. Leicester, England: Perpetuiy Research & Consultancy.

Gold, M., Siegel, J., Russell, L., & Weinstein, M. (1996). *Cost-effectiveness in health medicine*. New York, NY: Oxford University Press.

Greenwood, P., Karoly, L., Everingham, S., Houbé, J., Kilburn, M., Rydell, C., Chiesa, J. (2001). Estimating the costs and benefits of early childhood interventions: Nurse home visits and the Perry Preschool. In D. Welsh, D. Farrington & L. Sherman (Eds.), *Costs and benefits of preventing crime* (pp. 123–148). Boulder, CO: Westview Press.

Greenwood, P., Rydell, C., Abrahamse, A., Caulkins, J., Chiesa, J., Model, K., & Klein, S. (1994). *Three strikes and you're out: Estimated benefits and costs of California's new mandatory-sentencing law*. Santa Monica, CA: RAND.

Grey, C. (1979). *The costs of crime*. Beverly Hill: Sage.

Heckman, J., Moon, S., Pinto, R., Savelyev, P., & Yavitz, A. (2010). The rate of return to the HighScope Perry Preschool Program. *Journal of Public Economics, 94*, 114–128.

Knight, B. (1994). Possil Park Estate: Security scheme. In S. Osborn (Ed.), *Housing safe communities: An evaluation of recent initiatives* (pp. 88–95). London, England: Safe Neighbourhoods Unit.

Levin, H., & McEwan, P. (2001). *Cost-effectiveness analysis*. London, England: Sage.

Mankiw, G. (2001). *Principles of economics*. Sydney, Australia: Harcourt College.

Manning, M. (2004). *Measuring the costs of community-based developmental prevention programs in Australia*. (Unpublished master's thesis). Griffith University, Brisbane.

Manning, M. (in press). Cost-benefit analysis. In G. Bruinsma & D. Weisburd (Eds.), *Encyclopedia of criminology and criminal justice*. New York, NY: Springer.

Manning, M., Homel, R., & Smith, C. (2006). Economic evaluation of a community-based early intervention program implemented in a disadvantaged urban area of Queensland. *Economic Analysis and Policy, 36*(1 & 2), 99–120.

Manning, M., Smith, C., & Homel, R. (2013). Valuing developmental crime prevention. *Criminology and Public Policy, 12*(3), 1–25.

Mayhew, P. (2003). *Counting the costs of crime in Australia: Technical report.* Canberra, Australia: Australian Institute of Criminology.

McIntosh, C., & Li, J. (2012). *An introduction to economic analysis in crime prevention.* Ottawa, Canada: National Crime Prevention Centre.

Meyer, P., & Hopkins, S. (1991). Making economically sound confinement decisions: A response to the Zedlewski thesis. *American Journal of Criminal Justice, 15*(2), 106–133.

Painter, K., & Farrington, D. (2001). The financial benefits of improved street lighting, based on crime reduction. *Lighting Research and Technology, 33*(1), 3–10.

Petrosino, A., Turpin-Petrosino, C., & Finckenauer, J. O. (2000). Well-meaning programs can have harmful effects! Lessons from experiments of programs such as Scared Straight. *Crime & Delinquency 46*(3), 354–379.

Reynolds, A., Temple, J., Robertson, D., & Mann, E. (2002). Age 21 cost-benefit analysis of the Title I Chicago Child-Parent Centers. *Educational Evaluation and Policy Analysis, 24*(4), 267–303.

Robertson, A., Grimes, P., & Rogers, K. (2001). A short-run cost-benefit analysis of community-based interventions for juvenile offenders. *Crime & Delinquency 47*(2), 265–284.

Rollings, K. (2008). *Counting the costs of crime in Australia: A 2005 update.* Canberra, Australia: Australian Institute of Criminology.

Roman, J.., Chalfin, A., Reid, J., & Reid, S. (2008). *Impact and cost-benefit analysis of the anchorage wellness court.* Washington, DC: Urban Institute Justice Policy Center.

Safe Neigbourhoods Unit. (1993). *Crime prevention on council estates.* London, England: HMSO.

Scheidegger, K., & Rushford, M. (1999). The Social benefits of confining habitual criminals. *Stanford Law & Policy Review, 11*(1), 59–64.

Schweinhart, L., Montie, J., Xiang, Z., Barnett, W., Belfield, C., & Nores, M. (2005). *Lifetime effects: The HighScope Perry Preschool study through age 40.* Ypsilanti, MI: High/Scope Press.

Welsh, B., & Farrington, D. (2000). Monetary costs and benefits of crime prevention programs. *Crime and Justice, 27,* 305–361.

Chapter 4

Case Studies in Reducing Violence and Disorder

Mateja Mihinjac and Danielle M. Reynald

Violence and disorder in public places are most visible and therefore often the most worrisome crimes. The chapter begins by briefly overviewing the effects of violence and disorder on society at large. Few experimental studies have measured and reported the effect of situational measures on these crimes. A selection of case studies is presented in this chapter which exemplify how physical and social aspects of some dangerous and fear-provoking places can be managed to change both their functioning and perception, thus reducing the high risk of violence and disorder while reducing associated levels of fear and anxiety. The chapter concludes by stressing the importance of context-appropriate place management practices for effective functioning of a place and advocates the need for evaluative experimental studies that support situational prevention of violence and disorder beyond mere anecdotal evidence.

Background

While public space crimes such as robbery and assault were relatively stable internationally in the 1990s, they have recently begun to decrease slightly in the past decade (Van Dijk, van Kesteren & Smit, 2007). Violence and disorder present a concern as they are difficult for police to control and they give vulnerable places a bad reputation. Fear and anxiety that characterise places with such physical and social features reduce the quality of life for all users, including residents, business owners and casual place users. Furthermore, direct or indirect victimisation from violence and disorder can entail a cost to the health system and multiple other public services (Mair & Mair, 2003). Conventional approaches to controlling crime are often ineffective in addressing these problems, are expensive and tend to divide the communities (Hale, 1996).

International victimisation surveys show only around half of robberies and a third of assaults and threats are reported to the police, revealing that these crimes are more prevalent than reported figures suggest (Van Dijk et al., 2007). Conventional approaches — such as arrest, punishment, incapacitation, deterrence and rehabilitation — focus predominantly on offender-based strategies which – often unsuccessfully – attempt to change the life-course of potential and existing offenders (Mair & Mair, 2003). Moreover, when violence is addressed through conventional approaches, resources often go into buying firearms to 'fight violence with violence', special policing practices, victim-sensitivity strategies, training programs, violence educating campaigns, and other often reactive strategies. While these practices have their place, and might in some cases be very necessary (e.g., domestic violence or suicide attempts), more needs to be done to address crimes of violence and disorder in public spaces using alternative or complementary strategies.

Indermaur (1999) suggests that there is 'value in attempting to change the situation rather than relying on education and treatment alone' (p. 13). Primary prevention strategies, such as the place-based prevention offered by situational strategies, aim to have a direct effect on offender decision-making by making explicit the immediate risks of offending in the immediate situation faced by offenders (Eck, 2002). Place-based prevention strategies avoid criminal sanctions and the economic costs associated with them; moreover, the costs of prevention are more evenly distributed among place owners and managers as 'the risk of crime at places is often under partial control of people who own these places' (Eck, 2002, p. 243). The direct and immediate circumstances of place-based crime prevention approaches may therefore be more effective than other more distal conventional crime prevention approaches and promises of sanctions (Eck, 2002).

In the context of public spaces, situational crime prevention techniques highlight the importance of guardianship, but tend to focus even more heavily on the role of place managers as crime controllers in this context. Place managers are people who regulate the functioning of a place through attention to situations that could lead to crime and disorder or through the indirect regulation of situations for good business (Felson, 1995). Place managers can therefore be doorpersons, building managers, receptionists, bus drivers, security officers or business owners. Management at places is designed to prevent unintended use of space while fostering intended uses (Felson, 1995). Place management is viewed as 'a set of four processes that owners, their employees, and others use to organise a location's physical and social environment' (Madensen, 2007; cited in Madensen & Eck, 2013, p. 566). These processes (Madensen & Eck, 2013, p. 566) aim to

1. *Organise space* — the organisation and design of the space or location, including location selection, construction, repair and upkeep.
2. *Regulate conduct* — the promotion and prohibition of activities, including activities that are sought after and those that are undesirable.
3. *Control access* — the inclusion and exclusion of individuals or groups of people.

4. *Acquire resources* — the acquisition of money and other resources that can be used to carry out processes 1 through 3, as well as to generate profit.

When applied as a place-based crime prevention strategy, situational interventions draw on these processes independently or in combination in order to address place-specific crime problems. Such approaches have been proven to be effective and can influence affective crimes such as violence and disorder, which are often considered impulsive and with disregard for opportunity structure (Indermaur, 1999).

The organisers of public events often take advantage of these principles when they aim to control the crowds and manage space to prevent aggressive behaviour and violent outbursts amongst the crowds. In public protests and demonstrations for example, access of the crowds to small and narrow streets is blocked to contain the activity to open public spaces and major roads, which allow both better supervision and police intervention if needed (Verma, 2007). Shearing and Stenning (1997) in their note on Disney World demonstrated how principles of effective place management such as formal surveillance, target hardening and compliance-assisting measures are implemented, intending to control visitors' behaviour and achieve their compliance.

Others have indicated that by taking venue, event and staff characteristics into account, effective crowd management and environmental modifications can reduce frustrations and stress in stadiums (Madensen & Eck, 2008) and entertainment districts (Homel, Hauritz, Wortley, McIlwain, & Carvolth, 1997). This is achieved by controlling and directing access as well as movement throughout the venue and by providing adequate and proper placement of essential facilities. Some authors also identified the importance of the physical layout of convenience stores (Amandus, Hunter, James, & Hendricks, 1995; Murakami, Higuchi, & Shibayama, 2004). They showed that the following aspects were negatively associated with robbery victimisation: good lines of sight, screened entry/exit points, reduced exterior escape routes, and clear rules about expected behaviour and sanctions, coupled with good cash handling practices. Libraries have also implemented programs which employed situational measures to reduce provocations or improve surveillance and guardianship, thus protecting staff and library visitors from violent encounters with disturbed and violent individuals (Cromwell, Alexander, & Dotson, 2008). Furthermore, public park designs have included 'self-management' approaches that improve functionality, use and perceptions of these places (Hilborn, 2009). These measures include guardianship opportunities, assisting natural surveillance and target hardening, and access control measures to control both movement and times of use. Facilities are also regularly maintained and provide support for intended activities.

Due to the nature of violence and disorder, these crimes are often characterised by measurement and detection difficulties. Accordingly, a limited number of empirical evaluations of situational interventions have been conducted, some of which are reviewed below. They illustrate how place management processes have been successfully activated in various public domains to reduce violence and disorder.

Case Studies

Operation Cul-de-Sac

This operation was an initiative employed between 1990 and 1991 in the neighbourhoods of Los Angeles to reduce opportunities for gang-related violence (Lasley, 1996). The most worrisome crime problems at critical hotspots included drive-by shootings, gang homicides, street assaults and street-based drug trafficking. These activities were supported by major thoroughfares that allowed easy vehicular access to targets and escape routes. To control access to these areas, all 14 major roads leading to and from the hotspots were blocked off with road barriers (fixed iron fences with a lock that could only be opened for emergency vehicles) to create cul-de-sacs with one-way access. This intervention blocked violent gang encounters, including drive-by shootings, and achieved the objective of restoring the area's defensible space properties.

The evaluation employed an interrupted quasi-experimental design with data for one year before the intervention, one year during, and two years after, covering a ten block area. A comparison area was also chosen to account for other potential factors that could contribute to the outcome or show displacement effects. The reported results of the analysis were as follows:

1. A 20% decrease in predatory and property crime rates in the first year and a 14% decrease in the second year of the program (compared to the rate before implementation).

2. A reduction in a number of homicides for the experimental area (from seven before the implementation to one within the two years of the program).

3. A reduction of aggravated assault in both years after the implementation (8% and 37% respectively).

4. Property crime was found not to have been affected by the road barriers.

5. Displacement was not detected.

Soon after the program ended and the barriers were removed, the overall crime rate increased by 14% compared to the initial levels before the intervention. Homicide in particular experienced a significant rise, mainly as a result of drive-by shootings by gangs from both sides of the barriers. The assaults remained constant. Overall, crime levels in the comparison area remained constant over time attesting to the effect of the barriers in the intervention area.

Improved Lighting in Dudley

This study examined victimisation and the perception of safety in a neighbourhood night-time environment as a result of improved visibility in the dark (Painter & Farrington, 1997). The study was conducted in 1992 in two adjacent public housing estates in the English town of Dudley in the West Midlands. While residential roads in the experimental area were selected for improved lighting, the adjacent area served as a control area with no changes introduced. Prevalence and incidence of crimes in each of the areas were measured through non-equivalent control group quasi-experimental design with before and after measures using a victimisation survey. A total of 431 randomly selected participants from the experimental area were interviewed before the intervention and 372 re-interviewed 12 months after the intervention. In the control area, 448 residents were interviewed before and 371 re-interviewed for the purposes of after-intervention measures. The interviewees were not told about the purpose of research and the intervention was not specifically disclosed to them, although most participants discussed the intervention of their own volition during the interviewing process. They were asked about victimisation, perceptions of improvements in visibility, and about their attitudes and behaviours in their neighbourhoods at night time. Unfortunately, only the results for overall crime rates were reported in the after-intervention measures (Painter & Farrington, 1997, pp. 220–224):

1. Prior to the intervention, residents in the experimental area experienced slightly higher prevalence of crime than those in the control (42% compared to 39.1%), with a significant difference in personal crime victimisation that included robbery, snatch theft, assault, threatening behaviour, sexual assault, sexual pestering (13.5% compared to 8.9%).

2. 12 months after the intervention, residents from the experimental area reported a 23% reduction in victimisation for all crimes (from 42% to 32.3%); and the incidence of crime (measured as an offence rate per 100 households) decreased by 41% (from nearly 115 to 68 crimes/100 households).

3. 12 months after the intervention, residents from control area experienced a 3% reduction in crime overall (from 39.1% to 38%); and the incidence of crime decreased by 15% (from just over 82 to nearly 70/100 households).

4. Overall, 'in the experimental area, there was a substantial and significant decrease in the incidence of all categories of crime after the improved street lighting' (p. 221).

5. The residents of the experimental area expressed increased satisfaction with their estate in the after-interviews.

6. The interviewees in the experimental area reported changes in night time occupancy of the streets due to reduced levels of fear (22.1% increase for males and 27.7% increase for females), thus increasing their personal presence and opportunities for informal supervision.

Similar findings to these were reported in a replication study in Stoke-on-Trent (Painter & Farrington, 1999), where three comparable areas (experimental, adjacent and control) were used to measure and control for changes in the prevalence and incidence of crime. Using interviews, the authors found that the prevalence of overall crime decreased by 26% in the experimental area and by 21% in the adjacent area, but increased by 12% in control area. In terms of incidence, there was a 43% reduction in crime across the experimental area, a 45% reduction across the adjacent area, and a 2% reduction in control area. The dramatic change in the incidence of crime in the adjacent area could be attributed to the diffusion of benefits.

Open-Street CCTV in Scotland

This study was conducted to evaluate the overall crime prevention effect of open-street CCTV installation on crime in a town centre of Glasgow (Ditton & Short, 1999). Thirty-two cameras were positioned throughout the city in 1994. Police crime data were used for two years prior to the intervention and a year postintervention. Regression analysis was performed that controlled for confounding factors such as seasons and population composition trends. The results showed an overall 9% increase in crime a year after the intervention. However, this was not consistent across different groups of offences:

1. The most violent crimes including murder and serious assault decreased by 22%.

2. Crimes of arson and vandalism decreased by 8%.

3. Petty assault, drunkenness and other crimes of disorder decreased by 7%.

4. Reckless and drunk driving decreased by 12%.

5. Crimes of sexual assault and prostitution increased by 17%.

6. Crimes of theft, burglary, fraud and similar property offences increased by 23%.

7. Crimes against the public and drug-related offences increased by 32%.

Despite a great deal of variation in crime rates, some potentially violent offenders appeared to have been deterred by the sight of CCTV. The variance might also suggest that a consistent positive effect of CCTV could be compromised due to an increased sense of anonymity in large cities such as Glasgow.

'Mobile Places'

This case study describes how 'mobile places' such as public buses also require good place management practices to provide a good image and a safe environment. The study was conducted on double-decker buses in Manchester, UK, where CCTV surveillance systems were implemented to suppress a re-occurring problem of vandalism by children and teenagers (Sturman, 1980). Vandalism primarily included damage to seats by slashing and paint spraying, and window smashing. Since the damage was greatest at the rear on the upper deck and back seats, it was speculated that supervision of those particular areas had to be increased.

First, the materials inside 99 double-decker buses were replaced with materials that would prevent visible damage or easy removal of parts of the seats. CCTV and conductors were introduced on some of the buses to increase surveillance and its perception. After the buses were inspected for damage, the results revealed a significant reduction in vandalism on buses with conductors, attesting to the importance of formal supervision on one-person-operated buses. Furthermore, the internal layout of the buses proved important in predicting vandalism — particularly on the buses without conductors where concealed parts of the buses, rear areas and upper decks suffered most damage. In fact, buses without a conductor suffered nearly twice as much damage on upper decks compared to those with a conductor. Conversely, those seats that were positioned so that they offered good visibility to the driver and CCTV were less damaged.

Similar outcomes were also observed in a North English study, where the costs of vandalism and graffiti cleaning dropped by two thirds over nine months across the whole fleet of 80 buses despite CCTV only been installed on two of those buses (Poyner, 1992). Verbal and physical assaults on drivers also dropped, as did fare evasion.

Victoria's Travel Safe Program

A Travel Safe program in Victoria, Australia, was introduced in 1990 to address problems of vandalism and assaults, and associated cancellations of public transportations services (buses, trams and trains; Carr & Spring, 1993). Elevated levels of fear amongst passengers also led to declining use of transportation services. The main problems included unclean vehicles, stations and stops; perception of poor safety due to damaged property; the presence of offensive groups; and negative media coverage. To address these problems, the program was designed to

1. rapidly remove signs of graffiti, vandalism and littering to improve positive perceptions of places and deny benefits to graffiti 'artists'
2. implement customer-oriented upgrades at selected stations including shelters at bus stops
3. improve aids to security, including public telephone; improved illumination at bus shelters, train and tram stops and stations; and have office-based staff circulate through trains and around stations to provide an authoritative presence
4. enhance surveillance opportunities via CCTV on stations, buses and trains
5. improve image by repairing damage from graffiti and vandalism and from unintentional damage; and removing litter
6. increase Transit Patrol and police presence in problem areas
7. regionalise Transit Patrol to make it more accessible and customer-oriented
8. allow staff to escort travellers to their parked cars
9. mobilise the community to participate in the repair program, and assist in landscaping and other activities to enhance a sense of ownership
10. incorporate the community's interests and concerns in modifications
11. form partnerships between the community, local government and private sector.

The results after two years of the program included a reduction of crimes against persons, primarily assault, by 42% (from an average of 57.3 to 33.1 incidents per month); and increased availability of trains (from 65%–70% to 98% of operational services during peak periods). A more reliable service was also provided on a daily basis due to reduced vandalism and improved safety. Additionally, the community's sense of ownership was increased and was further encouraged through community and education programs, community involvement in seminars and multi-partnership liaison.

Surfers Paradise Safety Action Project

In 1993 the Surfers Paradise Safety Action Project on the Gold Coast in Queensland, Australia, highlighted the importance of situational factors and environmental precipitators for crime. The initiative has had important implications for the development of policies regarding responsible drinking practices in Queensland and Australia (Homel et al., 1997). The project was a community-based initiative designed to reduce violence within and around licensed venues in the major tourist area of the Gold Coast. A holistic multipartnership approach was undertaken that included the control and reduction of irresponsible alcohol drinking practices by eliminating discounted drinks and service of alcohol to intoxicated individuals. Greater focus was also given to alcohol-free entertainment. Improvements in security and safety included training of security staff to increase their patron management capacity. Internal and external layouts of the clubs were also manipulated to reduce crowding and associated frustration and aggression. Special attention was also given to organised transportation policies after pub closure times, to ensure the safety of patrons and reduce chances of violent and disorderly behaviour.

Observations were conducted on 18 nightclubs over two summers prior to, and two summers after, the interventions. The analysis of these qualitative field observations of patrons' behaviour within and outside the premises revealed significant reductions in the incidents of verbal abuse (81.6% reduction), arguments (67.6% reduction) and physical assaults (52% reduction; Homel et al., 1997, p. 70). These positive effects endured until 1996, when management of the program and maintenance of the strategies was reduced.

In 1994, the project was replicated in three North Queensland cities: Cairns, Townsville and Mackay, with similar findings (Hauritz, Homel, Mcllwain, Burrows, & Townsley, 1998). Research conducted on licensed premises in Sydney in 1991 also showed the importance of place management practices with internal and external design factors that reduce the potential for crowding, as well as operational practices that focus on entertainment rather than drinking (Homel & Clark, 1995; Homel, Tomsen, & Thommeny, 1992).

Australian Motorcycle Grand Prix

Planning for the 1989 Australian Motorcycle Grand Prix at Phillip Island, Victoria, Australia, included a key objective of effectively managing large crowds and preventing violence (Veno & Veno, 1993). In particular, organisers were concerned to avoid repetition of events at the Bathurst Grand Prix in 1986. The annual Bathurst event was associated with chronic violence, disorder and crowd management problems. In 1987, a major riot was associated with overly forceful policing tactics — including numerous roadblocks and ticketing for minor traffic violations — and alcohol restrictions. Frustration levels of riders and spectators were also affected by poor camping and entertainment facilities, which provided few relaxation options. Media sensationalism was seen as exacerbating the problem.

At the Phillip Island event, policing tactics were changed from a militaristic approach to community inclusive practices, with less direct police involvement. Families and middle-class persons were welcomed to the event with the intent of providing mixed demographics to reduce the risk of violence. Instead of stopping and searching motorbike riders, police accompanied them and cleared the path to the venue. Set rules for police interventions were designed to prevent discretionary actions which could provoke violence. In cooperation with private operators, the organisers also provided better facilities, including camp sites. Media reporting was more restrained and responsible.

After the event, the spectators were asked to rate the quality of police work. The great majority (80%) rated police as 'good' or 'very good', compared to only 13% at Bathurst. Crime and disorder problems were also significantly lower compared to previous events, which resulted in fewer arrests (36 of 240,999 spectators arrested compared to 23 of 4,297 at Bathurst in 1987). Finally, 92% of the 350 randomly selected and interviewed residents at Phillip Island responded affirmatively to the question whether they wanted this event to be repeated in 1990 (Veno & Veno, 1993, pp. 169–171).

'Building for Life' Housing Developments

This study is a good illustration of the design-crime relationship despite the absence of pre- and post-program evaluation. The study was conducted on 12 housing developments between 2009 and 2010 (Armitage, Monchuk, & Rogerson, 2011). Six 'Building for Life' developments were initially selected from three parts of England. The developments were built according to CPTED principles, as described in chapter two of this book. The CPTED principles covered road layouts, car parking, house design, surveillance, territoriality, communal space, management and maintenance, and physical security. A matched comparison was created from the same number of corresponding nearby non-Building for Life developments, providing a total of 2,193 properties for evaluation. The study included a detailed analysis of design features and their influence on victimisation across the 12 developments.

The main part of the study relied on field observations by using the 'Design Features Checklist' for assessing the risk of victimisation for each property (Armitage et al., 2011, p. 36). The checklist covered environmental features of dwellings and surroundings — including footpaths, roads and parking facilities. Special attention was given to (a) through-movement traffic flow that could contribute to outsiders' knowledge of criminal opportunities and escape routes; (b) provision of parking facilities and residents' car parking habits; and (c) identification of places that lacked proper territorial definition, such as footpaths, play areas, open spaces and public buildings. Interviews with key personnel who were responsible for safety at each of the housing developments were also conducted on sites prior to field observations in order to understand how place was designed and managed.

A 3-year crime analysis was conducted jointly for all 12 study sites. Statistical analyses showed that, overall, 94% of the variation in crime was explained at the property level — meaning that physical features played an important role in predicting victimisation of locations and dwellings. Among other findings, the Armitage et al. (2011, p. 48) study showed that

1. Disorderly behaviour and violence accounted for the highest proportion of crime: 39% were criminal damage offences; and 22% were crimes against a person, including assault, theft from a person and robbery.

2. The type of street was an important predictor of victimisation: properties on through roads and those on 'leaky' cul-de-sacs (with through footpaths) experienced 93% and 110% more crime respectively that those on a true cul-de-sac (no connecting formal or informal footpaths) — which successfully controlled access to dwellings and blocks.

3. Properties that were overlooked by three to five neighbouring properties experienced lower victimisation than those that had no properties overlooking from the rear, thus diminishing opportunities for informal supervision.

4. Parking facilities were inadequate overall: they were distant from housing and poorly thought-out, resulting in rear-house or illegal on-street parking. According to the authors' assessment this posed increased security risks by providing concealment opportunities and assisted access to dwellings.

Implications

The case studies above have illustrated how situational measures have an important role to play in preventing violence and disorder. The techniques that were implemented were dependent upon the contexts and crime problems that were targeted. The techniques included combinations of highly visible target hardening and access control methods — such as the barriers in Operation Cul-de-Sac — or they relied more on perceptions of surveillance capabilities — as with the CCTV systems on Manchester buses. Moreover, some problems required the implementation of a comprehensive multi-partnership approach, as evident in the Surfers Paradise and Phillip Island projects. This seems a common practice, especially when situational measures are implemented in conjunction with problem-oriented policing, with the intention of addressing nuisance behaviours before they evolve into serious criminal incidents (Goldstein, 1979). Consultation between planners and the police was fundamental in the Building for Life housing developments. The importance of context-specificity in addressing violence and disorder is therefore vital (Ekblom, 2011).

A place manager needs to account for differences between settings, and needs to first identify the particular circumstances that give rise to specific types of crime problems. This facilitates the implementation of appropriate crime prevention techniques. Effective place management requires the regulation of functioning at places by providing support for intended activities, and managing the potential crime opportunities resulting from characteristics of places (Madensen & Eck, 2013). While the importance of guardianship should not be overlooked, it is effective place management that addresses the problems in contextually different public settings (Ekblom, 2011). This is best considered in the planning stages of a new development, and implementing strategies so that they intensify the effects of each another. For example, in housing developments, surveillance opportunities for the most vulnerable properties, such as those on through roads, might need to be intensified by planning multiple residences that 'neighbour' each other from the rear (Armitage et al., 2011).

The variability of effective interventions in the case studies highlight how place management practices and situational strategies should not be seen, automatically, as directly transferrable from one situation to another. Application should instead embrace the context or 'analytic generalization' of sites (Yin, 2009, p. 38). Theoretical propositions and frameworks resulting from the case studies should serve as a guide — rather than 'instructions' — during a design phase regarding on how and what strategies could be implemented.

It is also evident from the case studies that, while situational measures were implemented across public, semi-public and somewhat also private settings, they often concurrently impacted multiple types of crime. However, when implementing multiple strategies concurrently, care must be taken that prevention of one crime does not inadvertently encourage other forms of crime or generate heightened fear of crime (Clarke, 2004; Weisel, 2002). For example, 'Building for Life' residential developments were planned with the intention of deterring multiple crimes and enhancing residents' feelings of safety.

Another issue highlighted in the case studies was the methodological problem of isolating cause and effect relationships. Single interventions — such as road barriers, street lighting or CCTV — could be assessed fairly confidently as the factor responsible for reductions in crime. In the other case studies, the adoption of multiple interventions was probably necessary, but it did mean it was difficult or impossible to say which interventions were the most effective.

Finally, it is also important to note that maintenance of successful interventions is essential. The tendency to regression was shown following withdrawal of the interventions in Operation Cul de Sac and the Surfers Paradise

Safety Action Project. In the case of the road blocks in Los Angeles, lack of maintenance of damaged barriers and 'mixed messages' about their effectiveness led to their removal (Lasley, 1996, p. 29). In the Surfers Paradise Project, lack of ongoing self-regulation, community monitoring and formal enforcement caused the return of violence to levels prior to the project (Homel et al., 1997).

Conclusion

Using a selection of case studies, this chapter has demonstrated the potential of situational interventions and their advantage over regular policing strategies, in reducing violence and disorder. A positive crime reduction link between situational interventions and crimes of violence and disorder was illustrated across contextually-different settings. More is needed to ensure that places are managed so that they support intended use of space, are liveable, safe and socially sustainable to reduce fear and crime. It has also been shown that program evaluators need to conduct more systematic crime prevention intensity and impact measures.

References

Amandus, H.E., Hunter, R.D., James, E., & Hendricks, S. (1995). Reevaluation of the effectiveness of environmental designs to reduce robbery risk in Florida convenience stores. *Journal of Occupational and Environmental Medicine, 37*(6), 711–717.

Armitage, R., Monchuk, L., & Rogerson, M. (2011). It looks good, but what is it like to live there? Exploring the impact of innovative housing design on crime. *European Journal on Criminal Policy and Research, 17*(1), 29–54.

Carr, K., & Spring, G. (1993). Public transport safety: A community right and a communal responsibility. In R.V. Clarke (Ed.), *Crime prevention studies, vol. 1* (pp. 147–155). Monsey, NY: Criminal Justice Press.

Clarke, R.V. (2004, October). *Twenty five techniques of situational crime prevention: What they forgot to tell you in the police academy.* Paper presented at the Problem-Oriented Policing Conference, Charlotte, North Carolina.

Cromwell, P., Alexander, G., & Dotson, P. (2008). Crime and incivilities in libraries: Situational crime prevention strategies for thwarting bibliobandits and problem patrons. *Security Journal, 21*, 147–158.

Ditton, J., & Short, E. (1999). Yes, it works, no, it doesn't: Comparing the effects of open-street CCTV in two adjacent Scottish town centres. In K. Painter & N. Tilley (Eds.), *Crime prevention studies, vol. 10* (pp. 201–223). Monsey, NY: Criminal Justice Press.

Eck, J.E. (2002). Preventing crime at places. In L.W. Sherman, D.P. Farrington, B.C. Welsh & D. Layton MacKenzie (Eds.). *Evidence-based crime prevention* (pp. 241–294). London, England: Routledge.

Ekblom, P. (2011). Deconstructing CPTED ... and reconstructing it for practice, knowledge management and research. *European Journal on Criminal Policy and Research, 17*(1), 7–28.

Felson, M. (1995). Those who discourage crime. In J.E. Eck & D. Weisburd (Eds.), *Crime prevention studies, Vol. 4* (pp. 53–66). Monsey, NY: Criminal Justice Press.

Goldstein, H. (1979). Improving policing: A Problem-oriented approach. *Crime and Delinquency, 25*, 236–258.

Hale, C. (1996). Fear of crime: A review of the literature. *International Review of Victimology, 4*, 79–150.

Hauritz, M., Homel, R., Mcllwain, G., Burrows, T., & Townsley, M. (1998). Reducing violence in licensed venues: Community Safety Action Projects. *Trends and Issues in Crime and Criminal Justice, No. 101.* Canberra, Australia: Australian IC.

Hilborn, J. (2009). Dealing with crime and disorder in urban parks. *Problem-oriented guides for police series, guide no. 8.* Washington, DC: U.S. Department of Justice. Retrieved from http://www.popcenter.org/Responses/pdfs/urban_parks.pdf

Homel, R., & Clark, J. (1995). *The prediction and prevention of violence in pubs and clubs.* Retrieved from http://www.griffith.edu.au/__data/assets/pdf_file/0016/13327/prediciting.pdf

Homel, R., Hauritz, M., Wortley, R., Mcllwain, G., & Carvolth, R. (1997). Preventing alcohol-related crime through community action: The Surfers Paradise Safety Action Project. In R. Homel (Ed.), *Crime prevention studies, vol. 7* (pp. 35–90). Monsey, NY: Criminal Justice Press.

Homel, R., Tomsen, S., & Thommeny, J. (1992). Public drinking and violence: Not just an alcohol problem. *The Journal of Drug Issues, 22*(3), 679–697.

Indermaur, D. (1999). *Situational prevention of violent crime: Theory and practice in Australia.* Retrieved from http://www.crc.law.uwa.edu.au/__data/page/50334/Situational_Prevention_of_Violent_Crime.pdf

Lasley, J. (1996). *Using traffic barriers to 'design out' crime: A program evaluation of LAPD's Operation Cul-de-sac.* Retrieved from http://www.popcenter.org/library/scp/pdf/104-Lasley.pdf

Madensen, T.D., & Eck, J.E. (2008). Spectator violence in stadiums. *Problem-oriented guides for police series, guide no. 8.* Washington, DC: U.S. Department of Justice. Retrieved from http://www.popcenter.org/problems/pdfs/spectator_violence.pdf

Madensen, T.D., & Eck, J.E. (2013). Crime places and place management. In F.T. Cullen & P. Wilcox (Eds.), *The Oxford handbook of criminological theory* (pp. 554–578). New York, NY: Oxford University Press.

Mair, J.S., & Mair, M. (2003). Violence prevention and control through environmental modifications. *Annual Review of Public Health, 24*, 209–225.

Murakami, M., Higuchi, K., & Shibayama, A. (2004). Relationship between convenience store robberies and road environment. In J.P. van Leeuwen & H.J.P. Timmermans (Eds.), *Recent advances in design & decision support systems in architecture and urban planning* (pp. 341–356). Dordrecht, the Netherlands: Kluwer Academic.

Painter, K., & Farrington, D.P. (1997). The crime reducing effect of improved street lighting: The Dudley project. In R.V. Clarke (Ed.), *Situational crime prevention: Successful case studies* (pp. 209–226). Guilderland, NY: Harrow and Heston.

Painter, K., & Farrington, D.P. (1999). Street lighting and crime: Diffusion of benefits in the Stoke-on-Trent project. In K. Painter & N. Tilley (Eds.), *Crime prevention studies, vol. 10* (pp. 77–122). Monsey, NY: Criminal Justice Press.

Poyner, B. (1992). Video cameras and bus vandalism. In R.V. Clarke (Ed.), *Situational crime prevention: Successful case studies* (pp. 185–193). Guilderland, NY: Harrow and Heston.

Shearing, C.D., & Stenning, P.C. (1997). From the panopticon to Disney World: The development of the discipline. In R.V. Clarke (Ed.), *Situational crime prevention: Successful case studies* (pp. 300–304). Guilderland, NY: Harrow and Heston.

Sturman, A. (1980). Damage on buses: The effects of supervision. In R.V. Clarke & P. Mayhew (Eds.), *Designing out crime* (pp. 31–38). London, England: HMSO.

Van Dijk, J., van Kesteren, J., & Smit, P. (2007). *Criminal victimisation in international perspective: Key findings from the 2004–2005 ICVS and EU ICS.* The Hague, the Netherlands: Boom Legal. Retrieved from http://www.unicri.it/services/library_documentation/publications/icvs/publications/ICVS2004_05report.pdf

Veno, A., & Veno, E. (1993). Situational prevention of public disorder at the Australian motorcycle grand prix. In R.V. Clarke (Ed.), *Crime prevention studies, Vol. 1* (pp. 157–175). Monsey, NY: Criminal Justice Press.

Verma, A. (2007). Anatomy of riots: A Situational crime prevention approach. *Crime Prevention and Community Safety, 9,* 201–221.

Weisel, D.L. (2002). Graffiti. *Problem-oriented guides for police series, guide no. 9.* Washington, DC: US Department of Justice. Retrieved from http://www.popcenter.org/problems/pdfs/Graffiti.pdf

Yin, R.K. (2009). *Case study research: Design and methods.* Thousand Oaks, CA: Sage.

Chapter 5

Case Studies in Reducing Property and Financial Crime

Tim Prenzler

The case studies in this chapter illustrate large reductions in crime through a range of situational interventions. Many of the cases involve collaboration between stakeholders, including police, security providers, business groups and residents. A number also illustrate the value of an experimental approach and running pilots before full implementation. The chapter concludes by drawing out lessons from the case studies, including the benefits of diagnostic research and the need for comprehensive impact measures.

Background

Most of the big gains in the global downturn in crime have been in property crime; in areas such as theft, burglary and motor vehicle theft. As we saw in chapter 1, much of this can be attributed to the expansion of situationally-based security measures, or 'securitisation'. A good deal occurred through market-driven private-sector adoptions of security. In other cases, governments have intervened in the market by mandating security. Examples include legislated standards for home security and vehicle security.

Target hardening, access control and increased surveillance have been shown to have strong effects against property crime. A 1996 US study of commercial burglary found that the probability of a property without an alarm being burgled was 4.6 times that of an alarmed property (Hakim & Shachmurove, 1996, p. 43). Security devices have been shown to be particularly effective against burglary when used in combination. For example, a British Crime Survey showed that:

> Households with 'less than basic' home security measures were six times more likely to have been victims of burglary (5.8%) than households with 'basic' security (0.9%) and ten times more likely than households with 'enhanced' home security measures (0.6%). (Flatley, Kershaw, Smith, Chaplin, & Moon, 2010, pp. 2–3).

'Basic security' referred to window locks and double/deadlocks on external doors; while 'enhanced' security included these and one other device, such as sensor lights, security grills or an alarm.

The case study summaries in this chapter cover a small number of studies on property crime reduction, selected to indicate something of the range of possible approaches and settings. The variety of cases available on the record is now extensive, including some highly inventive interventions. For example, a project in New York City in the 1980s was successful in eliminating graffiti on subway trains through a systematic cleaning program. The approach included a commitment to keeping defaced carriages out of circulation, thereby removing the rewards for offenders (Sloan-Howitt & Kelling, 1990). It is sometimes the case that very simple changes have large effects on crime. In a UK study, for example, thefts from bags at a busy market were significantly reduced by widening aisles to improve surveillance (Poyner & Webb, 1997).

There are fewer cases of large reductions in financial crime on the record. The spread of the internet has created enormous new opportunities for fraud and embezzlement. Nonetheless, there are studies showing potential for large gains; and simple measures, applied systematically, are sometime very effective. One example is 'proof of purchase' requirements to stop refund fraud (Challinger, 1996). Blais and Bacher (2007), in a study of insurance fraud, found that suspected 'claim padding' was reduced by simply including warnings about prosecution policy on company letters.

The focus of the present chapter is on property and financial crimes, but it must be said that crime prevention projects are often aimed at reducing these and other crimes simultaneously. This is especially the case with place-based projects, with success measured across both violent and property crimes.

Property crime

Collective Security on Dutch Industrial Estates

In the late-1980s, at the 300-hectare Enschede-Haven industrial site, the Area Entrepreneur Association requested police increase patrols to reduce crime. Police analysed the offence profile for the area and suggested a partnership in which the police would support on-site private security. From that point, the following steps occurred (van den Berg, 1995):

Step 1   The association formed a cooperative from the majority of the 410 companies.

Step 2   Police established a Project Agency, which coordinated the cooperative, the police and local government.

Step 3   A successful submission was made to a national government crime prevention body to subsidise the start-up costs of the project.

Sept 4   A government employment agency supported the recruitment of unemployed persons as security guards.

Sept 5   Police provided the guards with training.

Step 6   Sufficient funds were collected to station a security guard on the estate outside business hours.

Step 7   All alarm activations were channelled through one security firm's monitoring station.

Step 8   The on-site guard checked activations before contacting police, thereby minimising false call outs.

Step 9   The project was advertised on signage around the site.

Step 10 The local council improved lighting and the general appearance of the area.

Van den Berg's (1995) evaluation does not describe how the project worked in terms of arrests or deterrence. However, security incidents were reduced by 72%, from 90 per month in the year-and-a-half before the project began to 25 per month in the year-and-a-half after it was established. The partnership continued as a self-funded project once the initial subsidy expired. A similar partnership on the Vianen industrial estate produced a 52% reduction in burglary (van den Berg, 1995).

The Kirkholt Project

One of the most famous anti-burglary initiatives on the record is the Kirkholt Project in the UK (Forrester, Frenz, O'Connell, & Pease, 1990). The project targeted repeat victimisation on a housing estate, and involved several strategies. Within a few days of a burglary, a crime prevention officer would conduct a security survey of the premises, with security hardware upgrades funded by the local council's housing department. Another measure involved the removal of coin operated fuel meters, which attracted burglars. A specific form of 'neighbourhood watch' — 'cocoon watch' — was also introduced. This involved asking victims' immediate neighbours to report suspicious activity. Cocoon watch participants were also given free security upgrades. Cocoon surveillance was based on a finding that 70% of burglary entry points were visible to neighbours. Burglary rates declined by 75%, from 44 per month before the project began to 11 per month in the third year after implementation, with no observable displacement. Multiple victimisations were reduced almost to zero. Burglaries in neighbouring areas declined by 24%. When savings from reduced burglaries were set against costs, the project produced an estimated overall saving of £1.2 million (see also chapter 3 on financial aspects).

The Leicester Small Business and Crime Initiative

This project was focused on commercial burglary (Tilley & Hopkins, 1998). It was managed by a committee, with representatives from the city council, police and chamber of commerce. Funding was provided by a bank charity. Initial survey research informed a focus on repeat or 'chronic' victims. Security audits were carried out by a project officer following a police incident report. A mix of security devices was usually installed, including alarms and CCTV. Portable alarms were installed in some cases. These could be shared with other premises once risk periods for repeat offences had expired. Silent alarms were also used, with a view to capturing and incapacitating offenders after research found numerous offenders could complete a burglary following the activation of an audible alarm. The project resulted in very few arrests. However, burglary was reduced by 41%, from 735 incidents in the year before the project to 433 in the second and final year of evaluation. Criminal damage was reduced by 36%.

Stopping Prolific Burglars in Boggart Hill

A project targeting prolific burglars in Boggart Hill, in the UK, was successful in arresting repeat offenders in an initial 'crackdown' period, using profiling techniques that matched known offender methods with offence characteristics. In a traditional police operation, 'the response to the burglary problem would have ended there' (Farrell, Chenery, & Pease, 1998, p. 7). In the case of the Boggart Hill project, a 'consolidation phase' saw the installation of security hardware on burgled homes. The approach generated a 60% reduction in burglaries, from an average 44.9 per month preproject to 18.5 in the consolidation phase. A 'hallow effect' or 'diffusion of benefits' was evident in a 36% drop in burglaries in adjoining areas.

Operation Identification in Wales

This was a UK Home Office demonstration project involving the large-scale application of property marking as a defence against domestic burglary in a small community (Laycock, 1991). Police and special constables visited residences offering free use of property marking equipment. On a second visit, officers took an inventory of the marked property. Window and door decals advertised the fact that property inside the home was marked. There were further visits and letters, and participation extended to 72% of households. The project received extensive media coverage, and known burglars were included in the home visits. In the 12 months before Operation Identification, participating households were the victims of 91 burglaries. This fell 61% to 35 burglaries after the operation began, with no evidence of displacement. For nonparticipants, the victimisation rate was stable, with 37 incidents before and 39 after the operation.

CCTV in Newcastle upon Tyne

The Newcastle upon Tyne City Centre Partnership Security Initiative is one of the few open space CCTV programs showing significant reductions in crime (Brown, 1995). The system was set up in 1992 with a combination of local private sector money and a government grant. Sixteen cameras were installed with zoom, pan and tilt capability. Police managed the system, with the CCTV control room linked by radio to patrol officers and retailers. Data about the concentration of crimes was used to locate cameras.

According to Brown (1995, p. 26), the system had a 'strong deterrent effect'. Cameras assisted rapid interventions by police, and the rate of arrests per criminal incidents increased. The system also assisted with convictions: 'Almost all of the 400 people arrested as a direct result of the scheme admitted guilt after being shown video footage' (in Brown, 1995, p. 26). The evaluation reported the average number of incidents across a range of crime types for 26 months before the program was fully implemented, and compared these with the average number for 15 months after implementation. Key findings for the area within the CCTV system were as follows (Brown, 1995, p. 17):

- Burglary was reduced by 57% from 40 incidents per month to 17 per month.
- Theft from motor vehicles declined 50% (18 to 9).
- Theft of motor vehicles declined 47% (17 to 9).
- Criminal damage declined 34% (32 to 21).
- Other theft declined 11% (223 to 198).

While the rate of arrests increased relative to the number of recorded offences, the overall number of arrests decreased as offences decreased. In addition, a diffusion of benefits was observed in adjoining areas, which experienced substantial, albeit smaller, reductions in crimes.

Business Improvement Districts in the United States

Business Improvement Districts — or BIDs — stimulate commerce by attracting people to an area with improved amenities and security. Funds from government and business groups are used for cleaning, repairing vandalised property, graffiti removal and security patrols. Cook and MacDonald (2011) reported there were approximately 1,000 BIDs in the US in 2010. Evaluations show some significant successes in crime reduction without displacement, including burglary and motor vehicle theft. One review reported that 'most neighbourhoods with established BID security programs have experienced double-digit reductions in crime rates (sometimes up to 60%)' (Vindevogel, 2005, p. 237). Police back up is considered essential to success. A recent economically-focused assessment found BIDs could provide substantial public benefits, including significantly reducing the costs of criminal justice processing of offenders (Cook & MacDonald, 2011).

Strike Force Piccadilly: Combating Automatic Teller Machine Ram Raids and Bam Raids

Strike Force Piccadilly was set up in 2005 by the New South Wales Police Property Crime Squad to counter a dramatic upsurge in ATM ram raids in the greater Sydney area. The Strike Force won two Australian Crime and Violence Prevention Awards and the 2013 international Herman Goldstein Award for Excellence in Problem-Oriented Policing.

Police were initially overwhelmed by the attacks on ATMs (Figure 5.1). In some of the more destructive raids, gangs smashed through shopping centres in stolen vehicles and knocked over ATMs in central atriums. In mid-2006, the Piccadilly team convened a stakeholder forum, which led to the establishment of an ongoing partnership between police and security managers from the ATM Industry Association, the Australian Bankers' Association, cash-in-transit firms, and the Shopping Centre Council of Australia (Prenzler, 2011). Research and information sharing identified key vulnerabilities around machines, including easy vehicle access and frequent false alarm activations that delayed police responses. The analysis led to a commitment to implement the following measures:

1. A police priority response 1800 number (based on multiple alarm activations).
2. The installation of situational prevention measures, including ATM relocations, specialist bollards (with anti-cutting technology) and anti-ramming devices (such as flexible base plates).
3. E-mail circulation of intelligence reports.
4. Publication of an ATM risk assessment and reduction guide.
5. On-site CPTED-based advice by police crime prevention officers.

These changes were effective in producing large reductions in 'successful' raids (where cash was obtained) and 'unsuccessful' raids (involving considerable property damage). The rapid response system closed the raiders' time frame, the relocations reduced access, and the bollards and anti-ramming devices increased target hardening. The reduced time frames assisted investigations, which led to the arrest and incapacitation of 97 persons between August 2005 and June 2007.

Criminal gangs then adopted a new technique, which had spread overseas (Prenzler, 2011). Explosive gas attacks — or 'bam raids' — involve pumping combustible gases into ATMs and setting them alight, destroying the machine and allowing access to the cash canister. The outbreak of bam raids included 19 attacks in November 2008. Strike Force Piccadilly 2 was formed in July 2008. The strategies used in Strike Force Piccadilly 1 were maintained, including the stakeholder meetings and 1800 hotline. In addition, ATM operators installed gas detection equipment. The detectors would trigger:

1. a back-to-base alarm that alerted police on the priority system,
2. an audible alarm and release of smoke designed to act as deterrents, and
3. release of a gas that mixed with the explosive gas, making it inoperable.

The capture and incapacitation of a small group of specialist offenders was facilitated by CCTV footage and assistance from commercial partners in the preservation of crime scenes.

Figure 5.1 shows the number of successful and unsuccessful ram raids on a three month (quarterly) basis from October 2005 to March 2013. Over the longer term, there was a 100% reduction in successful raids, with no cases since August 2009. Unsuccessful raids declined by 84% from the initial peak period. Figure 5.1 also shows there was a 100% reduction in successful bam raids, with no cases recorded since April 2009. Unsuccessful attacks declined by 95% from the peak period.

Financial Crime

Combating Fare Evasion on Public Transport in the Netherlands

The previous chapter included a case study of enlarged guardianship on public transport, targeting 'fare dodging, vandalism, and aggression' (van Andel, 1989, p. 47). Increases in these crimes were widely attributed to cost-cutting measures, including removing the position of conductor.

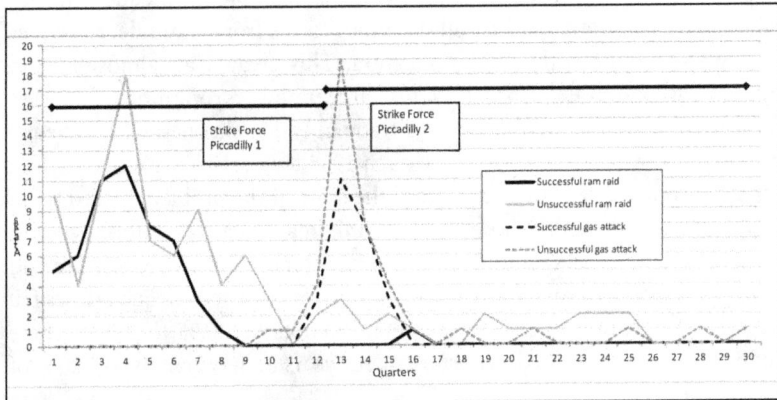

Figure 5.1

ATM ram raids and bam raids, Greater Sydney area, October 2005 to March 2013. *Source:* Data provided by the New South Wales Police, August 2013. (Used with permission.)

Opportunities for fare evasion were also enlarged by the introduction of additional doors on trams. In response to escalating problems, in 1984 the Ministry of Transport and Public Works supported the employment of 'safety, information and control' officers – or VICs – on the tram and metro services in three cities to provide patrols and check tickets. In addition, from 1985, bus drivers were required to check all tickets as passengers boarded through the front door.

Evaluation of the fare evasion component of the project occurred through random checks on passengers; and a survey of passengers and staff. The results were complex, across three cities and three modes of transport. Overall, large reductions were found in the first year, with further drops in most cases in following years. The largest estimated declines in fare evasion in the first year were on the Amsterdam Metro, from 23.5% of passengers to 6.5% (-17%), and Rotterdam buses, from 14.1% to 2.4% (-11.7%) (pp. 50-51). The Hague tram system, where VICs could not impose fines, had an initial drop but without subsequent falls. Surveys showed that passengers noticed more inspections and were strongly supportive of the changes because they improved the fairness of the system. Staff were also supportive.

The new boarding procedures on buses involved a delay factor, which necessitated the assignment of extra buses. In two cities, the savings were estimated to almost completely cover the costs. The VIC program cost about three times the money that was saved, but the goals were not exclusively financial.

Reducing Cheque Fraud in Sweden

Knutsson and Kuhlhorn (1997) illustrate the relative ease of some forms of crime — and crime prevention — with the example of cheque fraud in Sweden. In the 1960s, banks would honour losses from fraudulent cheques up to 300 kronor without identification. This created an almost perfect opportunity for fraud, especially for large numbers of minor forgeries. Stockholm saw the proliferation of a trade in stolen cheques, where cheque crimes grew by 500% from 2,663 cases in 1965 to 15,817 in 1970. Banks and retailers were resistant to change until the scale of the problem forced them to negotiate with police. In 1971, the bank guarantee was withdrawn and proof of identity was required for all cheque transactions. The measure had a dramatic effect. Across Sweden, the number of reported cheque crimes fell 82% from 1970 to 1972. In Stockholm, offences fell 86% to 2,198. These reductions were sustained over subsequent years at between 10 and 20% of the peak levels.

Data-Matching Against Welfare Fraud in Sweden

Kuhlhorn (1997) reported on the introduction of a data-matching program for housing subsidies in Sweden. One database consisted of income estimates for recipients of housing subsidies (the target group). The other contained income estimates for recipients of sickness insurance. In the first database, applicants were motivated to understate their income with a view to increasing their subsidy. In the second database, applicants were motivated to overstate their income to increase their sickness benefit. The data-matching system was introduced in 1979. In the first year of operation, 39,408 households lost all or part of their subsidy (6.1% of checked households). Over two years there was a large increase in voluntary corrections. Kuhlhorn's study did not describe any prosecutions, nor were there any data on cost-benefit ratios. The study did, however, report the findings of an opinion poll on the program. The survey found that 94% of respondents thought the checks were appropriate, and 87% of housing subsidy clients in the sample supported the checks.

Centrelink and Early Intervention Against Welfare Fraud

In 2011–2012, Australia's main welfare distributor, Centrelink, introduced a system of personal contact with clients to identify error and embryonic fraud. Introduction of the system was prompted by a major legal case that reduced the criminal liability of customers who failed to inform Centrelink of changes in their eligibility. A set of pilot projects, mainly involving telephone communication, supported the roll out of a system that included SMS and e-mail 'reminders' about obligations to report changes in circumstances that might affect payments (Department of Human Services, 2012, p. 222). Centrelink already had a complex array of anti-fraud measures in operation — including identity verification procedures, covert surveillance and data-matching. However, the rates of detected fraud and prosecutions had been stable, and Centrelink was losing tens of millions of dollars each year to fraud (Prenzler, 2012). Part of the problem was that administrative processes allowed 'noncompliance' to go undetected and unremedied for too long. Losses built up, and the cases were then treated criminally as 'fraud'.

When the new program was introduced, several anti-fraud strategies were also stepped up. However, direct contact was the main innovation in the period. The government reported that, in a 5-month period, there were over 120,000 contacts under the 'front-foot initiative', saving an estimated $37 million (Carr, 2012). The legal case also prompted a major downgrade of criminal matters. Overall, The number of fraud cases referred to the federal public prosecutor declined by 73%, from 4,608 in 2009–2010 to 1,235 in 2011–2012 (Centrelink, 2010, p. 71; Department of Human Services, 2012, p. 229).

Chip and PIN Security and Plastic Card Fraud

In the UK, the replacement of signature and magnetic stripe security with 'chip and PIN' technology began with a trial in 2003 (Levi, 2008). (The computer chip on the card authenticates the PIN entered by the customer.) The trial was initiated in response to the growing problem of card misuse — including forging signatures, theft of cards, and skimming and cloning. A survey of consumers in the trial area showed 83% supported the new technology. A national roll out, funded by the card companies, began later in 2003, which involved issuing approximately 140 million cards to 42 million customers, and upgrading hundreds-of-thousands of ATMs and retail terminals.

An evaluation by Levi (2008) covered 2 years of data across a number of categories. In relation to UK-issued cards in UK retail 'face-to-face' transactions, losses from fraud declined by 67%, from £218.8 million in 2004 to £72.1 million in 2006. The fraud category 'mail nonreceipt' (mainly misuse of cards stolen from letters) saw an 81% fall from £79.9 million to £15.4 million. Other categories saw less dramatic falls. 'Counterfeit (skimmed/cloned) card fraud' fell by 23% and ATM fraud by 17%. Victimisation of UK cardholders abroad, where the new system did not operate, increased 43%.

Implications

As in the previous chapter on violence and disorder, the case studies outlined in this chapter demonstrate the benefits of introducing situational prevention methods into diverse opportunity structures for crime. Techniques included target hardening, target removal, property identification, reducing anonymity, enlarged surveillance and guardianship, removing excuses, and rule setting and communication. These techniques were often implemented in various combinations. Benefits were also apparent from focusing on repeat victimisation, repeat offenders (to a lesser extent), and crime hot spots. The benefits of focused geographical place management were evident in the property crime cases. For example, one of the main explanations for the success of the Newcastle upon Tyne CCTV project, in comparison to similar but less successful projects, was that business activity was highly concentrated in the town centre, and camera coverage of likely crime locations was high. Industrial estates and small communities also included a defined area of responsibility, with limited access and reduced anonymity.

A number of the case studies were notable for using start-up funds to employ security officers, or to fund or subsidise security upgrades. Sources included taxpayer monies from government, business collectives where each member paid a small share, or charitable trusts. Initial success then led to self-sustaining programs. The Dutch cases were part of a wider crime prevention program facilitated by the national government, with planning and financial support. In that regard, the anti-burglary cases can be compared with an unsuccessful Australian project. The Beenleigh Break and Enter

Reduction Project, set up in the late 1990s, sought to apply lessons from the successful UK projects, but interventions were largely limited to free security advice and encouragement of property marking (National Crime Prevention, 2001). The lack of financial support most likely explained the failure to install security hardware. While the evaluation identified a decrease in repeat victimisations, overall incidents of burglary increased.

Another important lesson from the case studies concerns the role of police. The first chapter in this book referred to research showing the limited impact of police on crime prevention. However, this assessment was done at an international comparative level. A good number of the cases analysed in this chapter showed local police in leadership and coordinating roles, and also playing a key role in providing rapid response and arrests in association with actions taken by private sector partners. While the cases illustrate the common view that 'police cannot prevent crime on their own', they also show police are often essential partners on successful projects.

Readers will recall that situational crime prevention has been accused of lacking a social justice dimension. Clearly, however, there was a general public benefit in all of the case studies, whether in reduced victimisation across a wide range of persons or reduced costs to taxpayers. The Dutch crime prevention programs also provided social benefits through enhanced employment. The VICs project gave work to approximately 1,200 persons: '50% had been unemployed, 30% were women, and 25% came from ethnic minorities' (van Andel, 1989, p. 49). Reduced crime opportunities also help potential offenders stay out of the criminal justice system.

Another lesson concerns the relative simplicity of many interventions, even when they involve advanced technology. In the case of mandated identification requirements for cashing cheques, Knutsson and Kuhlhorn (1997) describe how an 'expensive and ineffective system of formal control' — involving police investigations and prosecutions — was superseded by 'an inexpensive and effective situational control' based on reducing anonymity (p. 116). Anti-fraud data-matching, on the other hand, involves sophisticated computing technology, but via a very simple principle of comparing records to identify inconsistencies. Kuhlhorn (1997) described the cross-referencing capacity of data-matching technology as 'a crime prevention Eldorado' (p. 238). His analysis did not include cost-benefit estimates, but early research on data-matching against welfare fraud in the US found savings were approximately twice the costs (Greenberg, Wolf, & Pfiester, 1986).

Democratic accountability is also a value implicit in these case studies. This is particularly important where public-sector resources are involved; it is also relevant more generally because criminal victimisation has wide-ranging effects and crime prevention interventions often entail issues about privacy and civil liberties. Case studies generally represent efforts to take an honest and scientific approach to program evaluation, including stakeholder experience and opinion surveys. However, this approach tends to be the exception rather than the rule. In many jurisdictions, millions of dollars are spent on crime prevention projects without proper evaluation and accountability (see chapter 1). At the same time, most of the case studies in the chapter do not 'tick all the boxes' in terms of model practice. Postintervention data were often limited to one or two years, leaving open the question of sustainability. Financial data were often missing entirely. Although, it is not essential for crime reduction projects to show a profit (see chapter 3), financial data are important to full accountability.

Conclusion

Many of the cases summarised in this chapter showed exciting and quite extraordinary reductions in crime, with good evidence linking interventions to successful outcomes. Many of the projects exemplify democratic values of consultation and collaboration. Property crime and financial crime remain significant problems around the world, with many millions of victims each year. The small number of case studies selected for this chapter show that large reductions in these crimes can be achieved through determined efforts, including systematic program development and implementation.

References

Blais, E. & Bacher, J. (2007). Situational deterrence and claim padding: Results from a randomized field experiment. *Journal of Experimental Criminology, 3,* 337–352.

Brown, B. (1995). *CCTV in town centres: Three case studies.* London, England: Home Office.

Carr, K. (2012, December 18). *Media release: Prevention better than cure for social security system.* Retrieved from http://pandora.nla. gov.au/pan/65939/20130322-1615/www.mhs.gov.au/media/ media_releases/2012/12/18_dec_2012_-_prevention_better_ than_cure_for_social_security_system.html.

Centrelink. (2010). *Annual report, 2009–10.* Canberra, Australia: Author.

Challinger, D. (1996). Refund fraud in retail stores. *Security Journal, 7*(1), 27–35.

Cook, P.J. & MacDonald, J. (2011). Public safety through private action: An economic assessment of BIDS. *The Economic Journal, 121,* 445–462.

Department of Human Services. (2012). *Annual report, 2011–12.* Canberra, Australia: Author.

Farrell, G., Chenery, S., & Pease, K. (1998). *Consolidating police crackdowns: Findings from an antiburglary project.* London, England: Home Office.

Flatley, J., Kershaw, C., Smith, K., Chaplin, R., & Moon, D. (2010). *Crime in England and Wales 2009/10*. London, England: Home Office.

Forrester, D., Frenz, S., O'Connell, M., & Pease, K. (1990). *The Kirkholt Burglary Prevention Project: Phase II*. London, England: Home Office.

Greenberg, D.H., Wolf, D.A., & Pfiester, J. (1986). *Using computers to combat welfare fraud*. Westport, CT: Greenwood.

Hakim, S., & Shachmurove, Y. (1996). Spatial and temporal patters of commercial burglaries. *American Journal of Economics and Sociology, 55*(4), 443–456.

Knutsson, J., & Kuhlhorn, E. (1997). Macro-measures against crime: The example of check forgeries. In R.V. Clarke (Ed.), *Situational crime prevention: Successful case studies* (pp. 113–121). Guilderland, NY: Harrow and Heston.

Kuhlhorn, E. (1997). Housing allowances in a welfare society: Reducing the temptation to cheat. In R.V. Clarke, (Ed.), *Situational crime prevention: Successful case studies* (pp. 235–241). Monsey, NY: Criminal Justice Press.

Laycock, G. (1991). Operation Identification, or the power of publicity? *Security Journal, 2*(2), 67–72.

Levi, M. (2008). Combating identity and other forms of payment fraud in the UK. *Crime Prevention Studies, 23*, 111–131.

National Crime Prevention. (2001). *Lightning strikes twice: Preventing repeat home burglary*. Canberra, Australia: Attorney-General's Department.

Poyner, B., & Webb, B. (1997). Reducing theft from shopping bags in city centre markets In R.V. Clarke (Ed.), *Situational crime prevention: Successful case studies* (pp. 83-89). Guilderland, NY: Harrow and Heston.

Prenzler, T. (2011) Strike Force Piccadilly and ATM security: A follow-up study. *Policing: A Journal of Policy and Practice, 5*(3), 236–247.

Prenzler, T. (2012) *Responding to welfare fraud: The Australian experience*. Canberra, Australia: Australian Institute of Criminology.

Sloan-Howitt, M., & Kelling, G.L. (1990) Subway graffiti in New York City: 'Gettin' up' vs. 'Meanin' it and Cleanin' it'. *Security Journal, 1*(3), 131–136.

Tilley, N., & Hopkins, M. (1998). *Business as usual: An Evaluation of the Small Business and Crime Initiative*. London, England: Home Office.

Van Andel, H. (1989). Crime prevention that works: The Care of public transport in the Netherlands. *British Journal of Criminology, 29*(1), 47–56.

Van den Berg, E. (1995). Crime prevention on industrial sites: Security through public-private partnerships. *Security Journal, 6*(1), 27–35.

Vindevogel, F. (2005). Private security and urban crime migration: A bid for BIDs. *Criminal Justice: The International Journal of Policy and Practice, 5*(3), 233–255.

PART TWO

Advanced Security Management

Chapter 6

Principles of Security Management: Applying the Lessons From Crime Prevention Science

Rick Draper and Jessica Ritchie

The effective management of security-related risks relies on three basic principles: (1) understanding what may be at risk of loss or compromise, from whom, and in what context; (2) successfully assessing the range of factors that may make a risk event more likely and/or more harmful to stakeholders; and (3) making informed and defensible decisions about responses that may be appropriate in the circumstances. The chapter considers established security management practices and their theoretical underpinnings, drawn from the science of crime prevention. In doing so, this chapter explores the application of international standards in the assessment and management of security-related risks. The chapter concludes by reinforcing the need to make informed security management decisions, supported by documenting the evidence and assumptions behind the decisions.

Crime Prevention and Security

'Crime prevention' has been defined as 'the anticipation, recognition and appraisal of a crime risk and the initiation of some action to remove or reduce it' (National Crime Prevention Institute, 1986, p. xi). It is somewhat self-evident that it is not possible to initiate any informed preventative action unless the risk is first understood. Furthermore, not all security-related risks involve 'crime' in the statutory application of the term. Fischer and Green (1992, p. 3) highlight the fact that the term 'security' is much broader in its application: '[implying] a stable, relatively predictable environment in which an individual or group may pursue its ends without disruption or harm and without fear of disturbance or injury'. However, insofar as criminal sources of 'disruption or harm' can be anticipated, both for individuals and organisations, it is clear to see that the application of 'crime prevention' can and does contribute to 'security'.

McCrie (2004, pp. 15–16) observes that the practice of security management is able to draw on the theoretical foundations and substantial body of crime prevention research arising from the work of criminologists including

Ronald V. Clarke, Marcus Felson, Paul and Patricia Brantingham, and others. In a protective security context, Clarke's situational crime prevention (Clarke, 1997) and Cohen and Felson's (1979) routine activity approach both present practical hypotheses that can be applied in understanding specific security-related risks, and in making decisions about strategies that may reduce the likelihood that a risk event will occur (Draper & Rose, 2006).

The applicability of situational crime prevention theory to security risk management is further evidenced by the number of case studies illustrating the effectiveness of such measures (e.g., Clarke, 1997; see chapters 1–5 in this book). Similarly, the theoretical principles of CPTED (see chapter 2), as originally described by C. Ray Jeffery (1971), have been shown, along with other environmental factors, to reduce the likelihood of specific security risks being realised (see Hunter & Jeffery, 1992, p. 201).

Clarke's matrix of 25 situational crime prevention techniques is divided into five broad strategies (see chapter 1; Center for Problem-Oriented Policing, 2013):

- 'Increase the effort' the offender needs to apply to succeed
- 'Increase the risk' to the offender
- 'Reduce the rewards' to the offender
- 'Reduce provocations' that may encourage, facilitate or precipitate offending
- 'Remove excuses' available to the offender.

These five strategies are directly relevant to managing security-related risks. For example, fences, locks, safes and other 'target hardening' strategies are routinely associated with security to make it harder for a threat source to compromise an asset (see chapter 7). Similarly, CCTV systems and intruder alarms are intended to increase the likelihood of the threat source being detected and punished. For example, reducing the level of accessible cash and property marking are both security strategies designed to reduce the rewards available to potential offenders, thereby reducing the attractiveness of the target for robbery and theft, respectively. Effective security policies and procedures for dealing with disgruntled customers or staff are intended to reduce potential provocations that may lead to violence. Likewise awareness programs, which communicate security policies and procedures, reduce the range of excuses available for potential sources of threat in areas as diverse as fraud and embezzlement through to harassment and incident reporting.

Fundamental Security Questions

Irrespective of context, the fundamental questions that need to be answered in understanding and effectively managing security-related risks are:

1. What are we trying to protect?
   - What is it that might be 'at risk'?
   - What makes it attractive to a potential source of threat?
   - What is its importance to concerned stakeholders?
   - What is the full range of consequences for all stakeholders, given a specific threat scenario?
2. From what/whom are we trying to protect it?
   - What is the nature of the source of threat?
   - What are their objectives?
   - What are their capabilities?
   - What is their motivation?

The nature of what needs protecting in any given situation is going to be context-dependent and may span a number of specialised areas. For example, in the area of information security there are four aspects of information that may require separate consideration:

1. protection from unauthorised access
2. protection from unauthorised disclosure
3. protection from alteration or change
4. protection from loss or destruction.

While in this example the asset being protected may be one specific piece of information, it is clear that depending on the potential source of threat, very different strategies may be needed to effectively protect that information from the different modes of potential compromise. Understanding the nature of the asset being protected and the potential threats to that asset are fundamental to being able to develop and implement effective security risk management strategies. In considering 'what we are trying to protect', the following general categories should always be considered:

- People (not just limited to staff)
- Information (known, printed, digital — storage, transit and destruction)
- Property
- Activities/Operations
- Reputation/Goodwill.

Risk Management

The origins of structured approaches to managing security-related risks can be traced back to the late-1970s and early-1980s — the same period during which the initial work, referenced above, on opportunity based crime prevention was being done. Walsh and Healy (1982, p. 2–1) noted that '[no] security plan or program can be effective unless it is based upon a clear understanding of the actual risks it is designed to control'. This language differs a little from that used in published risk management standards (e.g., Standards Australia, 1995, 2006; Canadian Standards Association [CSA], 1997; International Organization for Standardization [ISO], 2009a, 2009b). Nonetheless, Walsh and Healy (1982, p. 2–1) highlighted the need for a clear understanding of:

1. The kinds of threats or risks affecting the assets to be safeguarded.
2. The likelihood or probability of those threats becoming actual loss events.
3. The impact or effect upon the asset or upon the enterprise responsible for the asset if the loss occurs.

As with all things that may be subject to analysis at some time in the future, with the benefit of hindsight, such as in litigation (Sarre & Prenzler, 2009, p. 190), consistency in approach and in terminology are important. Despite having published standards and reference documents for decades now, there is still a lack of consistency in the terms and definitions used by practitioners, as well as in security-related texts and articles (Garcia, 2006, pp. 509–510). To the casual observer, Walsh and Healy (1982) may appear to use the words 'threat' and 'risk' interchangeably in their reference to the assets to be safeguarded. However, while these two terms are related, they have clear and separate meanings when describing security-related matters.

The ISO defines 'risk' as the 'effect of uncertainty on objectives' (ISO, 2009a, p. 1). This implies that risk is the combination of the likelihood or probability that something will happen, and the outcomes of that occurrence. The Standards Australia (2006) handbook (*HB 167: Security Risk Management*) presents a range of formulaic approaches to quantifying or qualifying the level of risk, but consistently highlights the key parameters of 'likelihood' and 'consequences' as essential to describing risk (pp.163–168). Similarly, the CSA defines risk as 'the chance of injury or loss as defined as a measure of the probability and severity of an adverse effect to health, property, the environment, or other things of value' (CSA, 1997, p. 3).

The term 'threat', in a security risk management context, is often used to describe the risk event (i.e., what might happen [e.g. robbery, theft of stock, assault on staff, information compromise, etc.]). The likelihood of a given threat being realised can be assessed by identifying and understanding the factors relevant to a 'source of threat' (i.e., in crime prevention terms, the 'potential offenders'). These factors for consideration may be similar for some threat sources, but differ significantly for others.

For example, there will be different factors to consider in assessing the likelihood of theft of stock where the source of threat is managerial staff — compared to an external criminal threat source. The term 'vulnerabilities' is used to refer to weaknesses that increase the likelihood of a threat source successfully realising a threat against a specific asset, resource or function (Federal Emergency Management Agency [FEMA], 2005 pp. 1–3); for example, aspects of 'target suitability' and 'capable guardianship'). However, it must also be noted that the term 'vulnerability' is also applied to factors that increase the potential consequences arising from a risk event.

Whether or not a particular weakness represents a vulnerability is directly related to the nature of the threat source. A threat source making rational choices will logically weigh up the effort required and potential risk involved, against the perceived reward (Clarke, 1997). The capability and motivation of an offender to target a specific asset, resource or activity will be key factors in identifying vulnerabilities.

In summary, vulnerabilities contribute to the likelihood that a threat to a given asset, resource or activity will be realised and/or the consequences arising from such an event will be worsened. The actual risk is able to be defined by describing the nature of the threat in combination with a foreseeable consequence (i.e., if the 'threat' is robbery, the risk may be described as 'loss of cash through robbery').

There are however a range of potential consequences that may arise from any given risk event (Standards Australia, 2006, p. 72). For example, in a robbery of a convenience store, the range of consequences may include:

- physical injury to staff
- physical injury to customers
- psychological injury to staff
- psychological injury to customers
- loss of cash
- loss of merchandise
- loss of personal property belonging to staff
- loss of personal property belonging to customers
- disruption of operations
- reduced productivity (e.g., police and court time)
- damage to reputation (e.g., impacting staff recruiting).

The degree to which any of these consequences may be experienced will be influenced by the risk management strategies in place. For example, the risk of loss of cash through robbery may be mitigated by insurance; and the risk of harm to staff through robbery may be reduced by store layout, staff training, and/or physical barriers.

It should be noted that there may also be some potential for financial and productivity loss arising from civil litigation or prosecution for workplace health and safety breaches. For example, Sarre and Prenzler (2009, p. 209) note that, in the case of *Derrick v. ANZ Banking* Group [2005] NSWIRComm 59, the New South Wales Industrial Relations Commission fined the bank $156,000 'for not maintaining a safe workplace and failing to carry out adequate risk assessments'. While in this case the fine was not insignificant, the direct and indirect cost of being prosecuted added substantially to the overall consequences arising from the original robbery.

Clearly, it is impractical to attempt to assess in detail all consequences that may arise from every conceivable threat to every asset. The Standards Australia (2006) handbook (*HB 167*) notes that a 'criticality assessment is a vital step in the identification of risk as it provides a starting point for consideration of the pertinent threats ... and vulnerability to those threats' (p. 46). Care needs to be taken not to focus too much on events with high consequences but an extremely low likelihood. This might distract from other assessments of risk to assets, resources and activities that are vital to an organisation. In addition, the criticality of any asset should not be assessed only in terms of its direct financial value. Consideration may also need to be given to its social value and the time and resources that may be needed to recover from its loss or destruction.

The lead time to recovery following a risk event may be a key factor in considering criticality. For example, in gold mining the two critical inputs, besides ore and human resources, are power and water. If power and/or water supply are lost for a significant period of time, the processing of crushed ore will cease. There is in fact a finite period of time for disruption of either of these services after which the costs of resumption of production at the facility may simply not be financially viable.

The steps in the overall risk management process are now well defined and provide a sound basis for developing an understanding of security-related risks and the treatment of those risks (see ISO, 2009a). As noted above, terminology can be important in ensuring that there is not scope for misinterpretation. The steps listed summarise the standard risk management process as defined by the ISO (2009a, p. 14).

1. Establish the context
2. Risk assessment
   2.1 Risk identification
   2.2 Risk analysis
   2.3 Risk evaluation
3. Risk treatment

Note: All steps should involve 'communication and consultation' and 'monitoring and review'.

It should be noted that the term 'risk assessment' is the collective term embracing the separate steps of risk identification, risk analysis and risk evaluation. It is in the risk analysis phase that the likelihood and consequences of the risk event are qualified or quantified within the given contexts applicable to the risk assessment.

Sources of Threat

The potential sources of threat are very much dependent upon the context within which the at-risk asset, resource or activity may be found. Some references categorise sources of threat according to the type of threat, although some sources of threat should in fact be considered under multiple types. Some of the types of threat defined in the Standards Australia (2006, p. 53) handbook (*HB 167*) include:

- Malicious acts
- Greed or personal gain
- Terrorism
- Incidental acts.

The sources of threat for malicious acts may include disgruntled personnel, contractors or customers. They may also include general sources of threat such as vandals or propagators of computer viruses who might not have specifically targeted the owner of the asset per se, but rather exploited an opportunity that was available to satisfy their own malicious objectives. The other categories of threat are somewhat self-evident, with incident threats frequently arising through acts of negligence or as by-products of some other action.

Walsh and Healy (1982, p. 2–3) place risk events that security managers should consider in eight categories:

1. Nuclear war
2. Natural catastrophe
3. Industrial disaster
4. Civil disturbance
5. Crime
6. Conflicts of interest
7. Terrorism
8. Other risks.

Whatever categorisation method is used, it is important in considering sources of threat to understand as far as may be practicable their likely objectives. For example, an easy to identify source for the threat of robbery is external criminals (i.e., not a staff member). Their objectives in committing a robbery would appear to be to gain money or goods. However, they may also include, for example, satisfying an initiation test to join a gang. Understanding threat source objectives can be a vital contributor to developing risk management plans. If the threat source perceives that they will not be able to satisfy their objectives without undue risk or effort ('rational choice'), they may be deterred from prosecuting the threat.

At the centre of any determination of threat likelihood is an understanding of the potential capability and motivation of the threat source. The level of motivation for a threat source to prosecute the threat at any given *time and place* is likely to be contributed to by (a) the underlying rationale for pursuing the threat, and (b) the level of expectation regarding achieving the intended objectives (i.e. why? and will the expected outcomes for the threat source be achieved?).

For example, a staff member committing theft will want to have a reasonable expectation that they will not be detected and identified. The underlying rationale for theft may be to gain money to satisfy a gambling addiction. This might be a powerful motivation. However, if controls are such that the would-be criminal has no reasonable expectation of getting away with the theft, they are unlikely to proceed. They may be deterred by the potential shame of identification, loss of their job or a criminal conviction, fine or imprisonment. This can be contrasted with the risk entailed in suicide terrorism. A suicide bomber will have little or no concern about shaming, loss of employment or criminal justice processes. However, if it is possible to limit their expectation of achieving their objectives in prosecuting a threat against a given target, the target logically becomes less desirable.

Threats, Vulnerabilities and Layered Protection

Farrell and Pease (2006, p. 181) summarise Cohen and Felson's routine activity theory in the following terms: 'A crime occurs when a suitable target and a potential offender meet at a suitable time and place lacking capable guardianship'. In security risk management terms, this may be re-drafted as: 'A risk event will occur, when a source of threat is able to exploit vulnerabilities to adversely affect an asset, resource or activity'. The concept of 'capable guardianship', as advanced by Cohen and Felson, does not inherently require the physical presence of a human protector for the asset (see Farrell & Pease, 2006, p. 182). However, the key word here is 'capable', and this needs to be considered in the context of the applicable source of threat. For 'guardianship' to be capable in a protective security context, it will necessarily involve multiple layers of protection. This layering of protection has its origins in military strategy and is referred to as 'defence-in-depth' or 'security-in-depth' (see Kovacich & Halibozek, 2013, p. 340; Standards Australia, 2006, p. 59; Van Maanengerg, 1995, pp. 83–84).

The basic principle of defence-in-depth is that the security of the asset is not reliant on any one layer of protection. The layers of protection may be physical or mechanical in nature, such as fences, walls, and security enclosures (Kovacich & Halibozek, 2013, p. 341). Examples of situational techniques here include target hardening, and controlling access and egress. Protections may be procedural, such as policies and procedures, codes of conduct, pre-employment screening and supervision (Van Maanengerg, 1995, pp. 83–84). Situational examples include rule setting and alerting conscience. They may be technical, such as alarm systems, CCTV, firewalls, and analytics — involving strengthened surveillance and access control. Protections may also involve greater human guardianship, such as static security officers and response teams. These layers of protection should also be derived from design elements or usage characterises that are incorporated to support operational and behavioural objectives (Crowe, 2013, p. 28).

As noted in the Standards Australia (2006) handbook (*HB 167)*, the goal in assessing the vulnerability of any given asset to a range of possible sources of threat is to consider the vulnerabilities in each layer of protection for that asset (Standards Australia, 2006, p. 59). The fact that one security strategy is not 100% effective does not mean there is automatically an increase in the likelihood that the threat will be realised. An unlocked door is not automatically a vulnerability (Johnston, 2010, p. 38.). The role and contribution of each strategy needs to be considered. A key question here: Does the combination of strategies represent capable guardianship for the subject target (asset) for a given category of offender (threat source) at a given time and place?

Risk Analysis and Risk Assessment

The ISO 31010:2009 presents an expansive range of risk assessment techniques and guidance regarding their selection and use (see ISO 2009b). It is important to note that risk assessment techniques can vary significantly in terms of complexity and applicability to particular types of risk. For example, the 'Bow Tie' analysis (ISO, 2009b, pp. 64–66) — focused on a single adverse event in the centre of a flow chart of causes and consequences — is found more commonly in health and safety risk assessments than in security, as it is has limitations in dealing with multiple interrelated causation factors. In contrast, the 'Layers of Protection Analysis' technique (ISO, 2009b, pp. 59–60) appears to align more closely with the defence-in-depth approach, commonly found in security applications, and the 25 techniques of situational prevention. In practice, the most common technique found in security risk assessments in Australia and New Zealand is the

'Consequence/Probability Matrix' (ISO, 2009b, pp. 82–86). This is largely due to the presentation of this technique as an example in the original risk management standard (see Standards Australia, 1995, Appendix E).

Quantitative and qualitative versions of the Consequence/Probability Matrix have been used to varying extents to analyse security-related risks. An example of a qualitative matrix is shown in Figure 6.1. One of the keys to successfully using this technique is ensuring that the rationale for assessed levels of likelihood and consequences are well-documented. Notwithstanding that subjectivity in assessments is a limitation of this technique, it can be used to deliver reliable and consistent risk analyses across multiple facilities (Draper & Rose, 2006). The more granular and refined the inputs, the more consistent and reliable the output.

It should be noted that the scales used for risk factors in a Consequence/Probability Matrix may be linear, logarithmic or some other form as applicable to the risk assessment criteria being used. For example, in analysis of risks to human life, it is not uncommon to apply a weighting to the consequence scale, resulting in a higher level risk descriptor than might otherwise be seen with a linear scale.

Drawing on routine activity theory (Cohen & Felson, 1979) and rational choice perspective (Cornish & Clarke, 2011) as a theoretical base for evaluation, it is possible to estimate the level of likelihood of a specific location being a target for a robbery. The relative 'attractiveness' of the location will be influenced by the perceived level of reward available and the opportunities to commit the crime with the least effort and least risk to the offender. For example, if there is likely to be a low level of cash held at the facility and the perceived guardianship at the location is high, the 'attractiveness' of the location may be assessed as being 'very low' (see Figure 6.2).

It is somewhat self-evident, and supported by Cohen and Felson's routine activity theory, that irrespective of how attractive a target may be for a crime, such as robbery, there will be no likelihood of the crime occurring if there is no offender. Figure 6.3 illustrates how consideration of the level of similar crime in the area (base crime weighting) can be overlaid on a measure of 'attractiveness' to derive the likelihood of a location being targeted for robbery.

Risk Treatment

A range of physical security strategies is discussed in detail in chapter 7. However, it should be noted that regulatory requirements and guidelines exist in some sectors and these must be taken into account when developing risk treatment plans (Draper, 2013, p. 283). Notwithstanding any statutory obligations, there are other risk management options beyond seeking to

Risk		Potential Consequences				
		Insignificant	Minor	Moderate	Major	Catastrophic
Likelihood	Rare	Low	Low	Moderate	High	High
	Unlikely	Low	Low	Moderate	High	Extreme
	Possible	Low	Moderate	High	Extreme	Extreme
	Likely	Moderate	High	High	Extreme	Extreme
	Almost Certain	High	High	Extreme	Extreme	Extreme

Figure 6.1
Qualitative consequence/probability matrix example.
Source: Draper & Rose, 2006, p. 463. (Used with permission.)

Example

Attractiveness		Opportunity				
		Very Low	Low	Moderate	High	Very High
Cash Level	Very Low	Very Low	Very Low	Very Low	Very Low	Very Low
	Low	Very Low	Very Low	Low	Low	Low
	Moderate	Very Low	Low	Moderate	Moderate	High
	High	Very Low	Low	Moderate	High	Very High
	Very High	Very Low	Low	High	Very High	Very High

Low	Low	=	Very Low
Robbery Opportunity Descriptor	Cash Level Descriptor		Attractiveness Descriptor

Figure 6.2
Determining the relative attractiveness of a target for robbery.
Source: Draper & Rose, 2006, p. 463. (Used with permission.)

Likelihood		Base Crime Weighting				
		Very Low	Low	Moderate	High	Very High
Attractiveness	Very Low	Rare	Rare	Rare	Rare	Rare
	Low	Rare	Rare	Unlikely	Unlikely	Unlikely
	Moderate	Rare	Unlikely	Possible	Possible	Likely
	High	Rare	Unlikely	Possible	Likely	Almost Certain
	Very High	Rare	Unlikely	Likely	Almost Certain	Almost Certain

Figure 6.3
Determining likelihood based on attractiveness and availability of offenders.
Source: Draper & Rose, 2006, p. 465. (Used with permission.)

reduce the likelihood of a risk event and/or reduce the consequences. These options include:

- Accepting the risk (an informed CB decision)
- Avoiding the risk (eliminating all exposure)
- Redistributing the risk (decentralising the target/loss potential)
- Transferring the risk (though insurance or transferring functions).

While some authors opt for other terms, it is generally accepted that strategies to reduce exposure to security-related risks fall into three categories of control or 'sub-systems' (Garcia, 2013, p.18; Standards Australia, 2006, p.64):

- Delay strategies
- Detection strategies
- Response strategies.

Some reference sources add 'deterrence' and 'recovery' strategies to this list (Standards Australia, 2006, p.64). However, it can be argued that the three categories in the list may act as a deterrent to a potential threat source, either individually or in combination. Similarly, during the recovery phase following a risk event, strategies falling into one or more of the three generally accepted categories will be used.

Irrespective of how risk treatment strategies may be categorised, it is important that the objectives for those strategies be well defined and documented. For example, a CCTV camera may be used to provide wide area detection capability or images to enable clear identification of persons entering the field of view. These are very different objectives, and if both are required this may require the use of two cameras or a very high-resolution megapixel camera and supporting software capable of delivering both requirements.

Security Risk Management in Practice

Managing security-related risks involves a range of considerations that are anchored in the various contexts within which the applicable risks arise. For example, large corporations and government agencies will routinely have senior personnel in dedicated security management roles and may have mandated risk management requirements that must be followed (Attorney-General's Department, 2012). Smaller organisations, such as a small business, will not have the capacity or risk profile to justify the appointment of dedicated staff. In these cases, security management responsibilities will be formally or informally assigned to other roles. In any case, the successful management of security-related risks relies on all staff, and potentially other stakeholders, understanding and accepting their individual roles and responsibilities with respect to security (see chapter 8).

Whatever the size of the organisation, senior executives across all areas must ensure that security-related risks associated with their area of influence are identified and understood. Effective security risk management requires informed decisions to be made in relation to planning for proactively addressing security needs as well as to support appropriate responses to threats that may be realised. Senior executives must be seen to not only be setting security policy, but also leading by example in the implementation of key principles of security management; including: clearly assigning security responsibilities and ensuring accountability, integrating security across all aspects of the organisation, conducting regular risk assessments, assessing the impacts of protective measures, and maintaining a flexible approach to changing threats. Security strategies also need to be compatible with the organisation's goals and philosophy. They need to be operationally appropriate and workable, and they need to represent fiscally responsible choices.

Conclusion

This chapter showed that crime prevention and security management are not exactly synonymous. However, the theoretical foundations and research around routine activity and situational crime prevention contribute to a defensible basis for security management practices. Furthermore, the available international standards for risk management and risk assessment provide a clear and robust structure for understanding and treating security-related risks. Those responsible for security risk management can adapt and use the models presented to deliver accurate and consistent assessments across a wide range of risks.

References

Attorney-General's Department. (2012). *Protective security policy framework: Securing Government business.* Canberra, Australia: Author. Retrieved from http://www.protectivesecurity.gov.au/pspf/Pages/default.aspx.

Canadian Standards Association. (1997). *CSA Q850:1997 — Risk management: Guideline for decision-makers.* Ottawa, Canada: Author.

Center for Problem-Oriented Policing. (2013). *Twenty five techniques of situational prevention.* Retrieved from http://www.popcenter.org/25techniques/

Clarke, R.V. (Ed.). (1997). *Situational crime prevention: Successful case studies.* Guilderland, NY: Harrow and Heston.

Cohen, L.E. & Felson, M. (1979). Social change and crime rate trends: A Routine activity approach. American Sociological Review, 44, 588–608.

Cornish, D.B., & Clarke, R.V. (2011). The rational choice perspective. In R. Wortley & L. Mazerolle (Eds.), *Environmental criminology and crime analysis* (pp. 28–47). Abingdon: Routledge.

Crowe, T.D. (2013). Crime prevention through environmental design (Rev. ed. [L. Fennelly]). Waltham, MA: Butterworth-Heinemann.

Draper, R. (2103). Standards, regulations, and guidelines: Compliance and your security program. In L. Fennelly (Ed.), *Effective physical security* (pp. 283–291). Waltham, MA: Butterworth-Heinemann.

Draper, R., & Rose, E. (2006). Development of robbery risk analysis tools: Using the Australian and New Zealand Standard. *International Journal of Risk Assessment and Management, 6*, 456–471.

Farrell, G., & Pease, K. (2006). Risk management. In M. Gill (Ed.), The *handbook of security* (pp. 179–199). Houndmills Basingstoke, England: Palgrave Macmillan.

Federal Emergency Management Agency. (2005). *FEMA 452 risk assessment: A How-to guide to mitigate potential terrorist attacks against buildings.* Washington, DC: Author.

Fischer, R.J., & Green, G. (1992). Introduction to security. Stoneham, MA: Butterworth-Heinemann

Garcia, M.L. (2006). Risk management. In M. Gill (Ed.), *The handbook of security* (pp. 509–531). Houndmills Basingstoke, England: Palgrave Macmillan

Garcia, M.L. (2013). Introduction to vulnerability assessment. In L. Fennelly (Ed.), *Effective physical security* (pp. 11–39). Waltham, MA: Butterworth-Heinemann

Hunter, R.D., & Jeffery, C.R. (1992). Preventing convenience store robbery. In R.V. Clarke (Ed.), Situational crime prevention: Successful case studies (pp. 194–204). Guilderland, NY: Harrow and Heston.

International Organization for Standardization. (2009a). *ISO 31000:2009 — Risk management — principles and guidelines.* Geneva, Switzerland: Author.

International Organization for Standardization (2009b). *ISO 31010:2009 — Risk management — risk assessment techniques.* Geneva, Switzerland: Author.

Jeffery, C.R. (1971). *Crime prevention through environmental design.* Beverley Hills, CA: Sage.

Johnston, R.G. (2010). Changing security paradigms. *Journal of Physical Security, 4*(2), 35–47.

Kovacich, G.L., & Halibozek, E.P. (2013). Physical security. In L. Fennelly (Ed.), *Effective physical security* (pp. 339–353). Waltham, MA: Butterworth-Heinemann.

McCrie, R.D. (2004). The history of expertise in security management practice and litigation. *Security Journal, 17*(3), 11–19.

National Crime Prevention Institute (1986). *Understanding crime prevention*. Stoneham, MA: Butterworth-Heinemann.

Sarre, R., & Prenzler, T. (2009). *The law of private security in Australia*. Sydney, Australia: Thomson Reuters.

Standards Australia. (1995). *Australian Standard/New Zealand Standard 4360:1995 — Risk management*. Sydney, Australia: Author.

Standards Australia (2006). *Handbook 167:2006 — Security risk management*. Sydney, Australia: Author.

Van Maanengerg, D. (1995). *Effective retail security*. Melbourne, Australia: Butterworth-Heinemann.

Walsh, T., & Healy, R. (1982). *The protection of assets manual*. Santa Monica, CA: Merritt.

Chapter 7

Best Practice in Physical Security

Rick Draper and Jessica Ritchie

As the term suggests, 'physical security' involves those aspects of protective security focused on tangible measures for the protection of assets such as structural, mechanical and technical security strategies. This chapter examines best practice in physical security through the process of undertaking a security survey as part of a security risk assessment, including the presentation of findings within a structured report format.

What is Physical Security?

As illustrated in Figure 7.1, physical security is one of four overlapping categories of what is more broadly known as 'protective security'. This is defined in the Australian Attorney-General's Department publication *Protective Security Policy Framework: Glossary of terms* as follows (2012b, p.15):

> Protective security is a combination of procedural, physical, personnel, and information security measures designed to protect information, functions, resources, employees and clients with protection from security threats.

There is some debate about which security strategies should or should not be included within the area of 'physical security', and variations in definition can even be found within the one organisation (e.g., Attorney-General's Department, 2012a, p. 32; Attorney-General's Department, 2012b, p. 13; Garcia, 2007, pp. 1–11; US Army, 2001). However, for the purposes of this chapter, physical security is defined by the authors as:

> Tangible security strategies used in combination with the design, layout and orientation of structures and spaces to reduce the likelihood of specific threats and/or reduce the potential consequences should the associated risks be realised. Physical security strategies are intended to prevent, delay, detect and/or respond to security related threats to people, information and property assets, as well as threats to the activities or reputation of the individuals or organisations at risk.

In the rest of this chapter, the term 'resources' will be used to collectively describe those things that may be exposed to security related risks, including staff, clients, visitors, contractors, information in its various forms, physical property, cash, the activities and operations of an organisation, as well as reputation and goodwill.

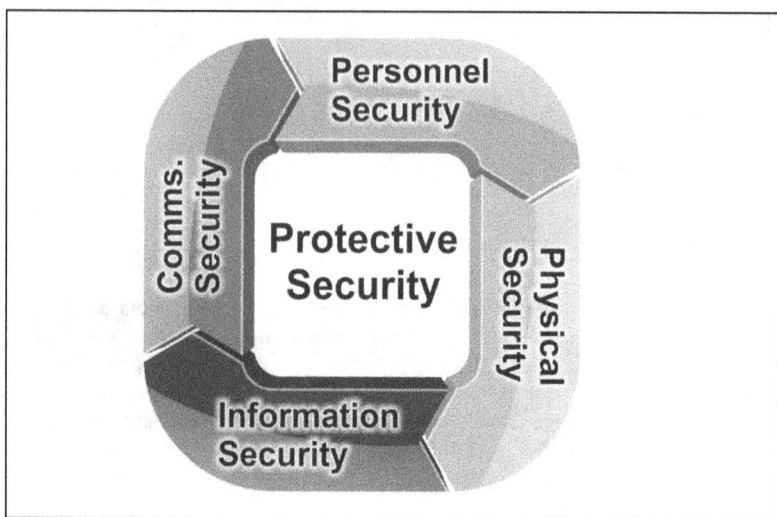

Figure 7.1
Elements of protective security.
Source: Draper, 2013. (Used with permission.)

Many physical security strategies are highly visible and easily recognised, while others may be overlooked by the untrained eye. Depending on the setting, physical security considerations may include the following (Fennelly, 2013a, pp. 77–359; Standards Australia, 2006, pp. 156–157):

- site selection and site layout
- fences and barriers
- projectile and blast protection
- signage and rules
- sightlines and buffer zones
- operational and defensive/offensive lighting
- vehicular and pedestrian traffic controls
- building design and layout
- personnel and mail screening
- X-ray and metal detectors
- structural material selection and concealed obstacles
- vaults and secure rooms
- glazing materials and protective films
- doors and other portal design
- mechanical and electronic locking

- keying and electronic access control
- location selection for higher risk activities
- service counter design and barriers
- alarm systems and CCTV
- annunciation and system monitoring
- automated and electronic response systems
- uniformed and covert security patrols
- static guards and response capabilities
- security training and drills/exercises
- personal protective security equipment
- safes and protective enclosures
- property marking and asset management
- ID cards and visitor management
- cash and asset handling
- tamper evident enclosures and security seals
- transport of cash and valuables
- incident recording and reporting
- incident notification and response.

As noted in the definition earlier, physical security strategies are 'tangible' or otherwise procedurally related to a tangible security strategy (e.g., standing orders for uniformed security officers, procedures for issuing keys, etc.). Thus, for the purpose of this chapter, they do not include strategies such as pre-employment screening (a personnel security strategy), anti-virus software (an information security strategy) or encrypted telecommunication (a communications security strategy). It should however be noted that there are overlaps across all categories of protective security, and the operation of one strategy may be reliant on protection from another in a different category. For example, protection on a computer server to provide authorised access to data is an information security strategy that is reliant on physical security strategies to prevent the server from being physically disconnected or stolen.

The categories of protective security should be regarded as a useful way to focus attention on the function of specific strategies. It is not necessary to be pedantic about labelling strategies in terms of their protective security category, and it can be counter-productive to waste energy doing so. For example, the encryption of data in transmission might be technically a communications security strategy, but the objective of such encryption may be for information security. Information can also be encrypted in storage, so it is an information security strategy in its own right. The important point here is to understand the scope of the risks being assessed and make any decision about whether or not to include a specific security strategy based on context.

The Physical Security Survey

A physical security survey is a systematic documented process by which the applications of security strategies are considered in the context of credible sources of threat against specific resources. Visual inspection of all resources, security plans and security devices is a key element of a survey. The objective is to identify deficiencies or vulnerabilities that increase exposure to security risks, as well as to ascertain where security strategies may be redundant or excessive in the current risk environment. The outcomes from a physical security survey inform the analysis of security risks and the development of defensible recommendations to mitigate those risks (Fennelly, 2013b, p. 41; Schaub & Biery, 1998, p. xi; Standards Australia, 2006, p. 59).

Physical security surveys should be undertaken within a defined scope. The scope of any survey may be set by geographical boundaries or specific functional areas within the site or sites, the types of threats or risks to be considered in undertaking the survey, or any combination of these. For example, the scope of a physical security survey for a convenience store might be limited to the risk of harm to staff through robbery at the checkout. This scope defines the nature of the risk, as well as the functional area to be considered. It therefore excludes other threats, such as shop lifting by customers, short-changing customers by staff, short-delivery by suppliers, theft of stock by staff, harassment of customers by gangs, or vandalism.

Failing to adequately define the scope of a physical security survey can inevitably lead to misunderstandings and potentially expose the person undertaking the survey to legal claims of negligence (Sarre & Prenzler, 2009, pp. 198–200). If there are constraints on time and resources, it is far better to focus on a specific set of related risks at one time, rather than to attempt to comprehensively cover all risks and not be able to adequately complete the task. However, in applying limitations in scope, anyone undertaking a security survey should be mindful that the effects of a security strategy may extend beyond the risks being considered. Consequently, care should be taken in making recommendations that may introduce vulnerabilities in other areas. This includes safety considerations. A classic example is to secure doors and windows in a way that prevents emergency escape during a fire.

Similarly, there may be vulnerabilities associated with some strategies due to the need to use the most cost-effective approach for managing a range of risks. As discussed in chapter 6, security risk management strategies are routinely arranged to provide defence-in-depth, where the protection of any given resource is not overly reliant on any one protective strategy. The overlapping of strategies and their associated vulnerabilities has been described as resembling slices of Swiss cheese (Standards Australia, 2006, pp. 59–60). Using this analogy, the objective is to arrange the slices of cheese in such a way that the holes (vulnerabilities) in one slice (strategy) do not overlap holes in the adjacent slices, thus preventing a path through the slices (increased risk exposure).

Stages of a Physical Security Survey

There are normally eight stages to a physical security survey (or audit), if a structured analysis of the level of risk is included:

1. Definition of scope and approach (preparation)
2. Resource appreciation (what is to be protected, within the scope?)
3. Threat assessment (from whom is it to be protected, within the scope?)
4. Audit of current strategies
   - What strategies are in place?
   - Are they appropriate?
5. Vulnerability identification (what might a threat source exploit and how?)
6. Security risk analysis (if applicable)
   - Likelihood of specific threats being realised
   - Consequences arising from those threats
7. Formulation of recommendations
8. Presentation of findings (e.g., report).

As noted previously, it is important to clearly define the scope of any physical security audit. Once the scope is determined, there are two general approaches to undertaking the survey: 'inward-out' and 'outward-in'. The 'inward-out' approach commences at the resource potentially at risk. With due consideration of the sources of threat and their likely objectives, it considers the physical security strategies radiating out from the resource. For example, if the resource being considered is tablet computers that might be stolen by opportunist criminals breaking into a school after hours, the physical security strategies placed in layers outward from the computer might include:

- property marking
- locked heavy-duty cabinet
- intruder alarm system with off-site monitoring
- locked classroom
- CCTV

- movement activated security lights
- perimeter fence with locked gates.

In an 'inward–out' survey it may not be necessary to continue beyond the point at which effective protection has been achieved. In the case of the threat described above this may be the locked heavy-duty cabinet in a locked classroom equipped with a monitored intruder alarm system. The property marking would deny maximum benefit to the offenders for re-sale and, as such, acts as a deterrent. The locked cabinet increases the effort required by the offenders, delaying access to the tablet computers. In combination with the monitored alarm system this increases the offenders' perception of risk of detection and apprehension (Clarke, 1980).

The 'outward-in' approach commences at the outermost layer of protection likely to be encountered by a given source of threat in targeting a specific resource. The effectiveness, applicability and vulnerabilities associated with those strategies all need to be considered. This approach requires thinking like the threat source and considering what effect various physical security strategies may have on decision making. One way of strengthening an 'outward-in' survey is through a 'penetration test', in which a proxy offender attempts to successfully access a resource from the outer perimeter. This technique can be very useful for identify vulnerabilities. There are, however, a number risks, including attacks by staff and false alarms to police, if the test is not properly managed.

The scope of the physical security survey will be defined in consultation with the owner of the premises or senior management within the organisation. It is self-evident that undertaking a physical security survey may reveal vulnerabilities that could cause harm to the business or organisation, were those vulnerabilities to be exploited. This makes the process of conducting the survey potentially sensitive and establishes the need to apply protective security strategies to the findings themselves. Whether or not you are undertaking a physical security survey as an external party or as an adjunct of your employment by the organisation concerned, it is important that the authority to undertake the survey and the agreed scope both be documented in writing. Other matters to take into account before commencing a physical security survey include:

- Contextual factors relevant to risk (e.g., local area crime rates)
- Organisational structure and positions of authority
- Stakeholders, their interest in the risks, and availability for consultation
- Operational factors and potential access constraints
- Health and safety issues
- Potential sources of information
- Format for the presentation of findings.

Physical Security Survey Report

The structure and format for reporting should be determined prior to the commencement of the physical security survey. Notwithstanding templates used within organisations, there are three formats that are routine used in presenting findings:

1. **The Brief:** A short narrative that includes an introduction describing the scope, a body with the substance of the findings, a conclusion based on the findings, and the recommendations.

2. **The Matrix:** A tabulated summary presenting the location/functional area, risk-related issues, findings and recommendations.

3. **The Narrative Report:** a comprehensive report that provides complete details of the physical security survey, findings, discussion, conclusions, recommendations and attachments. The structure of a typical narrative report includes:

   - Cover Page
   - Contents Page
   - Distribution List
   - Disclaimer
   - Executive Summary
   - Introduction and scope
   - Description of sites/areas reviewed
   - Findings
       Resource Appreciation
       Threat Assessment
       Existing Security Strategies (including strengths and weaknesses)
       Vulnerabilities
       Redundant strategies
       Risk Analysis (if applicable)
   - Conclusions
   - Recommendations
   - Attachments/Photos

The reader of the report should be able to clearly understand the scope of the review, the nature of threats and associated risks, the contribution of existing strategies to risk mitigation, and the rationale for all recommendations.

Wherever possible and relevant, drawings, diagrams and photographs should be included in a narrative style report to support the reader's comprehension. The reader should be able to understand both where the photo was taken and its significance. For example, a photograph of the front of a retail store may be taken for orientation purposes, to show the construction materials used or to highlight some specific vulnerability. Photos, maps, diagrams, tables, models and flowcharts can be included within the body of the text for immediate reference or be collected at the end of the report. If they are collected together in an attachment or annexure, they should be cross-referenced by number in the body of the report, making comprehension easier for the reader.

Subject to specified requirements by those authorising the review, all formats should include privacy markings (e.g., 'SECURITY-IN-CONFI-DENCE') and caveats as may be applicable for information security, along with a list of nominated recipients of the report.

Best Practice in Physical Security

As noted above, apart from identifying vulnerabilities, a physical security survey may also identify redundant security strategies, or strategies that are excessive or not cost-effective in the current risk environment. While recognising the need to be able to adjust security strategies in response to changes in the threat profile for specific resources, best practice in physical security demands prudent use of strategies to mitigate risks in the most fiscally responsible and operationally appropriate manner.

To use a medical analogy, most people would use simple first aid to treat a graze on a knee by cleaning the wound and applying a basic dressing. Additional treatment strategies, such as a plaster cast, precautionary antibiotics and bed rest are simply not justifiable in the circumstances, although they may contribute marginally to the healing process. It should be noted in this analogy that the additional treatment strategies will also add significant cost and be disruptive to the patient's daily activities. The same types of considerations exist with respect to physical security. Bigger locks and more sophisticated strategies do not necessarily translate to lower risk, and may even be detrimental to the goals and objectives of the organisation the strategies are intended to protect.

It is not possible, with any degree of reliability, to select physical security strategies, or determine their suitability, without being able to answer the fundamental questions that underpin security risk management (see chapter 6):

1. What are we trying to protect?
2. From what or whom are we trying to protect it?

For example, a safe may be an appropriate physical security strategy to protect a moderate amount of cash from theft by external criminal sources of threat, but it is not going to mitigate in any way the risk of financial loss through theft of that cash by a staff member with the combination of the safe. The answers to the two fundamental questions above provide the foundation for best practice in physical security.

Conclusion

Many physical security strategies are among the most visible in protective security, although not all may be obvious to the casual observer. In considering the selection or suitability of any physical security strategy, it is important to understand the nature of the risks it is intended to mitigate, with specific consideration to the sources of threat and their capabilities. It is also important to consider the contributions of related strategies that may form part of a defence-in-depth approach. There is no single correct method for undertaking a security survey as part of a security risk assessment, but preparation and understanding of what is to be protected, and from whom or what, is essential before commencing. The security survey report should be structured according to the scope of the review and in consideration of the audience to receive the report.

References

Attorney-General's Department. (2012a). *Protective security policy framework: Securing government business.* Canberra, Australia: Business Law Branch: Author.

Attorney-General's Department. (2012b). *Protective security policy framework: Glossary of terms.* Canberra, Australia: Business Law Branch: Author.

Clarke, R.V. (1980). Situational crime prevention: Theory and practice. *British Journal of Criminology, 20,* 136–147.

Draper, R. (2013) *Introduction to security management.* Unpublished lecture PowerPoint slides. 2008CCJ. Brisbane, Australia: Griffith University.

Fennelly, L. (Ed.), (2103a). *Effective physical security.* Waltham, MA: Butterworth-Heinemann.

Fennelly, L. (2103b). Security surveys and the security audit. In L. Fennelly (Ed.), *Effective physical security* (pp. 41–76). Waltham, MA: Butterworth-Heinemann.

Garcia, M.L. (2007). *Design and evaluation of physical protection systems.* Waltham, MA: Butterworth-Heinemann.

Sarre, R., & Prenzler, T. (2009). *The law of private security in Australia.* Sydney, Australia: Thomson Reuters.

Schaub, J.L., & Biery, K.D. (1998). *The ultimate security survey.* Worburn, MA: Butterworth-Heinemann.

Standards Australia. (2006). *Handbook 167:2006 — Security risk management.* Sydney, Australia: Author.

United States Army. (2001) *Field manual 3-19.30: Physical security.* Retrieved from http://www.globalsecurity.org/military/library/policy/army/fm/3-19-30/ch1.htm

Chapter 8

People Management in Security

Rick Draper and Jessica Ritchie

Fundamentally, all crime-related security risks originate from human based sources of threat. Similarly, and notwithstanding the array of technical and physical resources that may form part of a risk management program, the effective mitigation of crime-related risks fundamentally relies on people. This situation highlights the human imperative in security risk management. With this in mind, the present chapter discusses the importance of developing and implementing security policies and procedures as part of managing people. This applies to people within, and external to, organisations. The chapter concludes by highlighting the importance of effective communication of requirements through security awareness, and having strategies in place to facilitate compliance.

Security Planning

Within some industries and some sectors of government, there are regulatory controls and specified requirements for security planning that must be met (Draper, 2013, p. 283). However, irrespective of size, all companies, not-for-profit organisations, and government agencies can benefit from a structured approach to managing security-related risks that go beyond minimum legislated requirements. Security management plans do not necessarily need to be complex, but they do need to reflect a viable process for understanding and responding to the range of risks to which the organisation may be exposed. Like all good plans, it is important that objectives and implementation strategies are clearly defined, as well as having responsibilities assigned and processes in place for ongoing monitoring and review of all aspects of the plan (Golsby, 1996). However, care needs to be taken to ensure that security management plans are also flexible enough to respond to the dynamic nature of the threats to be addressed (Girard, 2004, pp. 418–419).

As discussed in chapter 6, security-related risks are inherently dynamic in nature and human sources of threat often bring with them considerations not evident in many other forms of risk. Nevertheless, security planning cannot be undertaken in isolation and any cursory analysis will show a significant overlap between planning for security management, and planning undertaken for occupational health and safety, crisis management and business continuity.

Dedicated Security and Non-Security Personnel

Security management plans, and associated policies and procedures must take into account differences in roles within the organisation. If the nature of the organisation is such that there is a need for a dedicated security function, the optimum position for the function within the organisational structure is a matter of some debate (Bamfield, 2006, pp. 496–497). Whatever the lines of reporting that may apply, from a management perspective the executives within the security function must clearly understand the priorities for the organisation, and be in a position to influence decisions that have a bearing on security risks.

As discussed later in this chapter, the dissemination of security related policies and procedures needs to be undertaken in accordance with need-to-know principles (Attorney-General's Department, 2012, p. 22). However, there are very specific considerations that need to be applied to persons with dedicated security roles. For example, security personnel in management and operational positions will be assigned tasks and duties, the details of which cannot be widely distributed without introducing vulnerabilities (e.g., response or investigation protocols).

Management of contracted security personnel is also an important consideration, where 'outsourcing' is used to replace in-house security staff or supplement in-house staff for security functions. The primary advantages seen in outsourcing are cost and resource flexibility. However, some organisations have found that outsourcing security roles can result in lower quality of service delivery and problems with demarcation of roles and authority (Bamfield, 2006, p. 501). But many of the same difficulties can be experienced with in-house and contracted security — including lack of clarity around roles, responsibilities and expectations.

The obligations of both employers and employees with respect to occupational health and safety are enshrined in legislation. As noted at the beginning of this chapter, some government department and agencies also have mandatory requirements with respect to security. For example, the Australian government requires that

> Agencies must provide all staff, including contractors, with sufficient information and security awareness training to ensure they are aware of, and meet, the requirements of the Protective Security Policy Framework (Attorney-General's Department, 2012, p. 10).

However, there is little to require most organisations to proactively consider many of the security responsibilities that fall to 'non-security personnel'.

Challinger (2006, p. 589) notes that '[some] management view security as an impediment to good business and efficiency'. This may in part be due to the view that inadequate attention is so often paid to 'non-security personnel' when considering security.

Security Policies, Procedures, Rules and Standing Orders

Good policies and procedures are the key foundations of effective management. They provide the basis for governance, communicate organisational values, and establish ethical and legal frameworks within which all aspects of the organisation are managed (Armstrong, 1990, p. 4). Policies and procedures document the actions members need to take to fulfil organisational purposes, and the appropriate authorities for managing and supervising tasks. In essence, they are a guide for decision-making, as well as a reference point for disciplinary issues.

In any organisation, there will be subjects for policy development that are uniquely related security, which need to be drafted separately. However, in areas where there are overlaps it is important to avoid the creation of separate security policies with potential for confusion or conflict. Where possible, security requirements should be incorporated into other policy areas so that the management of security risks associated with the function is seen as integral to those activities, rather than a separate function to be addressed by others.

For example, human resources policies dealing with recruitment and termination of employment will include a range of requirements that may vary for different positions. Clearly, the goal for any recruitment policy will be to locate and employ the best person for a given role. Security requirements, such as background checks and verification of qualifications, should be documented alongside what might be seen as the core aspects of the employment policy and procedures.

Golsby (1996, p. 7–1) notes that security policies 'will have an impact on the entire organisation as well as its customers, vendors, visitors, and even on the community in which it operates'. It is important that all policies and procedures are reviewed on a regular basis to ensure that they continue to meet corporate requirements and remain operationally viable. Failure to adequately document, review and maintain appropriate security policies can expose an organisation to claims of negligence and litigation (Sarre & Prenzler, 2009, p. 201). Similarly, any failure to maintain currency in policy areas related to regulatory controls may also expose the organisation to penalties or litigation.

In a security context there are some important distinctions that should be drawn with respect to policy, procedure, rules and standing orders. Appropriate definitions include the following:

- **Policies** are succinct statements of the organisation's philosophy and requirements within a specific area of its operations.
- **Procedures** support the implementation of policy through more comprehensive statements detailing required actions by nominated groups of people within the subject area of operations.
- **Rules** are concise statements of specific requirements under given policies.
- **Standing orders** — sometimes referred to as standard operating procedures or SOPs — are consolidated sets of procedures and rules presented in a format that facilitates easy reference and execution by specific groups of personnel (e.g., security standing orders).

Some organisations have distinct approaches to policy writing which frame the subject matter in structured templates for consistency. While consistency is highly desirable as a general concept for written policies, care needs to be taken that the core policy statement is not lost among verbose supporting material. Well-drafted security policies should include most, if not all, of the following features:

- Title (concisely describing the subject matter)
- Policy number (makes it easier to cross-reference when dealing with larger numbers of policies)
- Brief statement of purpose (why the policy has been drafted)
- Concise policy statement (effectively communicating the requirements)
- Definitions (any specific use of terms within the context of the policy, or terms that may be unfamiliar to readers)
- Nominated authority under which the policy has been approved (e.g. Board of Directors)
- Nominated position within the organisation with the primary responsibility for implementing and maintaining the policy
- Distribution list (detailing who should be given or have access to the policy – not all policies should be available to everyone)
- Key dates (Implementation/Effective Date, Last Reviewed, Next Review)
- Revision Number (including date revised).

For convenience and operational efficiency, the following features may also be considered for inclusion in security policies:

- a list of procedures through which the policy is to be implemented

- a list of related policies (e.g. a policy related to assault might include references to incident reporting, counselling / employee assistance program, etc.)
- a list of all reviews of the policy (including dates and responsible personnel/positions)
- a list of all revisions promulgated (including dates on which the revision came into effect).

Policies and their related procedures must not require actions that are unlawful or outside the control or competence of those tasked with implementation. For example, Post & Schachtsiek (1986, p. 127) provide a sample policy statement that might be used in a retail setting: 'All those who shoplift from the expensive department store will be prosecuted'. On the surface, the policy might seem appropriate. However, there are two key issues that will impact upon its implementation. Firstly, the policy assumes that all shoplifters will be detected. Secondly, although a private prosecution can be an option, decisions about prosecution are usually at the discretion of police and public prosecutors not store management. A more workable policy might be drafted as: 'The expensive department store will support the prosecution of all those identified as shoplifting from the store'. This would translate in implementation to an obligation for the store to provide personnel resources, such as CCTV footage, to support the prosecution of offenders by the relevant authorities.

Similarly, Post & Schachtsiek (1986, p. 127) provide the following example of a procedure related to the above hypothetical policy: 'Security personnel are to promptly notify police whenever a shoplifter is detained. Upon their arrival, the police are to make the actual arrest of the subject'. In Australia, there is a legal obligation for police to be notified immediately when a security officer detains a person on suspicion of an offence (Sarre & Prenzler, 2009, p. 110). Consequently, the sample procedure appropriately describes a legal requirement. However, at law the detention of the person on suspicion of committing an offence is an arrest. Thus, while the police may re-arrest the suspect in accordance with their own protocols, the second sentence in this sample procedure is technically invalid and potentially misleading.

Documenting the full range of security related policies and procedures applicable to any organisation may seem like a daunting task. However, to misquote the Chinese philosopher Laozi, a comprehensive approach to managing security risks starts with a single policy statement. There is no point in excessive delays waiting to publish an entire manual when core policies and procedures that have been drafted could be implemented and support the contribution of staff and others to effective security management.

Security Awareness

'Security awareness' is the means through which an individual is made conscious of, and accepts, his or her own role and responsibilities in the protection of the assets of an organisation (Draper, 1997). While the subject matter for security awareness programs will vary according to the organisation and the nature of the risks being managed, the goal of every security awareness program must be to engender protective attitudes and behaviours — both personally and on behalf of the organisation.

A common mistake in attempting to implement a security awareness program is failing to gain an understanding of how others in the organisation perceive security, before aspects of the program are developed. Interpretation of critical aspects of the 'security philosophy' or 'security message' may be influenced by:

- Observation
- Personal experience
- The experiences of others and/or
- Targeted communication.

Effective security awareness is therefore grounded in 'targeted communication'. As with Neighbourhood Watch, security awareness programs are intended to reduce the opportunity for security risks to be realised, through raising awareness about those risks, as well as improving attitudes about reporting incidents and suspicious behaviour (Mukherjee& Wilson, 1988, p. 2). However, it is important that there is alignment between the content of the message and what people are experiencing. Personal experiences can positively or negatively influence interpretation of security awareness messages, with past victimisation or offending behaviour having the greatest influence.

Security awareness programs frequently include the use of strategies that could be variously described as 'education' or 'training'. Education is generally seen as conferring general understanding, while training develops specific skills. Both are needed to enlarge awareness of general security vulnerabilities and responsibilities across an organisation, and task-specific obligations. The key here for security risk management is to recognise that while gaining 'attention' is important, it is only part of the equation in creating and maintaining awareness of security related issues.

Figure 8.1 illustrates the security awareness cycle, with corporate goals and security risks the key drivers in defining the rationale for an effective security awareness campaign. The five overlapping elements in the cycle reflect the need for security awareness programs to be thought of in terms of finite campaigns (i.e., they have a distinct preparatory phase before imple-

Figure 8.1
Security awareness campaign cycle.
Source: Draper, 1997. (Used with permission.)

mentation and, at a defined point the program is brought to a conclusion and evaluated). Lessons learnt should be fed back into future programs.

There is a danger that security awareness programs are overly inward-looking. For example, they might focus exclusively on employee dishonesty. This can have an extremely negative effect on the perceived role of security within the organisation. It is vital that awareness programs be deployed as tools to enhance all aspects of security organisation, not merely as a means of warning that 'security is watching you'. As noted above, security risk management strategies within any organisation impact on all people who come into contact with that organisation. Staff, contractors, suppliers, customers and visitors are affected by, or have a role in, the implementation of security policies. Consequently, all of these groups must be considered as potential targets for aspects of security awareness programs.

It can be argued that most organisations maintain a security awareness program of some description. In any organisation, a series of questions will reveal at least some basic level of security awareness on the part of staff:

- Who is responsible for locking the office?
- What would you do in an armed hold-up?
- Where is sensitive company information stored?
- Who is authorised to sign purchase orders?
- Where do you park your car when you are on night shift?

The answers to these questions and similar questions may or may not be appropriate, but what is also important is mode of communication. The answers are likely to have been communicated in some manner. That communication may have been formal and structured, utilising many of the strategies that we associate with security awareness, such as training sessions, meetings, posters, videos, booklets, newsletters, etc. Conversely, it may have been an unstructured series of apparently unrelated interactions, such as informal on-the-job instructions.

As noted above, the effectiveness of a security awareness program can be influenced by people's experiences inside and outside the workplace. For example, previous employment, neighbourhood watch meetings, and discussions with family and friends may all provide information that supports, or conflicts with, the security policies and procedures of the organisation. Problems arising from inappropriate attitudes, derived from outside the organisation, can be avoided by the manner in which the security environment is established. An informal approach to security awareness is likely to be too 'hit and miss' and fail to optimise the required level of consciousness. Factors such as management practices, organisational culture, corporate ethics, morale and discipline can all have an effect on the way an individual responds to messages about security awareness. A structured approach, however simple, will undoubtedly deliver more predictable and consistent outcomes when compared to informal approaches.

Conclusion

The management of security risks ultimately relies on the effective management of people; and not just those with dedicated security roles. All staff have roles and responsibilities related to security, as do contractors, and even customers and visitors in various ways. As with most aspects of business management, plans, policies and procedures are central to success. Managing security effectively, and in the most cost-effective way, is no exception. Clear definitions of roles and responsibilities are essential to address the range of security risks that an organisation may face. Equally important are the methods used to communicate requirements and obligations to those affected, and ensuring that processes are in place to facilitate compliance.

References

Armstrong, M. (2008). *How to be an even better manager.* London, England: Kogan Page.

Attorney-General's Department. (2012). *Protective security policy framework: Securing government business.* Canberra, Australia: Author.

Bamfield, J. (2006). Management. In M. Gill (Ed.), *The handbook of security* (pp. 485–508). Houndmills Basingstoke, England: Palgrave Macmillan.

Challinger, D. (2006). Corporate security: A cost or contributor to the bottom line? In M. Gill (Ed.), *The handbook of security* (pp. 586–609). Houndmills Basingstoke, England: Palgrave Macmillan.

Draper, R. (1997). *Developing and implementing a security awareness program — course notes.* Brisbane, Australia: International Security Management and Crime Prevention Institute.

Draper, R. (2103). Standards, regulations, and guidelines: Compliance and your security program. In L. Fennelly (Ed.), *Effective physical security* (pp. 283–291). Waltham: Butterworth-Heinemann.

Girard, C.M. (2004). Planning, management and evaluation. In L. Fennelly (Ed.), *Handbook of loss prevention and crime prevention* (pp. 418–430). Burlington, MA: Butterworth-Heinemann.

Golsby, M. (1996). *Developing and implementing a security management plan – course notes.* Brisbane, Australia: International Security Management and Crime Prevention Institute.

Mukherjee, S., & Wilson, P. (1988). *Neighbourhood watch: Issues and policy implications.* Canberra, Austrlaia: Australian Institute of Criminology.

Post, R.S., & Schachtsiek, D.A. (1986). *Security manager's desk reference.* Stoneham, MA: Butterworth-Heinemann.

Sarre, R., & Prenzler, T. (2009). *The law of private security in Australia.* Sydney, Australia: Thomson Reuters.

PART THREE

The Security Industry and the New Professionalism

Chapter 9

The Security Industry: Dimensions and Issues

Tim Prenzler

This chapter examines the security industry in terms of its functions, size and growth. It is fairly well known that the industry has gone through a large growth phase in the last few decades, but this expansion is often not well documented. In fact, the exact dimensions of change are difficult to map because in many countries, including Australia, there is no single set of comprehensive measures. Nonetheless, we can be confident that in many locations, in terms of personnel, the industry is close to parity with policing. In some places, private security outnumbers police. The chapter also examines a number of key issues associated with the spread of security into every aspect of people's lives. Topics covered include the privatisation of policing, inequality in security, private justice, quality-of-life effects, relations with police, and conduct issues. The chapter concludes with the view that the industry is a significant part of modern society and should be considered an equal partner with police in the task of crime prevention. While there are potential adverse effects of security, these need to be managed within an appropriate regulatory framework.

Categories

'Security' has been defined in a number of different ways. In general terms, it obviously refers to a condition of being 'secure'; that is stable; and free from fear, anxiety, threats, danger, crime or attack (www.thefreedictionary.com/security). The term 'security' is also often used to refer to international security, particularly in terms of the absence of the war and conflict. In this chapter it is used to refer to the work of 'the security industry', 'security services', 'protective security' or 'private police'. Related terms include 'loss prevention' and 'asset protection' services. Although the security industry tends to be focused on the prevention of crime, its work includes law enforcement (investigating crimes and bringing offenders to justice) and restitution (or loss recovery) after crimes have been committed (Strom et al., 2010).

Security services or the security industry can be categorised in different ways (Prenzler, 2004; Strom et al., 2010). The private or commercial contract sector is obviously a key grouping. These are businesses which sell security, including guarding services, monitoring and alarm services, and investigations. Customers include other businesses (such as retail or industrial firms), governments, NGOs (nongovernment noncommercial organisations like charities or clubs) or private citizens (e.g., householders and car owners). The other main sector is 'in-house' or 'proprietorial' security. This is where an organisation, such as a commercial retail chain or government department, directly employs its own security managers and security operatives. In-house security managers will usually need to buy in security equipment and may also contract in some security staff.

The industry is therefore best thought of as spanning both the private and public sectors. 'Private security' was often thought of solely in terms of the contract sector but is now widely seen as including in-house private sector services. For example, the ASIS International (2010) definition of private security is fairly broad:

> The nongovernmental, private-sector practice of protecting people, property, and information, conducting investigations, and otherwise safeguarding an organisation's assets.

Within the broad field of security, there are various occupational groupings and specialisations. Again, these can be defined in different ways. The following is a list of 18 'core elements that constitute the field of security', generated by experts at an ASIS symposium (ASIS Foundation, 2009, p. 4):

1. physical security
2. personnel security
3. information systems security
4. investigations
5. loss prevention
6. risk management
7. legal aspects
8. emergency and contingency planning
9. fire protection
10. crisis management
11. disaster management
12. counterterrorism
13. competitive intelligence
14. executive protection
15. violence in the workplace
16. crime prevention (general)
17. crime prevention through environmental design (CPTED)
18. security architecture and engineering.

A different set of 'functions' carried out by 'private security companies with a nonpublic police function' is provided by the Geneva Centre for the Democratic Control of Armed Forces, as follows (Born, Caparini, & Cole, 2007, pp. 3–4):

1. Prevention or detection of intrusion, unauthorized entry or activity, vandalism or trespassing on private property. This group of activities includes patrolling, guarding of private property, guarding of (nuclear) power plants, military installations and airport security;
2. Prevention or detection of theft, loss, embezzlement, misappropriation or concealment of merchandise, money, bonds, stocks, notes, valuable documents or papers, for example, protection of cash in transit;
3. Protection of individuals from bodily harm, e.g. bodyguards;
4. Adherence to, and enforcement of, established company rules, regulations, measures, policies and practices related to crime reduction;
5. Maintaining public order at events (concerts, football matches);
6. Reporting and apprehension of violators;
7. Transporting prisoners and guarding prisons; and,
8. Reporting on and responding to incidents and calls, including the conception, installation and maintenance of alarm systems and alarm centres.

Finally, in another version, Prenzler (2005) included a number of occupations in the areas of enquiries, location of persons, debt recovery and process service. These were included in a model of the industry based on four components, including an inner and outer 'core', and inner and outer 'layers'. These were categorised in part in terms of priority areas in the evolution of government licensing of security occupations (2005, p. 53):

1. The inner core consists of 'security firms, contract guards and investigators, and both contract and in house crowd controllers'.
2. The outer core consists of 'in-house guards, bodyguards, consultants, control room operators and trainers'.
3. An inner layer includes 'insurance investigators; in-house fraud prevention and crime prevention officers; and security equipment designers, manufacturers and installers (including locksmiths)'.
4. An outer layer consists of 'process servers and debt recovery agents, whose work is closely associated with that of private investigators, but who are normally licensed separately and often considered more in a commercial services or paralegal area of employment. These latter activities are part of a private justice system that intersects with the public justice system and arguably should be considered as part of the security industry'.

History

The long-range history of security, especially private security, has not been well documented. Certainly, though, it is clear that guarding and forms of target hardening go back to many of the earliest types of human society. Protection of property and persons was usually aimed at multiple threats; such as wild animals, and weather and temperature extremes; as well as thieves, robbers, rapists, murderers, bandits, marauding gangs, militias and armies. Ancient 'low-tech' protective devices included dogs, walls, fences, gates, trip wires and bells, strong boxes and secret compartments (McCrie, 2006). The use of mechanical locks has been traced back as far as ancient Egypt. In urbanised societies, town authorities would engage guards and night watchmen to provide collective security. In some cases, guarding duties were customary. In other cases, guards would be paid a wage. With the rise of capitalism and mercantile world trade in the 16th century, docks and transport networks became major targets for crime, and European-based trading companies began to employ their own security personnel to guard stock and warehouses (Johnston, 1992).

It has been argued that by the 18th and early-19th centuries, private means of protection and justice were dominant in the face of an entirely inadequate (often corrupt) public criminal justice system (Johnston, 1992). This included the services of 'private prosecutions and felons associations', in places such as England. These collectives were engaged in various forms of protection of members' property, including recoveries of stolen property such as sheep and horses (Johnston, 1992). Modern professional policing as we know it was introduced in the form of the 'New Police' in London in 1829. The model of trained uniformed public police was quickly adopted around the world. At the same time, including in colonial and frontier societies, private security remained the main source of protection and recovery of losses — increasingly on an outsourced contract basis (Johnston, 1992).

The invention of the burglar alarm in the mid-19th century drove developments on the technical side of security, while also stimulating growth in the 'manpower' sector (McCrie, 2006). Alarms initially alerted guards or other persons on premises. The spread of telephone lines allowed for monitoring off-site. In the US, westward expansion and the lag in government services spawned a number of famous security firms, including Wells Fargo and Pinkertons. The powers of private security came under scrutiny in the late-19th and early-20th centuries when Pinkerton agents engaged in industrial espionage and the violent suppression of strikes. Security received a further boost from the expansion of manufacturing during World War Two and the need for guarding services. However, it was during the postwar economic boom, mainly from the 1960s, that a 'rebirth of private security' occurred through the massive expansion of the industry (Johnston, 1992).

The growth of private security has been recognised as one of the most significant developments in policing generally since World War Two (Bayley & Shearing, 2001). Van Dijk (2008, p. 133) refers to the 'explosive growth of private security across the world'. Growth in this broad area, but especially in the private sector, has been associated with numerous influences, including increased litigation for security failures, the introduction of workplace health and safety legislation, the modern terrorist threat, and government policies of privatisation (Small Arms Survey, 2011). However, the strongest influence appears to have been the large upsurge in crime that occurred in many countries from the 1960s to the 1990s — driven by rising prosperity and freedom, and the proliferation of targets and opportunities for crime (Van Dijk, 2008). As we saw briefly in chapter one, this period was marked by a decisive shift away from reliance on police towards the self-provision of protection. Crime rates began to decline in many locations from the turn of the century, especially property crime rates. Nonetheless, the 'securitisation' process continued, and it continued to drive down crime rates (Van Dijk, 2008).

Securitisation addressed the separation of guardians from crime targets, which was the key factor in escalating crime rates. The employment of security guards provided a form of relatively cheap, site-specific, guardianship. The 1985 Hallcrest Report in the US found that private security officers began to outnumber police in the late-1960s or early-1970s, and by 1990 Hallcrest II put the ratio of private security personnel to police at 2.4:1. Expenditures on private security were estimated to have exceeded those for public police by 1977 (Cunningham, Strauchs, & van Meter, 1990, pp. 229–239). In other places, police continued to outnumber security guards into the 1990s and 2000s, although growth in the guarding sector tended to exceed growth in policing (van Steden & Sarre, 2007).

Despite enormous growth in security officer numbers, security personnel could not deliver sufficient cost-effective protection to close off crime opportunities. Alarms provided a more promising form of extending human guardianships through proxy technology that provided 24/7 coverage of vulnerable entry points on premises. Simple circuit breaker mechanisms were increasingly supplanted by motion detectors and other sensors from the 1970s. Despite major problems with false activations, by 2008, in the US, 92% of retail firms used an alarm system (Hollinger & Adams, 2009, p. 23). Globally, the 2004/5 International Crime Victim Survey found that household adoptions of burglar alarms across 30 countries averaged only 16%, up from 12% in 1989, but with levels up to 38% in Oslo and 34% in Sydney (Van Dijk, van Kesteren, & Smit, 2007, p. 136). Since the 1980s, alarms have increasingly been supplemented by CCTV. In 2013, the number of CCTV cameras in the UK alone was put at somewhere between 4 and 5.9 million (Reeve, 2013). Significant improvements have been made in recent years in picture quality, remote monitoring and interactivity (e.g., communication between monitoring station staff and persons on-site). Smart card technology has also become a popular, more convenient, alternative to mechanical entry control (Draper, Ritchie, & Prenzler, 2012).

Going from the 1990s into the 2000s, security in many places was upgraded into a broader risk management function (see chapter 6). In this view, 'security' should not just be about preventing burglary or theft, but concerned with predicting and pre-empting all threats to an organisation — including in the areas of safety, information technology, reputation, intellectual property and litigation (see chapter 6). Modern security managers now need to multi-task across physical and personnel security, fraud, health and safety, and legal powers and obligations.

Contemporary Industry Dimensions and Trends

Given the fact that the industry can be categorised in different ways, it is not surprising that there are different data sources that produce different pictures of the industry and trends over time. The following subsections report on four recent sources and areas of coverage, including one global report and information on the US, Europe and Australia.

Small Arms Survey

The 'Small Arms Survey' is managed by the Graduate Institute of International and Development Studies in Geneva, Switzerland. It is concerned with providing policy-relevant information at the global level on issues related to violence and small arms (Small Arms Survey, 2013). In 2011, the survey focused on private security in a report *States of Security*. Information on the industry was obtained from 70 countries, where there was an estimated 19.5 million people employed in private security. This was projected to include 25.5 million across all countries (Small Arms Survey, 2011, p. 101). Across the 70 countries surveyed, private security personnel were estimated to outnumber police by a ratio of 1.8:1. The industry was also valued at $US100-165 billion per annum, with an annual growth rate of 7% to 8%. Considerable variation was found in the size of companies, 'ranging from a dozen employees to several hundred thousand' (Small Arms Survey, 2011):

> For example, G4S has 530,000 staff in 115 countries, while Securitas employs 260,000 people in 40 countries ... Countless smaller firms are also active; about 30,000 companies are registered in the Russian Federation, while South African PSCs (private security companies) numbered nearly 7,500 in 2010. (p. 103)

Worldwide, private security companies were estimated to hold between 1.7 and 3.7 million firearms.

The Confederation of European Security Services

The Confederation of European Security Services (CoESS) is a security industry association that publishes periodic assessments of the size of the industry. Data are collected by a survey of CoESS country affiliates, other security industry associations and government departments. The report *Private Security Services in Europe — CoESS Facts and Figures 2011* (CoESS, 2012) covered 34 countries and found there was a total of 2,170,589 private security guards; 83% male and 17% female. The average number of security providers per 10,000 inhabitants was 31.1 (1/321), compared to 36.3 police (1/275; pp. 143-144). The financial turnover for the year was put at €35 billion, with a growth rate from 2005 to 2010 averaging 13.3% per annum. The market was dominated by three unnamed companies, with 55% of market share. These presumably included Securitas and G4S. It was estimated that the private sector accounted for 73% of the market and the public sector 25%. Considerable variation was found between countries in the relative sizes of the security and policing sectors. For example, the UK has a large private security sector, with an estimated security-to-population ratio of 1/170 compared to 1/382 for police. In Belgium, by way of contrast, the security/population ratio was 1/703 and 1/266 for police. In some countries, the ratios were fairly similar: for example, 1/294 for security and 1/290 for police in Lithuania.

The United States: ASIS International

In 2013, ASIS International published a report *The United States Security Industry: Size and Scope, Insights, Trends and Data*, based on a 2012 survey of 453 security executives and analysis of government labour statistics. This was the first major study of the industry since *Hallcrest II* in 1990 (above). The ASIS study estimated that US$350 billion was spent on security products and services in 2012. This included US$69 billon spent on Homeland Security, but it excluded expenditures on security products by public police. The total included US$80 billion for IT security and US$202 billion for 'operational security' (ASIS International, 2013, pp. 22–27). The security market was expected to grow by 6.6% in 2013, including growth of 9.3% in IT security. Apart from IT security, major growth areas included remote CCTV monitoring, biometrics and outsourced investigations.

The report put the number of private personnel 'dedicated to operational security' at between 1.7 and 1.9 million, including up to 760,200 persons (40%) in proprietary (in-house) security and up to 1,173,900 in the contract sector (60%) (ASIS International, 2013, p. 64). Personnel were broken down into the following categories and proportions (p. 65):

- Security officers 69.8% (26-31% armed)
- Administrative staff 2.0%
- 'Functional staff positions (specialists, coordinators)' 4.1%
- 'Functional management (operational security, executive protection, investigations, training, etc.)' 4.5%
- Executives/senior management 19.6%.

IT security staff numbers were put at approximately one million. Security officer numbers (private and government) were expected to grow by 19% from 2010 to 2020, and private investigators by 21% (pp. 65–67).

Australian Data and the 2011 Census

The category 'guards and security officers' was introduced into the Australian census in 1986, with 22,975 persons identified in this category, compared to 33,881 police (Prenzler, 2005, p. 54). Since that time, security categories have gone through several changes, making trend analysis difficult. In addition, a major limitation with the census is that it only measures persons' 'main occupation'. Prenzler, Earle, and Sarre (2009) accessed data from regulatory agencies and identified a total of 112,773 individuals who held one or more security licences in 2008. It was presumed that most of these were part-time, given the contrast with the 2006 census figure of approximately 39,000 individuals in core security functions. The 2009 study identified a number of points of comparison with police:

- Security personnel on average earned about half as much as police.
- Police were better educated than security personnel (e.g., only 16% of security personnel had a qualification above Certificate IV, compared to 52% of police).
- Police were concentrated in the 30 to 39 age bracket, whereas security had a broader age profile, with more younger and older members.

The Prenzler et al. (2009) study also found that in 2006 there were 5,478 security and investigative companies. Total income industry was $4.4 billion. Approximately 45% of companies were owner-operator, with no employees; another 42% employed between 1 and 19 employees, and 12% employed 20 to 199. In terms of market share, about half the market was serviced by a large number of small businesses and the other half was concentrated amongst five companies: Chubb, Linfox, ISS, Tyco and Signature.

Table 9.1 shows data from the 2011 Australian census for security-related occupations, including debt collectors. If we combine the last four security categories, which are the ones closest to the original 'guards and security

Table 9.1

Security Providers, Australian Census, 2011

Category	Number
Private Investigator	728
Security Consultant	874
Locksmith	2,574
Insurance Investigator	444
Debt Collector	8,487
Court Bailiff or Sheriff	639
Armoured Car Escort	535
Security Officer	38,147
Alarm, Security or Surveillance Monitor	766
Crowd Controller	866
Police	49,546
Population	21,507,717

Source: ABS, 2013.

officers', we can see there has been a 75% increase over 25 years from 22,975 in 1986 to 40,314 in 2011. Within the same time frame, the number of police increased by 46%, and the general population increased by 39% (from 15.6 million).

Issues

The growth of the security industry, especially the private sector component, has thrown up a range of social issues. These overlap with the critiques of situational crime prevention discussed in chapter one. Issues more specific to private security are examined now.

Privatised Policing?

Is the growth of the security industry part of a government privatisation agenda that reduces public ownership of core social services? This view was put forcefully in the following statement by an Australian police union official in the 1990s:

> There has been an abrogation of responsibility by governments of all political colours right across Australia away from their responsibility to provide the basics for the community to live in a safe and secure environment. The private sector has taken up the lag and the public is paying twice for what governments should provide. (*Lateline*, 1994)

In response to this, it can be said that the growth of private security generally occurred through market demand, as opposed to deliberate policies of outsourcing or downsizing policing (Johnston, 1992). The evidence shows that in many countries, from the 1970s to the 1990s, the proportion of police-to-population grew, while private security simply grew at a faster rate (Cunningham et al., 1990; Prenzler, 2004). Generally speaking, policing was insulated from privatisation policies because of political sensitivities about governments appearing soft on crime or reducing public protection.

More recently, since the 2007 global financial crisis, reductions in expenditures have affected police numbers, with some governments looking to partially replace police through private security contracts (ASIS International, 2013). In the UK, a new conservative government placed outsourcing on the agenda for policing in 2010. Police budgets were cut by 20%, and police managers were required to make savings through outsourcing and strategies for 'freeing up the police to fight crime more effectively and efficiently' (Home Office, 2011, p. 5).

Most notably, in 2011, Lincolnshire Police signed a £200 million 10-year contract with G4S. However, much of this involved noncore policing functions, including call centre staffing. The outsourced work closest to policing is a prisoner escort service termed 'Street to Suite', which allows police to remain on patrol or at a crime scene after an arrest. Lincolnshire Police and G4S have claimed a raft of successes to date, including improved customer service and reduced crime (Lincolnshire Police/G4S, 2013). The 2012 London Olympics also involved considerable outsourcing, with a £284 million contract to G4S. Last minute staff shortages generated some controversy, but security during the event was considered to have been well-managed, with no major adverse incidents and close cooperation between sectors (Hinton, 2012).

In Australia, a form of privatisation occurred through local governments acting on concerns about crime and ineffective policing by setting up security patrols and camera systems in town centres. Some of this was operationalised in-house, and some involved contracts with private firms (Sarre & Prenzler, 2011). Contracts can be attractive because they are seen as easy to terminate if the system is not working well, and they involve fewer direct liabilities for councils, such as insurance, superannuation and holiday pay. Airport security and stadium security have also involved considerable use of private contracts, but often in association with a significant public police presence (Sarre & Prenzler, 2011).

It has been argued that 'privatisation of policing' is a limiting concept. To capture properly the change process, it is more accurate to talk about the 'pluralisation' of policing, with various forms of self-provision of security involving private and public-sector organisations in diverse, changing and 'hybrid' forms, including specialist public sector agencies combating major and organised crime, white collar crime and corruption (Jones & Newburn, 2006). Pluralisation occurred in response to the inability of public policing to deal with the complex and evolving nature of crime. It could be argued, nonetheless, that public policing was not resourced to keep pace with demand – a type of privatisation by default. Governments should have invested even more tax-payers' money in policing.

The problematic assumption behind this view is that 'more police = less crime'. While this may be true in some cases, there is something of a law of diminishing returns in operation when it comes to police numbers (Kovandzic & Sloan, 2002). As noted in chapter 1, a routine-activity approach to crime highlights the impossibility of police having a natural monopoly on crime control because of the enormous gap between the number of police and the number of potential targets for crime. In addition, police are often limited in their legal capacity to enter premises to engage in preventive work (Prenzler & Sarre, 2014).

An associated view is that the effectiveness of security has shown police to be something of an expensive luxury. In many locations, police enjoy conditions that security officers can only dream about: 6 weeks holidays, rostered days off, generous shift and overtime allowances, generous superannuation, and career paths with well-salaried and excessive middle and upper management positions. What does the public receive for this? Outside clearance rates for homicide, police generally have only the most limited penetration of the crime problem. For many volume crimes, clearance rates are 10% at best (Prenzler & Sarre, 2012). As we saw in chapter 1, while police have a major role to play in containing crime, they appear to have an extremely limited capacity to make large reductions in crime — at least when they work alone.

With all this in mind, it could be argued that the evolution of policing and security in the last 40 years has followed a certain logic in terms of a rough but more efficient division of labour. Cheaper less-skilled security officers — public or private sector — carry out more mundane frontline guarding duties with police back up when required. The more expensive, well-trained, and armed public police provide emergency response and focus on more serious crimes and investigations. Police can also play a very effective role in reducing crime through facilitating public-private crime prevention partnerships (see chapter 5). Security services also provide more sophisticated technical and planning solutions to crime.

Inequality in Security

The issue of privatisation overlaps closely with the issue of inequality in security. Are the democratic principles of equality before the law and equal protection distorted by the operations and growth of private security? The answers to this question are difficult and subject to a number of qualifiers. One argument is that if the rich pay for security this frees up the public police to provide a better service to the poor (Prenzler, 2004). This is difficult to prove empirically, but it is reasonable to assume that the large reductions in property offences, resulting from increased security, give police more time to devote to disadvantaged areas and to more serious violent offences. As we saw in chapter one, at a global level, it appears that both the rich and poor have benefited from the growth of private security, but the rich have benefited to a greater extent, and there appears to be a growing security gap between the rich and poor. Ironically, then, one answer to this problem is not less security, but more — including more security aimed at disadvantaged sectors of society.

An associated argument involves a more developed 'social justice critique', which argues that expanded and privatised security compounds disadvantage by preventing marginalised groups from participating in mainstream life. Examples include the exclusion of homeless persons, and young people, from mass public private property. This view is expressed in the following quotation:

> The urban environment is a site of constant processes of social inclusion and exclusion. Issues of unequal power and resources are translated at a material level into, for instance, urban fortresses for the rich, no-go public zones for the poor, and an extensive apparatus of social control to regulate human interaction ... Attempts have been made to extend the range of surveillance, involving a variety of different groups... [including] employing private security guards ...

> Indeed, 'urban fortress' techniques and more subtle but highly intensive systems of surveillance and control tend to apply to selected sites: major shopping complexes; recreational and entertainment centres; luxury apartments and housing estates; modern office blocks. These areas can be rendered relatively safe and crime free. But at what costs? ... The social construction of urban space in a manner which reflects first and foremost the protection of private property and commercial interests of business people can lead to attacks on those groups who do not command the economic and social resources to 'use' such spaces in the 'appropriate manner'. (White & Sutton, 1995, pp. 84, 89–90)

This phenomenon is to some extent a regrettable effect of wider complex social inequalities that cannot all be sheeted home to greedy capitalists and private security. The authors also underestimate the natural concerns of ordinary people about crime threats. It seems reasonable to expect people to take precautions — in opting for secured accommodation for example — when self-protection is such a deeply instinctive part of our nature. In addition, as responsible citizens, people must take reasonable precautions (within their capacity) to protect themselves and their assets, as well as exercising a duty of care towards persons visiting their premises or in their employment. In that regard, the security industry provides a service in response to demand in a mature market economy, essential to freedom because monopoly government provision can be corrupt or inadequate. Access to private security, within a framework of law, could be considered an essential civil liberty, like access to private legal representation. Furthermore, re-engineering a more tolerant and equal society is a key role of government; but one way of doing that is by employing more security to protect vulnerable people.

Private Justice

Another area of criticism, closely associated with the social justice critique, has been defined more narrowly as a 'justice critique' (Prenzler, 2004, p. 273; Shearing & Stenning, 1983). With the growth of private security, more offenders are likely to be apprehended by private security. This may benefit some — unfairly — in terms of decisions not to inform police and enforce the law. At the same time, accused persons might suffer from the denial of due process. For example, an employee might be dismissed because of suspected, but unproven, theft.

This is another potentially problematic aspect of security, but the dimensions are largely unknown. The risk is certainly one that should be acknowledged and government processes put in place to guard against inequalities and injustices. Unfair dismissal laws are one example. Another example concerns mandatory disclosure laws, which require the reporting of suspected offences in the workplace, such as child abuse or misconduct. It could also be argued that police need to be more receptive to crime reports from the private sector or more encouraging of reporting. An important test will always be the harm done to victims, and the need to deter future offending, against the costs associated with a simple prosecute-and-punish model of justice. In addressing this question, one should also keep in mind the arguments made in chapter one, that reduced opportunities for crime, generated by private sector security services, can protect potential offenders from the negative effects of offending — including criminal justice processes, punishment and criminal stigma.

Quality-of-Life Impacts

Does security come at too high a price in terms of convenience, privacy and freedom? Fears of a 'dystopian' future have been expressed in concepts such as the 'new surveillance' (Marx, 2002) and the 'dispersal of social control' (Hoogenboom, 1991) — related to growth in security guards, CCTV, tracking devices, listening devices, X-ray scanning, computerised personal record keeping and data-matching. Again, as we saw in chapter one, this is an area of potentially adverse outcomes from the enlargement of security, but the risks need to be managed through a democratically-based regulatory system. Examples include up-dated privacy legislation (see chapter 11), freedom of information legislation, and codes of conduct for security providers — including for operators of surveillance equipment. Security providers are also pursuing convenience (and aesthetics to some extent) as a marketable product. A few examples include attractive security lighting, remote locking, plastic keycards, punch-in PINs (rather than a signature on paper), and plantings around bollards. CPTED applications should also seek to facilitate community relations between legitimate users of space (see chapter 3). Furthermore, available survey data suggest that people generally do not feel overly threatened by security, with a good proportion feeling safer as a result of visible security (Stenning, 1994; van Steden & Nalla, 2010).

Relations With Police

How should police and private security relate to each other? On the one hand, it would seem obvious that they should work closely together to reduce crime. This is increasingly the view adopted by governments and police (Prenzler & Sarre, 2014). On the other hand, the two operate on quite different principles and cooperation entails a number of potential conflicts of interest. Table 9.2 lists some key differentials that pose barriers to cooperation. For example, if police work closely with security firms — through information sharing or priority communications — then the clients of those firms may benefit unfairly. Police 'moonlighting' in the industry has also been identified a major problem (Born et al., 2007). This can involve officers owning their own security firms or working part-time in the industry. Police in this situation may be tempted to exercise police powers or make use of police resources.

Again, these issues need to be managed in a way that prioritises the public interest. Banning police from the industry, or requiring permission (subject to conditions), is one response (Born et al., 2007). More generally, the benefits of public–private partnerships in reducing crime have strengthened the case for closer cooperation. While there are risks that government resources are used to favour particular businesses or security firms, it appears that partnerships can be managed in a way that demonstrates a broad benefit (Prenzler & Sarre, 2014). In fact, it can be the case that groups who do not contribute to partnerships obtain benefits. Any tendering processes need to be properly competitive and transparent.

Table 9.2

Opposing Principles of Public Policing and Private Security

Taxpayer Funded	Profit Driven
Public interest	Client interest
Equal service (on triage basis)	Selective service
Offender oriented	Protection oriented
Reactive	Proactive
Specific powers	Agent and citizen powers
Centralised bureaucracy	Fragmented
Heavily regulated	Less regulated
Intensive training	Minimal (mandated) training

Source: Adapted from Prenzler and Sarre, 1998, p. 3.

Conduct Issues

Are the benefits of security services undermined by misconduct in the industry? Growth in the size of security services was accompanied by scandals and alarm over damaging behaviour by persons employed to protect people. Terms such as 'backyarders', 'cowboys', 'thugs' and 'criminals' have often been used to describe 'sections' of the industry (Prenzler, 2004). The following quotation from a 1992 newspaper report, under the headline 'Private police army grows: "Thugs" worry crime expert', exemplifies this view:

> Private security is Queensland's fastest growing industry after tourism, a leading criminologist says ...'Despite the real concerns that many hold about the increase in private police armies, it is inevitable that their size and functions will grow,' he said. However, Professor Wilson expressed fears about the training and selection criteria of security personnel, saying examples abounded of people with serious criminal convictions working in the industry. 'There are bouncers who act as thugs, burglar alarm "experts" who have difficulty in understanding one end of a plug from another,' he said. It was also possible that some security industry personnel were acting as fronts for professional thieves. (*The Courier-Mail*, 1992, p. 3).

The nature and extent of misconduct is addressed in detail in chapter 10. The chapter describes a wide range of abuses that can creep into the industry. However, there are also reputable firms that are easily tarred by the same negative brush of sensational media reporting of misconduct cases. While the finger of blame is often pointed at security providers as a group, the fact is that standards are only as good as government regulation. A diversified industry cannot police itself effectively, and it is not the duty of responsible firms to police irresponsible firms. Security associations try to improve standards but are limited to their membership and capacity (see chapter 12).

Security scandals and misconduct are therefore largely attributable to lazy and disinterested politicians who fail to recognise the value and risks in the industry and the need for basic regulation to ensure common standards (see chapter 12).

It should also be noted that scandals and misconduct in policing, in countries like Australia, have greatly eclipsed problems in the security industry. Abuses in public policing have necessitated highly complex and expensive regulatory systems. Despite this, various forms of corruption, negligence, assaults and excessive force by police continue to be major problems in many established democracies (Prenzler, 2009).

Conclusion

Responsibility for law enforcement and crime prevention is now dispersed across a wide range of agencies, both public and private, in-house and contract. The security industry has been growing at a significant pace since the 1960s and is now an established and prominent part of a complex 'policing' apparatus, with the private security component particularly prominent. The industry is not going away. In fact, it is likely to become further enmeshed with every aspect of people's lives. This fundamental social change has not been without its problems. There is a dark side to the industry. Security services are not distributed equally on the basis of need. Security can be inconvenient, ugly and oppressive. Security providers, like police, can betray their calling and engage in corruption, negligence and violence.

However, the industry is thriving because of the many benefits it provides to a very wide range of people in reducing criminal victimisation and helping people to feel safe. The downside issues should be addressed through the democratic process, with a focus on making the industry work in the public interest. 'Smart regulation' by government, in cooperation with the industry, discussed in chapter 12, is the key to maximising the benefits and minimising harms. Government also has a key role to play in making security work for disadvantaged people. This can be achieved in part through improving security in public housing and public institutions, in subsidising security, and in facilitating public-private crime prevention partnerships.

References

ASIS Foundation. (2009). *Compendium of the ASIS academic/practitioner symposium, 1997–2008*. Alexandria, VA: Author.

ASIS International. (2010). *International glossary of security terms*. Retrieved from https://www.asisonline.org/Membership/Library/Security-Glossary/Pages/Security-Glossary-P.aspx

ASIS International. (2013). *The United States security industry: Size and scope, insights, trends and data.* Alexandria, VA: Author.

Australian Bureau of Statistics. (2013). *2011 census of population and housing, customised data report (security-related occupations).* Canberra, Australia: Author.

Bayley, D., & Shearing, C. (2001) *The new structure of policing.* Washington, DC: National Institute of Justice.

Born, H., Caparini, M., & Cole, E. (2007). *Regulating private security in Europe: Status and prospects.* Geneva, Switzerland: Geneva Centre for the Democratic Control of Armed Forces (DCAF).

Confederation of European Security Services. (2012). Private security services in Europe: CoESS facts and figures 2011, Wemmel, Belgium: Author.

Cunningham, W., Strauchs, J., & van Meter, C. (1990). Private security trends, 1970 to 2000. Boston: Butterworth-Heinemann.

Draper, R., Ritchie, J., & Prenzler, T. (2012). Making the most of security technology. In T. Prenzler (Ed.), *Policing and security in practice: Challenges and achievements* (pp. 186–203). Houndmills Basingstoke, England: Palgrave-Macmillan.

Hinton, J. (2012). G4S donating £2.5m to armed forces. Retrieved from http://www.independent.co.uk/news/uk/home-news/g4s-donating-25m-to-armed-forces-8038567.html

Hollinger, R., & Adams, A. (2009). *2008 National Retail Security Survey.* Gainesville, FL: University of Florida.

Home Office. (2011). Annual report and accounts 2010–11, London, England: Author.

Hoogenboom, R. (1991). Grey policing: A theoretical framework. *Policing and Society, 2*(1), 17–30.

Johnston, L. (1992). *The rebirth of private policing.* London, England: Routledge.

Jones, T., & Newburn, T. (2006). Understanding plural policing. In T. Jones & T. Newburn (Eds.), Plural policing (pp. 1–11). London: Routledge.

Kovandzic, T., & Sloan, J. (2002). Police levels and crime rates revisited: A county-level analysis from Florida (1980-1998). *Journal of Criminal Justice, 30,* 65–76.

Lateline. (1994, 12 July). Sydney, Australia: Australian Broadcasting Corporation.

Lincolnshire Police/G4S (2013). The G4S Lincolnshire Police Strategic Partnership – One year on. Lincoln, England: Author.

Marx, G. (2002). What's new about the 'new surveillance'? Classifying for change and continuity. *Surveillance & Society, 1*(1), 9–29.

McCrie, R.D. (2006). A history of security. In M. Gill (Ed.), *The handbook of security* (pp. 21–44). Houndmills Basingstoke, England: Palgrave Macmillan.

Prenzler, T., & Sarre, R. (2012). The police. In H. Hayes & T. Prenzler (Eds.), *An introduction to crime and criminology* (pp. 258-274). Sydney, Australia: Pearson.

Prenzler, T. (2004). The privatisation of policing. In R. Sarre & J. Tomaino (Eds.), *Key issues in criminal justice* (pp. 267–296). Adelaide, Australia: Australian Humanities Press.

Prenzler, T. (2005). Mapping the Australian security industry. *Security Journal, 18*(4), 51–64.

Prenzler, T. (2009). *Police corruption.* Boca Raton, FL: CRC Press.

Prenzler, T., & Sarre, R. (1998). Regulating private security in Australia. *Trends and Issues in Crime and Criminal Justice, 98*, 1–6.

Prenzler, T., & Sarre, R. (2014, in press) The Role of partnerships in security management. In M. Gill (Ed.), Handbook of security. Houndmills: Palgrave-Macmillan.

Prenzler, T., Earle, K., & Sarre, R. (2009). Private security in Australia: Trends and key characteristics. *Trends and Issues in Crime and Criminal Justice, 374*, 1–6.

'Private police army grows: "Thugs" worry crime expert'. *The Courier-Mail,* (1992, November 30), 3.

Reeve, T. (2013). BSIA attempts to clarify question of how many CCTV cameras there are in the UK. Retrieved from http://www.securitynews-desk.com/2013/07/11/bsia-attempts-to-clarify-question-of-how-many-cctv-cameras-in-the-uk/

Sarre, R., & Prenzler, T. (2011). *Private security and public interest: Australian Research Council Linkage Report.* Adelaide, Australia: University of South Australia.

Shearing, C., & Stenning, P. (1983). *Private security and private justice: The challenge of the 80s.* Montreal, Canada: Institute for Research on Public Policy.

Small Arms Survey (2011). *States of security.* Retrieved from http://www.smallarmssurvey.org/publications/by-type/yearbook/small-arms-survey-2011.html

Small Arms Survey (2013). *About the small arms survey.* Retrieved from http://www.smallarmssurvey.org/about-us/mission.html

Stenning, P. (1994). Private security — some recent myths, developments and trends. In D. Biles & J. Vernon (Eds.), *Private sector and community involvement in the criminal justice system* (pp. 146–155). Canberra, Australia: Australian Institute of Criminology.

Strom, K., Berzofsky, M., Shook-Sa, B., Barrick, K., Daye, C., Horstmann, N., & Kinsey, S. (2010). *The private security industry*. Washington, DC: Bureau of Justice Statistics.

Van Dijk, J. (2008). *The world of crime*. Thousand Oaks, CA: Sage.

Van Dijk, J., van Kesteren, J., & Smit, P. (2007). Criminal victimisation in international perspective. Retrieved from http://www.unicri.it/services/library_documentation/publications/icvs/publications/ICVS2004_05report.pdf

van Steden, R., & Nalla, M.K. (2010). Citizen satisfaction with private security guards in the Nertherlands. *European Journal of Criminology, 7*(3), 214–234.

van Steden, R., & Sarre, R. (2007). The growth of privatized policing: Some cross-national data and comparisons. *International Journal of Comparative and Applied Criminal Justice, 31,* 51–71.

White, R., & Sutton, A. (1995). Crime prevention, urban space and social exclusion. *The Australian and New Zealand Journal of Sociology, 31*(1), 82–99.

Chapter 10

Legal Powers, Obligations and Immunities

Rick Sarre

On a daily basis in Australia security officers search bags, forbid entry, bar exits, ask probing questions, detain people, confiscate property, carry out inquiries and operate covert surveillance equipment, most significantly CCTV, without any clearly stated, or well understood, legal parameters. This chapter is designed to fill this gap. It examines the legal principles that apply to the activities that are routinely carried out on a daily basis by Australian security personnel. What will become immediately clear is that the legal powers, obligations and immunities of private security providers are not set out in an easily accessible statute, but are, rather, determined by a piecemeal array of common law principles, practical assumptions and legislative principles that were designed principally with other people in mind; for example, private citizens, police officers, journalists, landowners and employers. This chapter will explore these principles, and will seek to clarify what they mean for people carrying out 'policing' powers on behalf of other people.

What Legal Powers Exist?

Given the rapid expansion of the presence of private personnel in policing activities (Prenzler, Earle, & Sarre, 2009; Sarre & Prenzler, 2014), one might assume that careful attention would have been paid to the legal framework within which these activities take place. Sadly, this has rarely occurred. There are many aspects of the law relating to the protection of property, the use of reasonable force in self-defence, and the deployment of surveillance devices, for example, which are unsatisfactory and confusing for security providers and the public alike (McCahill & Norris, 1999; Sarre, Brooks, Smith, & Draper, 2014). Indeed, British academic Mark Button cites anecdotal evidence that some security personnel in the United Kingdom (as many as 10%) even believe that they possess the same powers as police officers (Button, 2007).

Security providers are not well inoculated against legal suit either. Let us compare the law that applies when public police make a mistake, or overstretch the mark. The law gives public police general immunity from any law suit in circumstances where their beliefs and acts are 'reasonable.' Private security personnel are afforded no such luxury. Private security thus remain vulnerable and constantly run the risk of being sued in the torts of assault, false imprisonment, intentional infliction of mental distress, defamation, nuisance and trespass to land. This is not to say that police do not run these risks, but because they have immunities in place, the police are far less likely to find themselves on the losing end of a law suit brought by an aggrieved person seeking compensation. Moreover, public police may act to prevent the commission of an offence before it actually happens (acting upon a suspicion). This concession is not granted to private security personnel.

Concerns about this confusion have been expressed in the past. Members of an Ontario, Canada, task force (Ontario & Anand, 1987) raised a concern over the fact that shopping mall owners and their private security personnel have virtually unfettered powers when it comes to directing the general public who frequent these places. They pointed out that the public police do not have similar powers in relation to conduct on public streets unless a person on a street is clearly committing an offence. The task force made two recommendations regarding reform. The first was rather radical, namely to make privately-owned malls, by legislation, equivalent to public streets for the purpose of policing people who moved through them. The less radical option was to amend trespass laws to require property owners to display signs indicating what behaviours would amount to conduct sufficient to attract the attention of their security personnel. The shopping mall owners associations in Ontario lobbied against both of the recommendations and the government of the day took no action. As Stenning (2009) points out, however, the report did raise the level of public debate over the issue, and negotiation over how 'public' shopping malls would be policed became a common point of negotiation in the planning approval process of new malls (Stenning, 2009, p. 28).

While it is true that there has been legislation passed in all Australian jurisdictions concerning the registration, licensing, identification and training of private legal personnel, the main aim of this legislation is to regulate those who operate within the industry, and to check those who wish to enter it against certain criteria and minimum training standards. The legislation does not deal with powers or immunities. There are two exceptions, but they are actually addressing the *lack* of power of security personnel rather than *actual* power. Section 8 of the *Security Industry Act 1997* (NSW) says that the holder of any licence can carry out the functions authorised by the licence but that '[a] licence does not confer on the licensee any function apart from a function authorised by the licence'. The South Australian *Security and Investigation Agents Act 1995*, section 15(1) goes a little further, stating that '[a] licence does not confer on an agent power or authority to act in contravention of, or in disregard of, law or rights or privileges arising under or protected by law'. Section 15(2) then repeats the New South Wales legislative proscription forbidding any attempt by any person to bluff the public: '[a] licensed agent must not hold himself or herself out as having a power or authority by virtue of the licence that is not in fact conferred by the licence'.

Legal Authority

The legal powers, rights and immunities of private security personnel are somewhat obscurely located across a range of fields: the criminal law; the law of property; the law of contract (both in terms of contracts of employment, and the contracts that apply to paying customers whenever they enter a private sports or entertainment venue); and employment law (Sarre & Prenzler, 2009, chapter 3). The principles of the criminal law, property law, contract law and employment law are, for the most part, located in what we refer to as the 'common law', that is, the reasoning that emerges from cases that come before the courts, where a judge has decided the case in favour of one party over another, for a particular reason. There may also be an Act of Parliament that assists the decision, and the judge may be called upon to interpret the wording of the Act. That interpretation then, also becomes part of the common law. By way of example, a property owner has a common law right to ask an unwelcome visitor to leave his or her home. There is legislation in each state that sets out how much force that property owner can use (see below) but the wording changes in each jurisdiction.

Starting from first principles, and speaking generally, unless there is specific legislation that empowers specialised security staff to undertake certain tasks for some particular event, such as the Commonwealth Games, the law confers no powers upon security personnel beyond the powers given to the ordinary citizen. That having been said, the powers of the private citizen are considerable. As explained above, the law in Australia that relates to property owners grants to these private individuals (or companies) the power to require visitors to leave the premises (using reasonable force if necessary), or to subject visitors to stipulations (such as a search) prescribed and advertised by the property owner. A shop-owner, therefore, can demand that persons entering his or her shop be prepared to open their bags for inspection prior to their leaving the store. Persons who are being served a summons by police can demand that those police leave their premises if it has been made clear to the police that they do not have permission to be on the premises (Sarre & Prenzler, 2009, ¶3.155). These rules emanate from an old English principle, dating from 1604, that 'a man's house is his castle' (Sarre & Prenzler, 2009, ¶3.140). Similar powers exist for employers over employees. Each of these powers can be delegated to agents (private security) who are entitled to wear uniforms, and even to carry a firearm if they have the correct licence. But the common law and the legislation that applies differs from jurisdiction to jurisdiction, as explained in the paragraph below entitled 'The use of force in defence of property'.

With this in mind, it is useful to look at some actual examples that apply to the sorts of activities undertaken by security personnel. Three areas of law are of particular interest, as they have prompted the parliaments to pass legislation that directly affects the tasks undertaken by security personnel. The first, the use of force in defence of property, is important, as personnel are often called upon to defend their clients' property. The second is the power of citizen's arrest, for, in the eyes of the law, security personnel are 'citizens.' Finally, we will have a brief look at surveillance law.

Use of Force in Defence of Property

In most states and territories, the common law power of property owners to defend their property from uninvited trespassers and not face criminal prosecution (which has been in place at least since 1604) has been reinforced by statute (Sarre, 2010a). The protection is provided by the defence of self-defence. Self-defence is generally available to persons who use force to prevent an assault on them, or their imprisonment or the imprisonment of another, to protect property from unlawful taking, damage or interference, or to prevent criminal trespass to any land or premises or to remove a person committing a criminal trespass (Sarre & Prenzler, 2009, chapter 4).

In South Australia, an amendment to the *Criminal Law Consolidation Act 1935* provides a subjective test to the law of reasonable force; the law now asks in section 15A: Did the accused have reason to believe that his or her life or property was in danger when acting in a defensive manner? If she or he did, then she or he will be able to establish a defence. If the accused can satisfy a judge or jury of his or her genuine belief, then he or she will not be found guilty of any assault or battery that may have occurred during that defence of person or property.

In the Queensland *Criminal Code Act 1899* there is a roughly equivalent section 277(1), but it persists with a more objective test. Note that, unlike the South Australian law, it extends the right to an agent (e.g., a security guard) of the property owner or occupier. It allows reasonable force to be used in self-defence provided that the person doing the defending does not do grievous bodily harm to the attacker. This legislative power also extends to those who are trying to prevent someone from thieving (s. 274).

There is a similar provision in Western Australia, both as to objectivity and extension to agents, under the *Criminal Code Act 1913*. Section 254(1) of this Act allows a property owner a fair degree of latitude in determining what amounts to reasonable force. Section 254(3) differentiates between the powers of landowners (who can use force up to grievous bodily harm) from those of their agents (who must not have intended any bodily harm).

The New South Wales Parliament, too, has legislated concerning the defence of one's property in sections 418–419 of the *Crimes Act 1900*. The prosecution has the onus of proving that the defendant was *not* acting in self-defence. Significantly, self-defence is not available in New South Wales if the death of the attacker has resulted (s. 420) but it may reduce murder to manslaughter (s. 421).

In Victoria, we find some variations on these themes. Section 462A of the *Crimes Act 1958* allows any person to use force 'not disproportionate to the objective as he believes on reasonable grounds to be necessary to prevent the commission, continuance or completion of' what is referred to in Victoria (and some other jurisdictions) as an 'indictable' (or very serious) offence, 'or to effect or assist in effecting the lawful arrest of a person committing or suspected of committing any offence'.

There is no provision in the *Crimes Act 1900* (ACT) for a defence of 'defence of property.' Under the Northern Territory *Criminal Code*, section 27, force in self-defence, defence of property and arrest is justified, however, provided it is not unnecessary force, and it is not intended and is not such as is likely to cause death or grievous harm.

Thus it is clear that, in Australia, legitimate force can be used to protect one's own property, and in self-defence, and, indeed, in effecting a lawful citizen's arrest (discussed below). But the provisions are inconsistent between jurisdictions, principally in relation to the amount of force that can be used, and rely upon vague wording such as *reasonable* force, and *not disproportionate* force.

Power of Citizen's Arrest

Private citizens (including security officers acting on instructions from their principals) have no power to detain or arrest any persons without their consent unless they are given authority to do so either by some specific legislative power or in circumstances where their actions are justifiable by virtue of the common law (Sarre, 2010b). Even then, the 'arrest' is limited to detaining the suspect until the public police arrive. That is, private citizens do not enjoy the immunities that public police officers have, and do not have a defence of reasonable suspicion or honest exercise of power if they make a mistake. But the legislation is clearer than the law of self-defence. One finds general citizen's arrest powers in the following legislation:

- Section 25 of the *Criminal Investigation Act 2006* (WA)
- Section 100 of the *Law Enforcement (Powers and Responsibilities) Act 2002* (NSW)

- Section 55(3) of the *Police Offences Act 1935* (Tas)
- Section 546 of the *Criminal Code Act 1899* (Qld)
- Section 441(2) of the *Criminal Code* (NT)
- Section 218 of the *Crimes Act 1900* (ACT)
- Section 271 of the *Criminal Law Consolidation Act 1935* (SA)
- Section 462A of the *Crimes Act 1958* (Vic).

Generally speaking, the force used in the detention cannot be dispropor-tionate to the threat. Where it is clear, on the evidence, that a private citizen, or security officer, in detaining a suspect, acted reasonably and the suspect unreasonably, then it is likely that the court will find in favour of the citizen or security officer (and against the suspect) if that suspect chooses, later, to sue the citizen for assault or false imprisonment. In other circumstances where, say, a property owner (or an agent) arrests a thief in a manner, and in circumstances, disproportionate to the likely harm to the victim, and in clear defiance of the rights of the suspect (e.g., to be taken forthwith to a police station), then the court is very likely to find in favour of the suspect (guilty or otherwise). The courts may order compensation for such suspects in appropriate circumstances.

Law of Surveillance

On a regular basis all around the country, insurance firms, and their con-tracted investigator businesses, covertly film and photograph suspected per-petrators of insurance fraud. The common law does not prohibit such filming, but the tapes may not be admissible as legal evidence if the person under surveillance can convince a court that there are public policy reasons to disallow such evidence.

Arguably, filming which intrudes upon intimate or private space (such as bathrooms, showers or change rooms) will most likely be deemed 'uncon-scionable conduct' in the absence of specific and informed permission. In that event, there may be a remedy in the torts of trespass to person, trespass to land, nuisance or defamation provided to any person adversely affected by such conduct. There may also have been a crime committed —'indecent filming' — as found in section 26D *Summary Offences Act 1953* (SA). But the elements of the particular tort must have been established by the plaintiff (Sarre & Prenzler, 2009, chapters 4–6) or the elements of the crime must have been proven beyond reasonable doubt by the prosecutor. If aggrieved plaintiffs can show that there is a clear case of unconscionable conduct by the person or authority authorizing the surveillance, and the potential damage to them is irreparable, the common law may assist. As general remedies for aggrieved persons, however, the law of tort and the criminal law are not particularly effective. It should be mentioned here that there is no general tort of invasion of privacy applicable in Australia (Sarre, 2003).

The criminal law may provide some assistance to those confronted by covert monitoring, but only in circumstances where other offences (such as stalking or criminal trespass) have been committed in the placing or monitoring of the camera. Note, however, an exception exists for licensed agents filming, albeit 'indecently', for the purposes of an investigation: section 26D (2)(b) *Summary Offences Act 1953* (SA).

In most jurisdictions in Australia different aspects of surveillance are now regulated by statute (see generally, Sarre & Prenzler, 2009, chapter 7). The Commonwealth *Surveillance Devices Act 2004* sets out the powers of national law enforcement agencies with respect to surveillance devices. In Western Australia, the *Surveillance Devices Act 1998* restricts the use of covert cameras generally. It prohibits the use of any optical surveillance device that records a 'private activity' or 'private conversation'. There is no infringement of the legislation if each 'principal party' consents to the use of the optical surveillance device, but this exception applies only where the person who uses the device is a party to the conversation.

Similar in breadth to the Western Australian legislation, the Victorian *Surveillance Devices Act 1999* prohibits, by criminal penalties, the use of an 'optical surveillance device', listening device or tracking device, such as a global positioning system (GPS) device, to communicate a private conversation or a 'private activity' where the person undertaking the surveillance is not a party to the activity. The enthusiasm for reform of this legislation (Victorian Law Reform Commission [VLRC], 2010) appears to have stalled, however. A previous government called upon the VLRC to undertake an enquiry into the laws related to surveillance in that State. The current government has shown no interest in acting upon the Commission's recommendations.

The *Surveillance Devices Act 2000* (NT), the *Listening Devices Act 1992* (ACT), Part 4 of the *Invasion of Privacy Act 1971* (Qld), the *Listening Devices Act 1991* (Tas) and the *Listening and Surveillance Devices Act 1972* (SA) all place similar restrictions on the public's ability to record conversations covertly, while the *Surveillance Devices Act 2008* (NSW) exists primarily for another purpose: it gives that State's law enforcement agencies the power to install such devices without a warrant.

In New South Wales (and only in that state) employees are specifically protected against unwarranted workplace surveillance by the *Workplace Surveillance Act 2005*. Specifically, it is now unlawful in NSW for an employer to engage in covert surveillance of an employee unless a magistrate has authorised the activity, and only for the purposes of checking on suspected *unlawful* activity by an employee. The type of conduct now illegal in New South Wales may include, for example, an employer (or an agent under the employer's direction) filming workers to prove that they are lying about their ill-health. Employers can escape liability, however, by showing that the covert surveillance was solely for the purpose of ensuring the security of the workplace or the persons working in it (Catanzariti, 2005). Note that this legislation does not cover emails, only electronic surveillance cameras. Email exchanges are viewable by employers by virtue of the contract of employment usually stipulating that any electronic transmissions made by employees can be monitored by employers.

Case Law

Most legal suits concerning private security are in instances where private security personnel are alleged to have exceeded their powers, or engaged in negligent acts or where an employee has sued an employer for failing to provide adequate protection for workers (see generally Sarre & Prenzler, 2009, ¶8.150, ¶8.250). It is instructive to examine briefly a few of these cases.

Exceeding Powers: Assault and False Imprisonment

In the two cases that follow, the courts found the employers of security officers responsible for the activities of their employees, who had engaged in inappropriate behaviour, by virtue of what is referred to in law as 'vicarious liability' (Sarre & Prenzler, 2009, ¶5.80); that is, the selection, training and supervision of these 'agents' was either inappropriate or insufficient.

Trenevski v. The Irish Bar & Restaurant Co Pty Ltd [2006] QDC 007

Robert Trenevski was repeatedly hit by security guards after celebrating his birthday. The Irish Bar, who had employed the guards, argued that their employees had embarked upon a 'frolic of their own' outside of their contracted employment duties. Judge Forde, however, found that the assault occurred while the controllers were attempting to recover stolen property (a hat that had been taken from the manager's head and dropped by the victim when pursued) and thus their employer was liable for their actions. Mr Trenevski was awarded $72,964, which was not overturned on appeal.

Myer Stores Ltd v. Soo [1991] 2 VR 597

A security officer in a department store saw a Mr Soo, who was suspected of having committed a theft earlier (by virtue of a recording on CCTV) re-entering the store. The officer called two police officers and together they confronted Mr Soo who was, in fact, an innocent man. The three of them alleged that he matched the description of the man they needed to speak to, and asked him to come with them to an office 'to sort the matter out'. Mr Soo refused, asking to be questioned there and then. The officers escorted him to the office nonetheless and interviewed him for an hour. Later they searched his home, finding nothing. They even asked him to go to a police station, which he did. He was finally exonerated. Myer Stores, as the employer of the security officers, was found liable to Mr Soo for their actions in the tort of false imprisonment. Mr Soo was awarded $10,000 in damages.

Negligent Acts by Security Officers

Crown Ltd v. Hudson [2002] VSCA 28

A patron of Crown Casino, one Mr Hudson, was attacked while at the casino. He sued the casino operators alleging negligence, arguing that their security had been lax. About 71 seconds had transpired between him being set upon by his assailant and security officers arriving on the scene. The question was whether the cause of the injury was the poor response time, and whether this delay was, in fact, negligent. Mr Hudson succeeded. He was awarded $50,000. The casino operators lost their appeal.

An Employer's Failure to Provide Adequate Training or Protective Security for Workers

This first case shows that an employer can be liable to its security guard employees for its poor training.

Anastasiou v. Chubb Security (Australia) Pty Ltd [2008] VSC 211

In April 2002, two security guards, one of whom was a Mr Anastasiou, were instructed to evict an intoxicated customer who was causing a disturbance. The guards led him down a very narrow corridor. The customer was abusive and struggling. This caused Mr Anastasiou to fall, seriously injuring his back. He sued his employer for failing to provide a safe system of work and in negligence. There should have been a clear understanding, said the plaintiff's lawyers, between the employer and the pub as to the demarcation of the roles of the personnel of each organisation. The Victorian Supreme Court agreed, finding that it should not have been the role of security guards to be the de facto 'bouncers' of licensed premises, since they had not been trained for that role. The damages were assessed at $720,790.

However, there have been a number of recent cases where similar arguments, on their facts, failed to succeed.

Lusk v. Sapwell [2011] QCA 59

A woman, while employed as an optical technician, was sexually molested by an elderly male customer. She sued her employer, alleging that she suffered psychiatric impairment as a result of the incident and that her resulting loss and damage were caused by their negligence and their breach of contract with her in not providing adequate security at the premises. The Supreme Court of Queensland, on appeal, disagreed, finding that the owners of the store were entitled to regard the magnitude of the risk of assault and the probability of its eventuating as singularly slight, and thus found for them.

Bainbridge v. James and Others [2013] VSCA 12

Mr Bainbridge, employed as Father Christmas for the festive season, was assaulted by a teenager en route to the change room. On this day, he did not have his escort with him. He claimed damages for an injury to his knee. The court found that the risk that he would be assaulted while performing his role, or while moving between his 'throne' and the rooms in which he changed clothes, was far-fetched and fanciful, and not foreseeable.

Cases such as these are useful for determining some legal parameters regarding the law of private security, but they rely upon parties launching litigation and thus allow only piecemeal and incomplete statements of legal principle to emerge.

Discussion

When exceptional authority is bestowed upon those who administer and enforce the law, it requires legislative action through parliamentary debate. For that reason, the rules regulating public policing are set out prospectively to authorise the taking of particular action, and also retrospectively to show interested others, such as the courts, parliaments and other accountability forums, that the action was justified in the circumstances. The public police have considerable powers to arrest, search and interrogate. Liberty is at stake if these powers are abused; hence they have been debated in parliaments and tested in courts for decades.

Private security personnel and private operatives are now undertaking many of the same roles, but the laws that apply to empower, restrict and protect them are not in the same league. Private security legal issues rarely come before the courts and there is little legislation that applies directly to nonpolice security personnel.

Where should we proceed from here? There is no broadly based legislation giving specific powers to all licensed agents. Parliaments have avoided such an approach other than to set up licensing regimes. They have not specifically set out immunities, preferring to infer that they apply only if the powers under legislation have been exercised appropriately. One can sympathise. It is a difficult task to specify private police powers across the board, given the many forms and varieties of private operatives and the multitude of activities in which they may be engaged at any one time or over a period of time. It would be well nigh impossible to write legislation capable of matching and accommodating all of the circumstances in which private personnel could be called upon to assist and to specify what they can or should do in certain circumstances, what they are required to *avoid* doing, and when they can safely rely upon immunity from legal suit. In addition, many private security firms are, or are becoming, national and transnational corporations, and thus any general attempt to set legislated rules which transcend national and international boundaries would be difficult to do, let alone to implement and enforce.

This would explain why the most common option is to do nothing. There are common law cases and some pieces of legislation that apply to issues such as citizen's arrest, use of force, trespass to land, defence of property and defence of another's property, search and seizure and covert surveillance which apply to all people including security personnel.

On the one hand, leaving these areas legally ambiguous encourages fewer law suits, forcing those aggrieved to negotiate more and litigate less. On the other hand, the levels of uncertainty and anomaly in this legal field are unsettling to many potential litigants, and may give rise to uncertainty especially when public and private operatives are working towards the same ends in the same locales simultaneously.

There is one idea that could be implemented immediately without too much difficulty. The idea of a person being protected from legal suit when exercising good faith is not novel. For example, section 74(2) of the *Civil Liability Act 1936* (SA) states that '[a] good samaritan incurs no personal civil liability for an act or omission done or made in good faith and without recklessness in assisting a person in apparent need of emergency assistance'. There is a similar provision is found in section 32 of the *Emergency Management Act 2004* (SA):

> (1) No civil or criminal liability will attach to the State Co-ordinator, an authorised officer or other person for an act or omission in good faith—
> (a) in the exercise or discharge, or purported exercise or discharge, of a power or function under this Act; or
> (b) in the carrying out of any direction or requirement given or imposed in accordance with this Act in relation to an emergency.
> (2) A liability that would, but for subsection (1), lie against a person lies instead against the Crown.

There is also legislation protecting people who offer apologies from being sued successfully on the basis of that courtesy (Sarre & Prenzler, 2009, ¶8.121). It would thus not be difficult at all to add, by legislation, a 'reasonable suspicion' and 'good faith immunity' for all people who engage in 'higher level' licensed security functions, thus protecting them, in appropriate situations, from the threat of legal suit.

Another idea that has captured some attention in Australia is the concept of a '2nd tier' security officer, one that evokes the spirit of the community support officer (CSO) concept that has become popular in recent times in the United Kingdom (Johnston, 2006, 2007). By way of example, in March 2007, the Labor government of Mike Rann introduced the *Protective Security Act 2007* (SA). Protective security officers (PSO) are not linked to any specific body of police, nor are they engaged just for a specific event. PSOs are appointed and managed by the South Australian Police Commissioner and are empowered to provide a first response to terrorist incidents and to protect buildings, vehicles, officials and designated places. They are resourced with a range of tactical options that can include the use of firearms, batons and capsicum spray. PSOs are not expected, nor are they required, to become involved in complex police activities or investigations. Nor do they have powers of a constable. They simply have the authority to give reasonable directions, refuse entry, or to direct a person to leave certain locations. They may also require persons to state their reason for being at a certain location, may require persons to state their name and address and to provide identification when requested. They are able to conduct searches on persons, vehicles or property (under certain circumstances), seize certain items and evidence, and detain a person for a 'protective security offence'. All of these powers and immunities are set out in the legislation. If it is possible for this to be done with respect of a certain cohort of security personnel, it should not be too difficult, one would have thought, to do the same in relation to other cohorts too.

Those who are tempted to think pessimistically about law reform in this field would do well to remember that it took over 50 years to persuade the English parliament to establish the 'new' police in the 19th century. Patience and perseverance may yet eventually be rewarded (Stenning, 2009, pp. 31–32).

Conclusion

As policing moves more and more into non-government hands, the traditional legal powers that apply to 'policing' are becoming quickly out-dated. Yet the powers and immunities of private security personnel are often unclear and inconsistent, if not anomalous, and are sometimes dependent upon fine legal distinctions. They differ markedly from those of the public police even though private personnel are often carrying out many of the same tasks. What should be done to remedy this situation is not entirely clear. Whatever path is chosen, the exercise in making the choices and debating the required legislation would, arguably, lift the profile of private operators and their associations, bolster training standards and accountabilities, improve public confidence, and enhance policing effectiveness and cooperation generally.

References

Button, M. (2007). Assessing the regulation of private security across Europe. *European Journal of Criminology, 4(1)*, 109–128.

Catanzariti, J. (2005, May 30). Big brother evicted — in the workplace. *CCH Daily Email Alert*, CCH Australia.

Johnston, L. (2006). Diversifying police recruitment? The deployment of police community support officers in London. *The Howard Journal of Criminal Justice 45(4)*, 388–402.

Johnston, L. (2007). 'Keeping the family together': Police community support officers and the 'police extended family' in London. *Policing and Society, 17(2)*, 119–140.

McCahill, M., & Norris, C. (1999). Watching the Workers: crime, CCTV and the workplace. In P. Davies, P. Francis & V. Jupp (Eds.), *Invisible crimes, their victims and their regulation*. London, England: Macmillan.

Ontario, & Anand R. (1987). *Task force on the law concerning trespass to publicly-used property as it affects youth and minorities*. Toronto, Canada: Ontario Ministry of the Attorney-General.

Prenzler, T., Earle, K., & Sarre, R. (2009). Private security in Australia: Trends and key characteristics. *Trends and Issues in Crime and Criminal Justice, 374*, 1–6. Canberra, Australia: Australian Institute of Criminology.

Sarre, R. (2003). Journalists, invasion of privacy and the High Court decision in *Lenah Game Meats*. *Australian Journalism Review, 25(1)*, 115–128.

Sarre, R. (2010a). Private policing: Some legal musings. *Journal of the Australasian Law Teachers Association, 3 (1/2)*, 45–54.

Sarre, R. (2010b). The law in Australia on citizen's arrest. *Australasian Policing: A Journal of Professional Practice and Research, 1(2)*, 9–10.

Sarre, R., & Prenzler, T. (2009). *The law of private security in Australia* (2nd ed.), Sydney, Australia: Thomson LBC.

Sarre, R., & Prenzler, T. (2014, in press). Private security trends and directions for reform. In A. Hucklesby & S. Lister (Eds.), *Private sector involvement in criminal justice*. Houndmills Basingstoke, England: Palgrave Macmillan.

Sarre, R., Brooks, D., Smith, C., & Draper, R. (2014). Current and emerging technologies employed to abate crime and to promote security. In B. Arrigo & H. Bersot (Eds.), *The Routledge handbook of international crime and justice studies*. London, England: Routledge.

Stenning, P. (2009). Governance and accountability in a plural policing environment — The story so far. *Policing: A Journal of Policy and Practice. 3*, 22–33.

Victorian Law Reform Commission. (2010). *Surveillance in public places: Final report.* Retrieved from http://www.lawreform.vic.gov.au/projects/surveillance-public-places/surveillance-public-places-final-report.

Chapter 11

Conduct Issues in Security Work

Tim Prenzler

As the security industry grows, more and more people become subject to the activities of security personnel and the impacts of security technology. As we have seen in previous chapters, industry growth has generated large reductions in criminal victimisation in many cases. There is, however, a dark side to security. Some references have already been made to adverse effects on privacy, aesthetics, convenience and inequality. This chapter examines the problem of illegal and unethical conduct and problems of incompetence. The chapter is structured in two parts. The first outlines 11 categories of misconduct, developed from analyses of scandals, inquiries and court cases. The second part illustrates some of these problems in greater depth using cases on the record in Australia. Overall, the chapter highlights the need for effective regulation of the industry: the subject of the final chapter of the book.

Background

The introduction of licence-based security industry regulation followed behind the spectacular growth of the industry in many countries, dating primarily from the 1960s and 1970s (see chapter 12). In some cases, forms of limited occupational registration preceded proper licensing. In the main, however, security firms and practitioners were free to conduct business and provide security services within a general framework of commercial, civil and criminal law.

Problems of misconduct in this early period have not been well documented. However, it appears that in many jurisdictions a set of overlapping concerns emerged about malpractice and the quality of security services. Private investigators had always been notorious for accessing confidential information and intruding on people's privacy, motivated in part by the legal requirement for applicants to show fault to obtain a divorce (King & Prenzler, 2003). As intruder alarms became more popular, false alarms activations and poor response procedures became a major headache for many property owners and police (Sampson, 2001). One of the earliest studies of the security industry was conducted by the RAND Corporation in the US in the very early 1970s. Based on case studies, litigation against security providers and complaints, the researchers identified the following problematic areas (Kakalik & Wildhorn, 1971b, pp. 57–61):

- Abuse of authority
- Dishonesty and poor business practices
- Access to confidential police records and gathering information from third parties
- Non-reporting of crime and the 'private' system of justice
- High false-alarm rates
- Personnel quality, training and supervision.

The RAND team also summarised complaints made to 17 regulatory agencies in one year in the following format (Kakalik & Wildhorn, 1971b, p. 54):

- Violation of regulation (413)
- Improper uniform or identification (369)
- Shootings (55)
- Impersonating a police officer (34)
- Theft (29)
- Failure to serve as agreed (29)
- Misrepresentation of services or fees (28)
- Violation of gun regulation (22)
- Illegal access to police records (18)
- Assault or use of excessive force (13)
- Negligence (13)
- Operating an unlicensed business (13)
- Drunkenness (12)
- Conviction of a crime (9)
- Offensive language (8)
- Killings (8).

There were also cases of 'false arrest, improper detention, invasion of privacy, improper search, improper interrogation, bugging, wiretapping, and extortion' (Kakalik & Wildhorn, 1971b, p. 54).

More generally, there was a growing recognition of the power of security providers over ordinary people (Shearing & Stenning, 1981). As the previous chapter showed, as agents of property owners, including on 'mass private property', security providers are able to deny entry and expel persons from places providing basic services — such as retail shopping centres. Security providers can also set conditions for entry — such as property searches and answering questions — and engage in surveillance. Security personnel can also engage in surveillance in public areas, and exercise citizen powers to arrest people and use force. Security providers are also able to deploy weapons — including dogs, batons and firearms. This array of powers and weapons can easily lead to abuses (Kakalik & Wildhorn, 1971a).

Categorising Misconduct

The two sets of dot point lists above show different ways of categorising misconduct in the industry. Another system was developed by Prenzler and Sarre (2008a, p. 1) in terms of a security industry 'risk profile'. The researchers developed their schema by integrating the findings of various secondary sources — mainly government reviews and academic research — and primary sources — including judicial inquiries, court cases, media reports and practitioner interviews. In some cases, misconduct has been longstanding and acute. Violence in entertainment and nightclub precincts is an obvious example. In some locations, private security has operated fairly openly like organised crime gangs, engaging in systematic graft and extortion (Button & George, 2006). This has been a particular problem in Russia and eastern European countries in transition to democracy and market economies, where the rule of law has lagged behind economic development. More generally, it is often very difficult to see how far problems extend beyond the immediate findings of a particular inquiry or the outcome of a specific case. There is a view, nonetheless, that documented cases often represent the 'tip of the iceberg', similar to the 'dark figure' of unreported crime. This suggests that it is appropriate to presume a general industry risk profile that needs to be addressed through government auditing and regulation.

The elements of the risk profile are not unique to security. Some types of malpractice are common to business, such as fraud and the black economy, and derive from the profit motive and temptations to cheat and avoid tax. In other cases, misconduct is similar to that observed in policing, including assaults and false testimony. These behaviours derive in part from frustrations with the end-means disjunction and legal limits on the exercise of authority and gathering evidence; i.e., law enforcement and crime prevention goals conflict with due process standards and human rights. These general and specific vulnerabilities are combined in the diverse nature of security work.

The following brief summaries of misconduct types were identified by Prenzler and Sarre (2008a).

1. Fraud

Clients of security firms are vulnerable to fraud because many of the services they contract in are provided outside their capacity for oversight. For example, a construction company might hire a firm to conduct physical inspections of a site during the night when the owner is asleep. The firm can easily falsify inspection records with the owner having no recourse if a theft occurs outside the alleged inspection times. This is an example of the classic problem of 'who will guard the guards?' or 'policing trust' (Shapiro, 1987).

2. Incompetence and Poor Standards

Prior to the introduction of security industry regulation, it was usually possible for security firms to set up business, and for individuals to work in the industry, with few protections for clients and the general public. The words used in a New South Wales Police Service (1995) inquiry state individuals and companies are 'able to "walk" into the security industry ... with little or no experience or expertise, no business acumen, no qualifications, no fidelity bond and no integrity' (p. 10). Even with regulation, training standards have often been limited to one day for operatives, with no qualifications required for security firm owners or in-house security managers (see chapter 12). For much of its existence, the industry also lacked adequate mandated technical standards to address the many deficiencies in the quality of alarms and CCTV. Basic security in areas such as transporting cash and valuables was also commonly deficient and often dangerous.

3. Under-Award Payments and Exploitation of Security Staff

Price competition and profit motive also drove a black economy in labour, involving under-award 'cash-in-hand' payments to security staff. This 'under-cutting' in tendering can involve fraud, where quotations provided to clients misrepresent labour costs; or it can involve security firms and clients colluding on cut-price contracts. Employees may see a benefit in tax-free payments, but they tend to lose in terms of loss of holiday pay, sick pay, penalty rates (e.g., night, weekend rates) and superannuation.

4. Corrupt Practices

Security firms can offer bribes to police and other agencies for preferential referrals for business, bypassing open and fair competition. Graft can also occur in tendering, purchasing of security equipment, and training.

5. Information Corruption

This type of corruption has primarily occurred in the enquiry sector, amongst private investigators, debt collectors and process servers. Bribe-payers will pay for confidential information about people's criminal records, location, contact details and assets.

6. Violence and Associated Malpractice

Assaults have constituted the most high profile and widespread problem in the industry, concentrated amongst security staff at hotels, nightclubs and other entertainment venues. Failure to protect patrons is part of the mix. Poor training and management also contribute to the victimisation of security staff.

7. False Arrest and Detention

Security officers are vulnerable to exceeding their powers and arresting persons — for shoplifting for example — without sufficient evidence. They can also misrepresent their powers to hold people in detention.

8. Trespass and Invasions of Privacy

Private investigators, process servers and debt recovery agents can trespass onto private property while seeking information, to serve court orders or recover property. Security officers can also engage in trespass by searching personal items without authorisation. Other breaches of privacy can include illegally accessing mail or other forms of communication, and accessing files or other data. Operators of CCTV systems can engage in voyeuristic abuses of privacy.

9. Discrimination and Harassment

Security officers are vulnerable to targeting young people and minority groups in ways that are discriminatory or racist, through intimidation and selective exclusion and eviction. Debt collectors have been known to exceed their powers by making threats and engaging in harassing tactics. Investigators can engage in surveillance, including tailing and filming people, which becomes harassment. Enquiry agents may also engage in intrusive questioning and threats.

10. Insider Crime

Security providers, including locksmiths and other technicians, have skills that can be used to commit crime rather than prevent crime — including burglary, theft and fraud. Security employees or contractors also have privileged knowledge about the vulnerabilities of their clients, including the location of assets, and the times of deliveries of valuables.

11. Misuse of Weapons

Security officers can carry an array of weapons including firearms, pepper spray, batons, handcuffs and dogs. These can be mishandled deliberately or negligently to inflict harm, including serious injuries and fatalities.

Case Studies

The following case studies illustrate many of the misconduct risks outlined above. The cases are taken from inquiry reports and media exposés in

Australia from the 1980s to the 2000s. A number of the cases stimulated major reforms in regulation of the industry, but the latter cases show regulatory strategies were not sufficiently sophisticated to prevent systematic abuses from developing. The cases were collected by Prenzler (1998, 2004), Prenzler and Sarre (2008b) and Prenzler and Milroy (2012).

Information Leads to Murder

A study of homicide in Victoria in the mid-1980s identified a case in which a man hired a private investigator to find his estranged partner who was hiding in fear of her life. The investigator located the woman and passed on the information to the client. The man went to the woman's new home and murdered her with several gunshots to the head. He then left the country and was never brought to trial.

Violence at Licensed Premises

In Victoria, a 1990 report by the Victorian Community Council Against Violence documented major problems with fights, brawls, assaults and harassment at licensed premises. The problem included approximately 800 serious assaults each year. Video evidence showed crowd controllers repeatedly bashing patrons into semiconsciousness and throwing them onto concrete. A survey of nightclub patrons found the large majority had witnessed violence. Thirty per cent claimed to have been victims of attacks, and crowd controllers were also victims of numerous attacks. Hotel and nightclub managers were blamed for encouraging or permitting aggressive tactics by security staff.

Selling Information

In 1992, the New South Wales Independent Commission Against Corruption found that private enquiry agents were engaged in a large-scale trade in confidential information, with an estimated turnover of $1 million over several years. More than 250 people were involved including police; officials from numerous government departments, including social security, tax, vehicle registration, Telecom, Australia Post and Medicare; and banks, insurance companies and other financial institutions. The information included passport and bank account details, correspondence and unlisted phone numbers. Some recipients were known criminals. The President of the Association of Investigators was involved, as were members and past and present office bearers of the Institute of Mercantile Agents.

The Neva Alone Scandal

In the mid-1990s in Queensland and New South Wales, the Trade Practices Commission investigated a 24-hour intruder and emergency alarm pendant system operated by Metropolitan Security Services. 'Neva Alone' — designed for elderly and infirm persons — often failed to activate properly. It was also found that on occasions the control room was left unmonitored.

Patrol Scandals

Also in the mid-1990s in Newcastle, Chubb employees revealed data readouts on patrol checks of clients' premises were falsified. The practice had allegedly been occurring for at least 10 years. In Brisbane, journalists revealed that 10 security firms were falsifying records of night-time security checks — in some cases patrol officers left business cards under premise doors all at once instead of at different times. In Perth, the Australian Competition and Consumer Commission found that Wormald consistently failed to provide mobile patrol checks at the levels agreed with clients. In 1996, Chubb (which took over Wormald) was obliged to accept court enforceable undertakings to provide sufficient staff and resources to fulfil contracts.

The 'Wedderburn Report'

The 'Wedderburn Report' by the New South Wales Police Service (1995) identified exploitative practices in under-award cash payments to security staff. Labour costs were understated in tenders, and a number of employers were found to have abused the federal government's Job Start subsidy by terminating employees once the subsidy expired. In a section titled 'Training the Criminal', the report described how persons with criminal records were trained and licensed in alarm installation, including techniques for bypassing security devices. The report included a case in which a guard licence was issued to a convicted armed robber on weekend detention.

Firearms Risks

The Wedderburn Report also found that the one day of mandated firearms training for armed security officers was highly inadequate. This was confirmed by a 1997 New South Wales Industrial Relations Commission report into safety in the cash-in-transit industry. The inquiry found that shooting incidents during cash-in-transit robberies were related to inadequate screening and training of guards and poor security procedures.

A Shootout in the Suburbs

In 1995, a woman was shot in the spine during a 'wild west'-style shootout between robbers and armoured car security guards in a busy street in the Brisbane suburb of Moorooka. A man aged 71 received an arm wound, a tourist was wounded in the leg, and a guard received a thumb wound. The woman shot in the spine was permanently paralysed. The bullet could not be removed, making it impossible to determine who fired the shot.

False Alarms

In 1997, a review of intruder alarms in Western Australia found that police were attending approximately 900 calls a week resulting from false activations. The causes included faulty equipment, improper installation, lack of maintenance and user error.

Corruption in Emergency Security Work

In 1998, the Victorian Ombudsman released the final report of Operation BART, which exposed a system of corrupt police preferences in emergency notifications to security firms. Firms paid police a kickback for bypassing the allocation system for repair work following burglaries and vandalism. The scam involved more than 550 police officers.

Australia's Largest Armed Robbery

In 1999, thieves escaped with $2.2 million in the robbery of a Brinks cash-in-transit vehicle in Brisbane. Suspicion centred on the driver of the armoured van, who was locked inside but opened the door and drove the van to a location where it was unloaded. The driver, who later vanished, was employed despite suspicions over his involvement in two thefts.

Theft of Firearms

In 2003/2004, a scandal erupted in New South Wales over the theft of firearms from security officers and security firm premises. Fifty-six firearms were stolen in a 3-month period. The incidents included the theft of 31 Glock pistols from a company called 'Obliging Security'. In one incident, security officers were robbed of cash and three semi-automatic pistols while servicing an automatic teller machine.

Outlaw Motorcycle Gangs in Nightclub Security

Also in 2003/2004, Adelaide became the focus of concerns over bikie gangs controlling nightclub security, engaging in money laundering, illicit drug sales, drive-by shootings and gang brawls. Police alleged that 'up to 80% of licensed premises in Adelaide's central business district (CBD) that employ security firms were using companies with links to outlaw motorcycle gangs' (Kelton, 2003, p. 1).

Prisoners Escape From Court Security

In Perth, in 2004, seven prisoners classified as dangerous escaped from custody at the Supreme Court while under the control of a private security firm. The men overpowered three unarmed guards, stole a key that allowed them to escape the building, and carjacked two vehicles. A massive police manhunt and high-speed pursuit followed, necessitating the closure of a freeway.

Chubb and Fraud

In 2004, Chubb was convicted in the Australian Federal Court of 26 charges it had misrepresented its ability to fulfil mobile patrol contracts in Sydney, the NSW central coast, Canberra and Tasmania. Chubb faced losing its licence but, after pleading guilty, was fined $1.5 million.

The Death of Cricketer David Hookes

In January 2004, high-profile cricketer David Hookes died after a physical altercation involving his friends and several security officers at a Melbourne hotel. An officer was charged with manslaughter, and it was revealed that at the time of the incident he was facing assault charges. A jury found the officer had acted in self-defence, but the sequence of evidence indicated security staff engaged in actions that were inappropriate and provocative.

Violence at Licensed Premises

The year 2004 saw numerous other reports of violence involving security officers. In Victoria, newspapers reported that over 50 people were suing security providers for assault, including cases involving brain damage and broken bones. *The Advertiser* in Adelaide reported that police had charged 87 crowd controllers with assault-related offences over the preceding two years. Inadequate training and supervision contributed to patterns of abuse concentrated amongst specific security officers and venues. A report by the South Australian Office of Consumer and Business Affairs referred to surveillance tapes held by police, 'showing extreme acts of violence by crowd controllers including vicious attacks on women and running street bashings. Assault data show that high proportions of the alleged assaults involve blows and kicks to the head region often requiring surgery' (2004, p. 5).

Shooting Death of an Armed Robber

The fatal shooting of an armed robber by a security officer in Sydney in 2004 revealed major weaknesses in the 'soft skin' cash-in-transit industry. This service operated outside the armoured transport sector to move valuables in unmarked vehicles. Many of the plainclothes officers were subcontractors who worked alone and carried large amounts of cash above legal limits with highly inadequate protection.

Airport Security Failures

A 2005 review of airport security by Sir John Wheeler identified substantial inadequacies in management and procedures. Regional and capital city airports were highly exposed to terrorist attacks, drug trafficking, theft, and infiltration by organised crime. System failures included inadequate screening and supervision of personnel; inadequate cargo screening, especially for explosives; and lack of entry–exit control at cargo and airside areas. Policing and security interactions were described as dysfunctional and beset by rivalries and lack of information sharing.

Sydney Transit Security

A 2005 inquiry by the New South Wales Ombudsman into the Sydney Transit Police found security officers exceeded their powers in the use of force and arrests. The RailCorp employees attracted large numbers of complaints, which were not adequately investigated. Serious breaches of security involving the theft of keys were also identified.

Criminal Infiltration of the Security Industry

In 2007, the Australian Crime Commission initiated a two-year investigation into criminal infiltration of the private security industry. The investigation was unprecedented in the use of surveillance, intelligence, solicitations for information, compulsory examinations, and data-matching. The commission found that most companies were legitimate and provided a quality service, but it also identified cases from across the country of organised crime groups obtaining control of security firms. Criminal activity included 'fraud, property theft, illicit commodity distribution (such as drugs), money laundering, trespass, assault, misuse of firearms [and] extortion' (Australian Crime Commission, 2011, p 4). In addition, the commission found there was a large black economy involving under-award cash payments to security officers, tax evasion, welfare fraud (by security officers claiming benefits while working) and breaches of visa conditions.

Operation Columba and Corruption in Security Guard Training

Operation Columba was carried out by the New South Wales Independent Commission Against Corruption in 2008. The investigation found that three registered training academies issued up to 9,000 false certificates to trainees with little or no instruction or assessment over a period of several years. The commission also identified a cash trade in first aid certificates and certificates for responsible service of alcohol.

The Fair Work Ombudsman's Special Audit of Security Employment Practices

In 2009, the Federal Fair Work Ombudsman initiated a special audit of employment practices in the security industry. The audit of 256 employers found that 49% were noncompliant with the *Fair Work Act 2009* (Cwlth). The main area of illegal conduct involved paying discounted 'flat rates' for weekends, shift work and overtime.

Miscellaneous

Prenzler and Sarre (2008b) also documented a number of lesser security breaches and scandals in Australia, indicative of an ongoing problem of inadequate professional development or oversight of the industry. These included the drug-related death of a woman on a cruise ship in 2002, revelations of poor security management practices at Parliament House, Canberra, in 2005 and the Australian Mint in 2006, mistreatment of a disabled person by security officers at a shopping centre in 2006, and repeated reports of inadequate security screening at mail centres and seaports.

Conclusion

This chapter has provided an account of the variety of malpractice that can occur in security. Although the extent and severity of misconduct appears to be highly variable, it also appears to be the case that the industry shares a common risk profile for illegal and unethical conduct. Some of the cases reported here involved long-standing abuses, including corruption and serious problems of assaults. These problems, combined with the growth of the industry, have spurred numerous innovations in industry regulation — the subject of the following chapter. Unfortunately, many of the cases in the present chapter occurred under standard licensing schemes, indicating that much stronger controls on the industry are needed in particular locations or in relation to specific types of misconduct risks.

References

Australian Crime Commission. (2011). Private security industry criminal infiltration. *Crime Profile Series*, July, 1–4. Canberra, Australia: Author.

Button, M., & George, B. (2006). Regulation of private security: Models for analysis. In M. Gill (Ed.), *Handbook of security*, pp. 563–585. Houndmills Basingstock, England: Palgrave Macmillan.

Kakalik, S.J., & Wildhorn, S. (1971a). *Current regulation of private police: Agency experience and views*. Santa Monica, CA: RAND.

Kakalik, S.J., & Wildhorn, S. (1971b). *Private police in the United States: Findings and recommendations*. Santa Monica, CA: RAND.

Kelton, G. (2003, October 18). Bikie gangs linked to 60 liquor venues. *The Advertiser*, p. 9.

King, M., & Prenzler, T. (2003). Private inquiry agents: Ethical challenges and accountability. *Security Journal, 16*(3), pp 7–17.

New South Wales Police Service. (1995). *Security industry review*. Sydney, Australia: Author.

Office of Consumer and Business Affairs. (2004). *Statutes Amendment (Liquor, Gambling and Security Industries) Bill 2004.* Adelaide, Australia: Government of South Australia.

Prenzler, T. (1998). La sécurité privée et le problème de la confiance: L'expérience Australienne. *Revue Criminologie, 31*(2), 87–109.

Prenzler, T. (2004). The privatisation of policing. In R. Sarre & J. Tomaino (Eds.), *Key issues in criminal justice*, pp. 267–296. Adelaide, Australia: Australian Humanities Press.

Prenzler, T., & Milroy, A. (2012) Recent inquiries into the private security industry in Australia: Implications for regulation. *Security Journal, 25*(4), 342–355.

Prenzler, T., & Sarre, R. (2008a). Developing a risk profile and model regulatory system for the security industry. *Security Journal, 21*(4), 264–277.

Prenzler, T., & Sarre, R. (2008b). Protective security in Australia: Scandal, media images and reform. *Journal of Policing, Intelligence and Counter-Terrorism, 3*(2), 23–37.

Sampson, R. (2001). *False burglar alarms.* Washington, DC: COPS (Community Oriented Policing Services), US Department of Justice.

Shapiro, S. (1987). Policing trust. In C. Shearing & P. Stenning (Eds.), *Private Policing*, pp. 194–220. Newbury Park, CA: Sage.

Shearing, C., & Stenning, P. (1981). Modern private security: Its growth and implications. In M. Tonry & N. Morris (Eds.), *Crime and justice: An annual review of research*, pp. 193–245. Chicago, IL: University of Chicago Press.

Chapter 12

Smart Regulation for the Security Industry

Tim Prenzler and Rick Sarre

This chapter addresses the issue of the best way to regulate security in terms of preventing misconduct and ensuring competency. In doing this, the chapter takes into account the interests — sometimes divergent, sometimes convergent — of different groups with a stake in the operations of the industry: the owners of security firms, security managers, security staff, security clients, and the general public. The chapter reviews a number of general accountability mechanisms that apply to the industry, including criminal and civil law, and commercial and other laws, and self-regulation. The limits of these mechanisms are outlined. They underscore the need for an industry-specific government licensing system. A model system is then advocated, based on the concept of 'smart regulation' — which entails using research evidence to find the most effective and efficient combination of regulatory mechanisms.

Regulatory Theory and the Security Industry

The term 'regulate', in the broad sense, refers to making something regular, reducing extremes, managing or controlling something, or ensuring reliability (thefreedictionary.com, n.d.). A good example is the use of prescribed minimum and maximum sentences to regulate judicial discretion in the courts. More specifically, 'industry regulation' refers to the control of an industry or business, usually by government, to protect customers, employees or the general public from faulty service, fraud, exploitation, and various other harms including pollution, disease, injuries and fatalities (Prenzler & Sarre, 2014).

Industry regulation typically includes two primary elements: (1) laws and associated rules, procedures or codes that define standards, and (2) regulatory agencies responsible for administering the rules. Compliance methods used by regulators are similar to those used in crime prevention, and normally include deterrence, incapacitation, facilitation of compliance and access control. Agencies deploy a range of specific strategies to obtain compliance, including the following (Ransley & Prenzler, 2012, p. 134ff):

- communication and education
- licensing and testing

- reporting requirements and auditing
- inspections and notices
- complaint investigation and resolution
- suspensions and orders
- prosecutions and litigation
- suspensions and bans
- fines and imprisonment
- agreements
- public disclosures and shaming.

A research literature has developed around issues of regulation. Much of the early work was concerned with documenting and explaining 'regulatory failure'. An example is the 1986 book, *Of Manners Gentle: The Enforcement Strategies of Australian Business Regulatory Agencies*, by Peter Grabosky and John Braithwaite. By the 1980s, many wealthy and established democracies, such as Australia, had built and maintained high standards for business and strong regulatory agencies. At the same time, these countries faced recurring problems of regulatory failure — evidenced in preventable injuries and deaths; pollution and environmental destruction; white collar crime and corporate fraud; and faulty, sometimes deadly, consumer products and medications. Grabosky and Braithwaite's (1986) research — using interviews and enforcement data — found that most Australian regulatory agencies were fairly well resourced, with considerable legal powers at their disposal. The problem of under-enforcement — or under-regulation — lay primarily with an organisational culture of deference (Grabosky & Braithwaite, 1986, pp. 1–2):

> Australian business regulatory agencies are of manners gentle. Not only is this reflected in the attitudes of the regulators, it also characterizes their polices and regulatory outcomes such as prosecutions, licence suspensions, plant shutdowns, injunctions, or the informal use of adverse publicity. Litigation or any kind of adversarial encounter with industry is commonly under-taken only as a last resort …

> In some ways, the subtitle of this book is a misrepresentation because so many Australian regulatory agencies are basically lacking in strategy. Rather, their conduct tends to take the form of:

> 1. Platitudinous appeals to industry to act responsibly;
> 2. Token enforcement targeted in a manner which bears no necessary relationship to failures to heed those platitudinous appeals;
> 3. Keeping the lid on problems which could blow up into scandals; and
> 4. Passing the buck to another agency within the labyrinth of Australian federalism when the lid cannot be kept on a scandal.

Subsequent to this report, a number of studies have focused more on the ingredients for effective regulation, developing and making use of concepts such as 'responsive regulation' (Ayres & Braithwaite, 1992), and 'regulatory craftsmanship' (Sparrow, 2000). These studies allege that zealous and committed regulators will be most effective when they:

1. have access to a broad set of strategies
2. apply a mix of strategies
3. are able to increase pressure on recalcitrant industries through an 'enforcement pyramid' (see Figure 12.1).

Responsive regulation includes the idea of different responses to different conditions. In other words, different industries require different forms of regulation, and more extreme problems require greater intervention. It also includes the idea of consultation with responsible stakeholders, including business leaders, managers, employees and unions. Insider expertise and experience should be a valued part of the regulatory process. A hierarchy like this allows for a graduated approach to compliance management. Regulators need to avoid underregulation, but also 'overregulation': when too many requirements and interventions create unnecessary or unfair burdens, adversely affecting the supply of needed goods and services. Regulators should first seek to facilitate compliance through education and communication. If these steps fail, they need to move to intermediate strategies, such

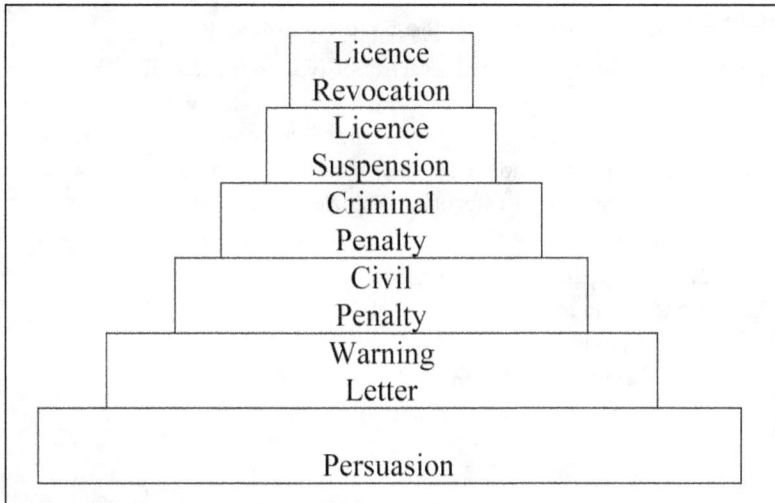

Figure 12.1
An enforcement pyramid.
Source: adapted from Ayres & Braithwaite (1992, p. 35)

as warnings and fines. If these are ineffective, they need to adopt top range interventions such as prosecutions, licence suspensions and business closures. Judgements about the types of strategies to deploy should also relate to the potential harms involved.

The concepts of responsive regulation and regulatory craftsmanship are usefully combined in the term 'smart regulation' (Gunningham & Grabosky, 1998). Being 'smart' about regulation means making use of all available evidence to assess the impact of regulatory strategies, and using this information to make adjustments to the regulatory mix to ensure optimal performance. Different types of evidence include test results of product samples, incident data (e.g., injuries, hospital admissions, compensation claims), complaints and allegations, and stakeholder surveys and interviews.

The type of regulation most relevant to the security industry is that of occupational licensing (Button & George, 2006). In modern democracies, almost all occupations that entail risks to workers, consumers and the public are licensed. Government agencies or professional associations issue a licence to operate, subject to criteria of integrity and competence. Unlicensed operators face fines and imprisonment. Competence is normally addressed through prescribed training and assessment. Integrity is usually addressed through reference checks, the creation of disqualifying offences, and complaints investigations and adjudication. But, before we look more closely at security industry licensing, we need to consider the case for regulation of the sector more generally.

The Rationale for Regulating the Security Industry

The previous chapter described a variety of types of misconduct that occur in security work. These problems have tended to escalate with the growth of the industry, as more and more people came into contact with security personnel and became dependent on, or subject to, security technology. These problems were listed in 11 categories (Prenzler & Sarre, 2008):

1. Fraud
2. Incompetence and poor standards
3. Under-award payments and exploitation of security staff
4. Corrupt practices
5. Information corruption
6. Violence and associated malpractice
7. False arrest and detention
8. Trespass and invasions of privacy
9. Discrimination and harassment
10. Insider crime
11. Misuse of weapons.

As we saw in the previous chapter, the degree of intensity and the prevalence of these problems are highly variable. Misconduct is often hidden from public view and only revealed when an incident occurs or when indicators lead to systematic investigations and public reportage follows. In other cases, like violence at entertainment venues, the problems are very much in the public eye, including through repeated media reports, but without effective action being taken. What we can say with certainty, however, is that the industry has an identifiable 'risk profile' (Prenzler & Sarre, 2008, p. 1). Part of the profile is common to many businesses and organisations: fraud, for example, and undercutting in tendering and under-award payments to staff. Others aspects are more specific to law enforcement agencies: assaults, for example, and misuse of weapons. Overall, security work involves various intrinsic pressures and temptations that can trigger abuses.

Regulation is designed to prevent these abuses and to protect potential victims. The clients of security firms need to be protected from fraud and insider crime. The general public need to be protected from violence, discrimination and harassment, corruption, incompetence, false arrest and trespass (Sarre & Prenzler, 2009, chapter 4). The potential for this is greatly enlarged, as we have seen, by the growth of 'mass private property', where large numbers of people are subject to the laws of private property and the authority of private security (Jones & Newburn, 2006). Security employees also need to be protected from under-award payments, other forms of exploitation, and threats to their safety. The owners of security firms need to be protected from unfair competition. Owners and managers need to be protected from the actions of unscrupulous operatives — including employee crime and violence.

Preventing deliberate malpractice is one target of regulation. Ensuring good practice in terms of competence and effectiveness is another. One of the big attractions of security is that frontline personnel are generally much cheaper than police. But this advantage can be undercut by incompetence. Similarly, the potential benefits of labour-saving security technology, including 24-hour electronic omnipresence, can be undermined by poor response times and false alarm activations.

The need for quality in security became particularly evident from the 1970s, with the rapid growth in crime rates. Added to this were the global terror tensions following the attack at the 1972 Munich Olympics, and then the more acute post-9/11 terror threat (Sarre & Prenzler, 2009). Private security plays a key role at critical infrastructure where security failures can be catastrophic. The 'reassurance policing' agenda, which sought to improve people's sense of safety, also included the deployment of security officers in public places (Crawford, Lister, Blackburn, & Burnett, 2005). In addition, given the major role of security in global reductions in crime, ensuring the competence of security providers is essential to reducing the security gap, especially for more vulnerable victims in lower socioeconomic groups (see chapter 1).

It has also been argued that professionalisation of security will support greater synergies in a 'plural policing' environment — given that partnerships have been an important part of successful crime prevention (see chapter 5). As one example, the introduction of security industry regulation in the UK in the early-2000s was in part driven by the view that greater professionalism would support public/private cooperation. The new Security Industry Authority (SIA, 2004) stated that:

> One of the reasons we came into being was to contribute as effectively as possible to a fundamental Government objective — reducing crime and the fear of crime ... But there is still a long way to go before the private security industry is viewed with trust by the general public, as a partner by other law enforcement authorities, and as making a real contribution to the fight against crime. (p. 2)

General Accountability and Regulatory Mechanisms

The following paragraphs briefly report on the benefits and limitations of what could be called general accountability mechanisms, or default regulatory systems, that apply to the security industry along with other industries. Chapter 10 provides more detail.

Criminal Law

All of the actions of security providers are normally subject to the criminal law. The threat of prosecution, and a fine or imprisonment, should deter security providers who might engage in criminal offences such as murder or homicide, assault and sexual assault, trespass, robbery, theft, fraud, and harassment and threats. In addition, if security providers do violate the law, the criminal courts should provide justice or recompense to victims; including through sanctions, victim of crime support units and financial compensation.

However, research shows clearly that criminal law, on its own, is deficient to address the potential for crimes by security providers (Davis et. al., 2003; Sarre & Prenzler, 2009). Criminal law involves a high standard of proof — beyond reasonable doubt — which can create difficulties in proving (to the requisite degree) offences by security officers. Witnesses are often absent or their memories may be faulty. In the area of assaults, for example, victims and witnesses might have been intoxicated. Criminal law is therefore inadequate as a regulatory mechanism to prevent abuses.

Civil Law

Security providers are also subject to civil law in areas such as assault, false imprisonment, harassment and negligence. The civil courts operate on a lower standard of proof than the criminal courts — the balance of probabilities, that is, that it is more likely than not that something had occurred — and security clients and ordinary citizens have successfully sued security providers on many occasions and obtained financial compensation (Davis et. al., 2003; Sarre & Prenzler, 2009). However, taking private legal action entails many risks. Outcomes cannot be reliably predicted, and unsuccessful litigants are usually left with the financial costs. Like criminal law, civil law is not sufficient to adequately regulate conduct and competency in the industry and protect vulnerable persons.

Commercial Law and Market Forces

The free market provides another dimension of partial regulation of the security industry. Economic competition, and government enforcement of contract law, should serve to deter or correct misconduct. Firms that fail to deliver services can be sued and ordered to compensate victims. An example would be a store that is burgled after a security system fails to work as claimed. In theory, firms that fail to deliver should have their reputations damaged and lose clients. In reality, as the previous chapter showed, clients can be defrauded in the delivery of security services, and market systems usually fail to detect breaches like under-award payments. Financial compensation for security failures may come too late to save a bankrupt business, as the commercial legal system is notoriously slow. The abuses documented in chapter 11 provide many other examples of 'market failure' (White, 2013).

Miscellaneous

Security work is also regulated by numerous other laws and regulatory agencies, including workplace health and safety legislation, privacy legislation and employment law. Some statutes include points of overlap with industry specific legislation. Examples include liquor licensing legislation that prescribes, for example, certain ratios of customers to security staff; and weapon licensing that allows licensed security officers to carry firearms under certain conditions (Sarre & Prenzler, 2009). Again, however, the misconduct cases on the record show that all of these mechanisms are generally inadequate to bring the industry up to reasonable standards of conduct and competency.

Self-Regulation

Numerous industries and professions seek to compensate for the deficiencies in the above mechanisms through self-regulation. To join an association, or remain a member, companies or individuals must meet standards of integrity and competency. Members can then use the badge of membership to promote themselves as credible and reliable operators. Examples of security associations in Australia include the Australian Security Industry Association Limited (ASIAL) and the Security Providers Association of Australia Limited (SPAAL).

The benefits of self-regulation are not well documented, but it would seem that effectiveness is highly dependent on the rigour of checks and enforcement of standards. Implementation can wax and wane with different executive groupings. It may be highly dependent upon the financial resources obtained from membership fees. Associations are likely to attract firms already committed to high standards, and disreputable firms can stay in business without membership. While associations are committed to self-regulation, this tends not to be an exclusive position. A common activity is to lobby for government regulation to ensure fair business competition and provide an additional layer of protection for security clients and the general public (Sarre & Prenzler, 2011).

The Introduction of Security Industry Regulation

Before the introduction of special security industry regulation, parts of the sector were, at times, subject to very limited forms of occupational 'licensing', 'registration' or government orders (Prenzler & Sarre, 2013; Weber, 2002). In a number of cases, private investigators, debt collectors, process servers and security guards would be required to obtain a licence from a court or police station by simply showing that they were not bankrupt or did not have a criminal history. The approach was largely tokenistic. Obtaining a licence was often 'as simple as filling out a form, paying a fee, and taking it to the local licensing sergeant ... after which you could strap a gun to your hip and protect premises, go on patrol and provide cash carrying services' (Cowan, 2009, p. 77).

Industry-specific legislation, and associated training and screening, was introduced on a piecemeal basis in different locations, mainly from the 1970s (Prenzler & Sarre, 2013). For example, statutory regulation was introduced in Ontario in 1966, Japan in 1972, New Zealand and Sweden in 1974, South Korea in 1976, New South Wales in 1985, and South Africa in 1987. In the US, licensing of some industry sectors has been traced back to the 19th century. By 1971, 38 of the 50 US states had regulatory statutes.

Button and George (2006) put forward criteria for describing regulatory systems with the concepts of 'width' and 'depth'. 'Width' refers to coverage of types of security work. For example, while licensing typically includes security firms and contract guards, it often leaves out 'in-house' guards, consultants and control room operators. 'Depth' refers to requirements for integrity and competency — primarily criminal history checks and minimum training standards. Depth also includes requirements related to uniforms, weapons and specialist training. The Button and George (2006) study included an assessment of regulatory systems in 16 countries. The systems generally lacked both breadth and depth. For example, many systems required only 8 hours of preservice training for security operatives.

Data on security industry regulation are generally not systematically reported at regional or federal levels. One exception is the periodic reports by the Confederation of European Security Services (CoESS). Table 12.1 includes data from the most recent report, for 2011, across the 34 countries. At first glance, the table might indicate considerable breadth of coverage. However, regulation, as reported, tends to be limited to the core elements of the industry, with few requirements specified in areas such as in-house security or private investigations. CoESS has adopted a six-level system for assessing the strength of regulation, from 'nonexistent' to 'very strict' (2012, p. 150). The largest group — 17 countries or 50% — was categorised as strict. Seven countries (21%) were classified as very strict: Belgium, Hungary, Luxembourg, Portugal, Spain, Sweden and Serbia.

In the CoESS assessment, variance in the depth of regulation is most evident in training. The average mandated basic training period was just under 100 hours (approximately three weeks; see Table 12.1). However, some countries had unspecified hours or very low training hours, while others had quite substantial requirements. Sweden required 288 hours of basic training for guards (approximately two months) and 44 hours for managers. Greece required a two semester diploma for basic training and a four semester diploma for managers.

In Australia, security industry regulation is state and territory based. Table 12.2 lists the relevant Acts in force in 2011. These Acts and accompanying regulations vary across almost every requirement. Table 12.3 lists the licence categories in Tasmania and New South Wales in order to illustrate some of the differences. There is also considerable variance in disqualifying offences, discretion concerning 'fit and proper' person criteria, fingerprinting, and drug and alcohol tests.

The evolution of regulation in Australia has tended towards comprehensive coverage, including locksmiths and the electronic equipment sector. Another positive development in recent years was an initiative by the Council of Australian Governments (COAG) for all jurisdictions to adopt common certificate-level pre-service competencies and qualifications. These include the following (Sarre & Prenzler, 2011, p. 47):

- Certificate I in Security Operations
- Certificate II in Security Operations

Table 12.1

Key Dimensions of Security Industry Regulation in 34 European Countries, 2011

Dimensions	
Total number of private security companies	52,300
Licensing for private security companies is mandatory by law	94%
Total number of private security guards	2,170,589
Licensing of private security guards is mandatory by law	88%
Competent national authority in charge of controls and inspections for the private security industry:	
• Police	41%
• Ministry of the Interior	38%
• Other	18%
• Ministry of Justice	3%
Entrance requirements at company level (owners):	
• Clean criminal record	88%
• Background screening and/or testimonial of good moral character	87%
Entrance requirements at personal level (operational staff):	
• Clean criminal record	97%
• Background screening and/or testimonial of good moral character	97%
When applying for an individual private security guard licence, the law requires the private security guard in question to undergo psychological examination	71%
When applying for an individual private security guard licence, the law requires the private security guard in question to undergo a medical examination	66%
Average minimum age for private security guards to be able to enter the private security profession as operational staff	18
There is an obligation for private security guards to follow basic guard training	97%
Average number of training hours	97
Mandatory specialist training exists (by law) for private security managers, i.e., operational managerial staff influencing operations (from site supervisor to CEO)	50%
Uniforms are mandatory	95%
ID cards are mandatory	98%
A special licence is required for private security companies providing armed private security services	82%
A special licence is required for private security guards providing armed private security services	96%
There are legal requirements for storing weapons after hours	85%

Source: *CoESS (2012, pp. 143–147)*

Table 12.2

Security Industry Regulation, Australia, 2011

Jurisdiction	Legislation
Australian Capital Territory	*Security Industry Act 2003*
New South Wales	*Security Industry Act 1997*
Northern Territory	*Private Security Act 1995*
Queensland	*Security Providers Act 1993*
South Australia	*Security and Investigation Agents Act 1995*
Tasmania	*Security and Investigations Agents Act 2002*
Victoria	*Private Security Act 2004*
Western Australia	*Security and Related Activities (Control) Act 1996*
	Security and Related Activities (Control) Amendment Act 2008

Source: Sarre & Prenzler (2011, p. 36)

- Certificate II in Technical Security
- Certificate III in Security Operations
- Certificate III in Technical Security
- Certificate III in Investigative Services
- Certificate IV in Security and Risk Management
- Diploma of Security and Risk Management.

The curricula attached to these certificates include key competences and associated units of study. For example, the Certificate II in Security Operations for crowd controllers consists of seven core units (Sarre & Prenzler, 2011, p. 48):

- Communicate effectively in the security industry
- Maintain workplace safety
- Work effectively in the security industry
- Work as part of a team
- Provide security services to customers
- Provide first aid
- Respond to security risk situation.

Four electives are also required. Normally these are:

- Control access to and exit from premises
- Monitor and control individual and crowd behaviour
- Screen baggage and people
- Protect self and others using basic defensive techniques.

Table 12.3

Licence Categories, Tasmania and New South Wales

Licence Categories

Tasmania

Commercial Agent

Inquiry Agent

Security Agent

Crowd Control Agent

Security Guard

Crowd Controller

Commercial Sub Agent

New South Wales

Master Licence (for corporation, government agencies and individuals)

Unarmed Guard

Bodyguard

Crowd Controller

Guard Dog Handler

Monitoring Centre Operator

Armed Guard

Loss Prevention Officer

Security Consultant

Security Seller

Locksmith

Security Trainer

Barrier Equipment Specialist

Electronic Equipment Specialist

Source: *Sarre & Prenzler (2011, pp. 40–41).*

Industry-Specific Regulation: How Effective is the Basic Model?

Industry-specific regulation is intended to fill the gaps left by criminal and civil law and the other mechanisms outlined above. It is not intended to work alone, but together with these mechanisms. As indicated, a basic model has emerged around the world (Button & George, 2006). Security firms must hold a specialist security business licence. Usually the owners are not required to have qualifications, but they must not be bankrupt, must have a physical address (not a post office box), must meet insurance requirements and must not have committed any disqualifying offences. Licences for 'operatives' — workers or employees (including owner operators) — are issued subject to minimum qualifications, and integrity criteria — primarily a clean criminal record. Operative licences are usually issued in categories. A separate weapons licence is usually required, and applicants must show a need for carrying a firearm.

The regulatory agencies which administer the licensing legislation are usually located within justice departments and fair trading or consumer affairs departments, or police departments. These agencies process applications and renewals, investigate and resolve complaints, and carry out inspections. They normally have the power to deny, suspend or revoke licences. They can also refer criminal matters to the public prosecutor.

The basic model has attracted very high levels of in-principle support in public opinion surveys and surveys of security providers — in the order of 80% to 90% or even higher (Prenzler & Sarre, 2013). However, a proper evaluation would need to triangulate as many data sources as possible. In theory, and controlling for other influences, the introduction of licensing should produce large reductions in adverse indicators like complaints, litigation, violence, injuries, fatalities and security breaches. There should also be improvements in public perceptions of, and experience with, the industry. Moreover, the specific system in operation should attract support from internal and external professional stakeholders — including security owners, managers and staff, police and legal groups. Subsequent additions to the width and depth of regulation should elicit further evidence of improvements.

Despite the promotion of this comprehensive model of evaluation, impact research has largely been limited to surveys of security providers. Some regulators report the numbers of licence rejections and revocations. These can be considerably higher in some cases. For example, in the UK, from its inception in 2003 to 2010, the SIA issued 345,442 'valid licences', revoked 19,120 licences, and rejected 21,242 applications (White, 2012, p. 6). This gives an indication of how many potentially inappropriate persons were excluded from working in the sector. It does not, however, evidence real changes in conduct.

The following paragraphs provide recent examples from the UK and Australia of practitioner surveys that have sought to assess the effects of regulatory systems. In the UK, an SIA (2010b, pp. 28, 30) survey of security 'suppliers' and 'operatives' found that:

- 76% agreed 'the buyers of security guard services recognise the value licensing has on the industry'
- 82% agreed 'there is trust in staff because of criminal records checks'
- 72% agreed 'there is greater awareness of the role that security guards can play in providing security and community safety'

- 64% agreed 'there is respect for staff because they hold a recognisable, national licence'
- 63% agreed that 'licensed staff are sufficiently trained to meet the requirements of the job'.

Of those operatives who had worked in the industry prior to regulation, 78% agreed 'there is more trust in security guards because of criminal records checks', and 72% agreed 'the training has improved my ability to do my job' (2010b, pp. 46–56). Very few suppliers reported licensing having had a negative effect on business, with 56% reporting increased business in the preceding 2 years.

In another survey conducted in the UK, 'door supervisors' were asked about their personal safety. Two-thirds (67%) of respondents said that they had experienced violence, with 54% stating they had been physically attacked and 22% experiencing an injury (SIA, 2010a, pp. 50–54). Of those who had worked in the sector for five years or more, 94% reported having been attacked. Nonetheless, 76% of all respondents agreed that training 'has improved my ability to do the job', 83% felt that 'licensing has increased the professionalism of those working in the door supervision sector', and 79% said that licensing had 'decreased criminality' in the sector.

A 2010 Australian survey of security managers and security firm owners found strong support for the main elements of existing licensing systems, but with mixed views on particular aspects (Sarre & Prenzler, 2011, pp. 53-81). In terms of pre-licence training, a majority felt that courses were adequate in teaching basic security procedures (83%), occupational health and safety (78%) and knowledge of law (60%). However, skills training was considered inadequate for self-defence (75%), communication (73%), conflict resolution (69%) and physical restraint (69%). In addition:

- 66% believed the system had reduced assaults by security personnel
- 60% believed regulation had reduced injuries to security personnel
- 67% felt that compliance with standards was not effectively monitored
- 59% thought the system was highly ineffective in removing disreputable operators
- 62% believed there was still a problem with competitors under-cutting tenders through cash-in-hand payments to staff.

A similar survey of security operatives found that 57% felt regulation helped reduce assaults by security officers on members of the public, but only 24% believed the system had helped reduce assaults on officers (Sarre & Prenzler, 2011, p. 131).

Smart Regulation

The limited data reviewed in the section above suggest that security industry regulation can produce improvements in conduct and competency in the industry. At the same time, there appears to be considerable room for improvement, especially in preventing violence. These data, and more general critiques, indicate that regulatory systems are characterised by many of the problems of under-regulation and token enforcement discussed in the first section of the chapter (Button & George, 2006; White, 2013). A big part of the problem is that the potential 'smart' aspects of regulation are under-developed: data-rich feedback on what works and doesn't work, what's appropriate and inappropriate, what's fair and unfair, and what supports the legitimate activities of the industry and what stymies these functions.

With this issue in mind, Prenzler & Sarre (1998) developed six key points — listed — which they argued should apply to security industry regulation in federal systems like Australia. Most of these points describe minimum requirements designed to ensure the most basic levels of integrity and competency in the industry, but some of the points make explicit the requirement that regulation be consultative and based on evidence (p. 6):

1. Comprehensive licensing would cover all occupations involved in security work and reflect and recognise the high levels of trust and client vulnerability entailed in security...

2. Regulation would be national, with States and Territories endorsing a model Act and Regulations. This would allow interstate portability of licences and removal of 'havens' for licence applicants rejected in other jurisdictions.

3. Development and administration of amended legislation would be consultative, with standing industry and stakeholder committees advising the regulatory agencies ...

4. Regulation would involve exclusion of personnel through a national system of criminal history checks and power over licensees through an enforceable Code of Conduct.

5. Mandated training standards would be based on analysis of security tasks and establishment of basic competencies for all categories ...

6. Regulatory agencies would be proactive, holding a mission both for research and professionalisation. Compliance monitoring and complaints investigation would need to be vigorous, including innovative approaches such as behavioural observation studies and other forms of research into the conduct of security staff ...

In Australia, some of the recent scandals described in the previous chapter prompted the introduction of a number of advanced regulatory strategies that could also be described as 'smart' (Sarre & Prenzler, 2011, pp. 43–46). Western Australia introduced drug testing for crowd controllers, and South Australia introduced random drug and alcohol testing across the board. Most jurisdictions stepped up identification checks, including photo ID, and fingerprinting and palm printing in some cases. In a bid to prevent the influence of criminal gangs, all jurisdictions introduced 'close associates' checks as part of their determination of a 'fit and proper' person. The impacts of these innovations have not been properly documented. However, at first glance, they illustrate the principle of adaptive or responsive regulation that seeks to match interventions to risk in a dynamic and changing environment.

Conclusion

This brief review of issues associated with security industry regulation shows that a common licensing model has emerged in many countries, including Australia, based upon prescribed training regimes and disqualifying criteria. Various academic and survey sources suggest that this is an appropriate mechanism to address the industry risk profile in regard to conduct and competency requirements. Part of this minimum model relates to the breadth of licensing, and the principle that all areas of security work should be subject to the minimum model. In countries like Australia this has been largely achieved. Considerable improvements can also be seen in the depth of regulation. However, the recent scandals and inquiries outlined in the preceding chapter suggest that depth of regulation has not been optimal. Smarter strategies are clearly needed, including more comprehensive evaluation methods. Smart regulation should ultimately lead specifically to more effective crime prevention across the industry, and, more generally, to the entrenchment of best practice models in security management.

References

Ayres, I., & Braithwaite, J. (1992). *Responsive regulation.* New York, NY: Oxford University Press.

Button, M., & George, B. (2006). Regulation of private security: Models for analysis. In M. Gill (Ed.), *Handbook of security* (pp. 563–585). Houndmills Basingstoke, England: Palgrave Macmillan.

Confederation of European Security Services. (2012). *Private security services in Europe: CoESS facts and figures 2011.* Wemmel, Belgium: Author.

Cowan, R. (2009, August/September). Celebrating 40 years, ASIAL 1969–2009, Then and now: Licensing and training. *Security insider,* 76-78.

Crawford, A., Lister, S., Blackburn, S., & Burnett, J. (2005). *Plural policing.* Bristol, England: Policy Press.

Davis, R., Ortiz, C., Dadush, S., Irish, J., Alvarado, A., & Davis, D. (2003). The public accountability of private police: Lessons from New York, Johannesburg, and Mexico City. *Policing and Society, 13*(2), 197–210.

Grabosky, P., & Braithwaite, J. (1986). *Of manners gentle: The Enforcement strategies of Australian business regulatory agencies.* Melbourne, Australia: Oxford University Press.

Gunningham, N., & Grabosky, P. (1998). *Smart regulation.* New York, NY: Oxford University Press.

Jones, T., & Newburn, T. (2006). Understanding plural policing. In T. Jones & T. Newburn (Eds.). *Plural policing: A comparative perspective* (pp. 1–11). New York, NY: Routledge.

Prenzler, T., & Sarre, R. (1998). Regulating private security in Australia. *Trends and Issues in Crime and Criminal Justice, 98,* 1–6.

Prenzler, T., & Sarre, R. (2008). Developing a risk profile and model regulatory system for the security industry. *Security Journal, 21*(4), 264–277.

Prenzler, T., & Sarre, R. (2013). Regulation. In M. Gill, (Ed.), *Handbook of security, Vol. 2.* Houndmills Basingstock, England: Palgrave Macmillan.

Ransley, J., & Prenzler, T. (2012). White collar crime. In H. Hayes & T. Prenzler (Eds.), *An introduction to crime and criminology* (pp. 125-140). Sydney, Australia: Pearson.

Sarre, R., & Prenzler, T. (2009). *The law of private security in Australia* (2nd ed.). Pyrmont, Australia: Thomson LBC.

Sarre, R., & Prenzler, T. (2011). *Private security and public interest: Exploring private security trends and directions for reform in the new era of plural policing. Report for the Australian Research Council.* Adelaide: University of South Australia.

Security Industry Authority. (2004). *Annual Report 2003/4.* London, England: Author.

Security Industry Authority. (2010a). *The impact of regulation on the door supervision sector.* London, England: Author.

Security Industry Authority. (2010b). *The impact of regulation on the security guard sector.* London, England: Author.

Sparrow, M. (2000). *The regulatory craft.* Washington, DC: Brookings Institution Press.

Weber, T. (2002). *A comparative overview of legislation governing the private security industry in the European Union.* Birmingham, England: ECOTEC Research and Consulting.

White, A. (2013). The impact of the *Private Security Industry Act 2001. Security Journal,* online pre-print, 118.

www.ingramcontent.com/pod-product-compliance
Lightning Source LLC
Chambersburg PA
CBHW062028270326
41929CB00014B/2361